Air transport
A marketing perspective

schémas:
p 3
p 64
airline mark.
p 226

p 166
p 183

95

Air transport
A marketing perspective

Stephen Shaw

School of Business Studies
City of London Polytechnic

Pitman

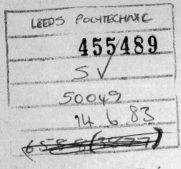
PITMAN BOOKS LIMITED
128 Long Acre, London WC2E 9AN

PITMAN PUBLISHING INC
1020 Plain Street, Marshfield, Massachusetts 02050

Associated Companies
Pitman Publishing Pty Ltd, Melbourne
Pitman Publishing New Zealand Ltd, Wellington
Copp Clark Pitman, Toronto

© Stephen Shaw 1982

First published in Great Britain 1982
Reprinted 1982

British Library Cataloguing in Publication Data

Shaw, S.
   Air transport: a marketing perspective.
   1. Aeronautics, Commercial
   2. Marketing
   I. Title
   387.7'4'0688   HE9781

ISBN 0-273-01760-8

Text set in 10/12 pt Linotron 202 Times, printed and bound
in Great Britain at The Pitman Press, Bath

Contents

Preface

In writing this book, I have been helped greatly by having the opportunity to discuss the ideas contained in it with a wide cross-section of those currently working in the civil aviation industry. It is therefore appropriate that I should thank the former students of our Air Transport and other courses for their willing contribution of ideas and comments. I should also like to thank my employers at the City of London Polytechnic, both for the encouragement they have given in the development of aviation training programmes, and for the time which has been allowed to me to write the book.

With regard to the manuscript itself, I am most grateful to Tom Bass, Barry Humphreys, Phil Shearman, Ernie Strangeway, Peter Smith and Rigas Doganis for their helpful comments on it, although of course all responsibility for any errors or omissions remains my own. I would also like to thank the numerous other members of the aviation industry with whom I have discussed particular aspects of the text. The points where I have not heeded their advice, and errors of interpretation remain, will be obvious.

Two particular people need to be thanked. I have worked closely with Andy Hofton, Lecturer in Air Transport at Cranfield Institute of Technology, for a number of years. In all the progress which has been made, my debt to Andy is very large indeed. He has worked on some of our courses, and has been very helpful in the provision of information on the technical aspects of aviation. He has also assisted with the preparation of some of the tables which are included in the book. However, important though these things have been, his most significant role has undoubtedly been in his uncanny ability to generate stimulating and useful ideas, many of which I have unashamedly incorporated into the text. Whatever merits it has will have come largely from Andy's contribution, and he deserves my warmest appreciation. Finally, I would like to thank my wife Gill, to whom I dedicate this book with great affection. The book has been written almost entirely at home, during a supremely busy period of domestic life. All this time, she has managed to keep three very young children quiet, in order to provide what has been a very good working environment. This is an achievement besides which even some of the giant strides of the contemporary civil aviation industry pale into comparative insignificance.

Stephen Shaw

Introduction

For those who have either a professional or a private interest in the world airline industry, it must be a feature apparent to all that the industry is characterized by an intense debate over its policy problems. Arguments occur over such aspects as the growth prospects for the aviation market, the resource implications of allowing for growth, appropriate directions for government regulatory policies, the needs of the consumer in terms of service provision, the requirements of a correct pricing policy for the industry, the role to be played by travel agents and freight forwarders in airline marketing—and so on.

The aim of this book is not to 'solve' these problems. Rather, it sets out to improve the climate within which policy debate can take place. For some time, our work at the City of London Polytechnic has been concerned with the provision of management training for airlines, airport operators and government regulatory agencies. In building up this part of our activity, our search has been for a logical, unifying framework within which to view the different aspects of the aviation industry and the links between them. This framework we have found in the theory of marketing. We now believe that such theory can be a key to understanding of the industry, and a necessary framework for industry managers to be able to review the problems which face them. We very much hope that, following the publication of this book, such an opinion will become more widely shared, and that the potential benefits of a broadly-based application of marketing theory to the industry will be accepted.

The book's aims are therefore unambitious, but we hope that there is thus a good chance of their being achieved. In an initial section, the intention is to give a brief coverage of the principles of marketing. Reading this section, plus a selection of the suggestions for further study which are made in it, will, we hope, ensure a wider familiarity than we currently find with the nature of marketing as a discipline. Then, in Chapters 2 to 8, we look in turn at each of the subfunctions of marketing in an airline context, and provide the basic information necessary to adapt the theoretical system to the real world of the airline industry. We also look briefly at each of the main decisions which will need to be made, and provide discussion of the factors which should be considered in formulating policies for each of the decision areas. Finally, in Chapter 9, a concluding section is given, where a number of the policy problems of the industry are discussed, and where a selection of the personal views we have formulated are put forward. This section is intended to demonstrate the practical application of the theory, and also to provide a stimulus to the discussion and debate which we very much hope will follow the book's publication. As a further aid to this debate, we have aimed at all stages of the book to give clear references to the sources of our information. Further reading of these sources will then be available to interested readers as an additional way of increasing the book's value.

Overall, therefore, the book is intended to provide a platform—in simple, non-technical language—on which our own management development and training programmes—and those of others—might be based. Indeed, as is so often the case, the initial reason for its preparation has been that no suitable source has previously become available to provide such a platform. If you are reading the book as an interested member of the public, or as someone who works in the industry, our hope is that you will come to the end of it feeling better informed than when you began, and that your interest in the industry and its problems will have been stimulated. If this has happened, you may then wish to attend one of our courses, in which case we suggest that you write to us at the Polytechnic. If you are reading it as a manager with responsibilities for training, it should give you an outline of the areas where it can be useful in your development programmes, and suggest which of your staff can benefit from it. As far as the City of London Polytechnic is concerned, we will be using the book as preliminary reading on our management training and development courses. This will allow us to use our courses, in consultation with clients, to explore in detail some of the aspects which can only be treated superficially in the general survey which the book sets out to give. If you feel that your own staff would benefit from a programme of this type, then we should be delighted to hear from you.

1 The Nature of Marketing

1.1 Marketing Defined

It will be a useful starting point for the book to give three definitions of the nature of marketing:

> 'Marketing is the management process responsible for identifying, anticipating and satisfying customer requirements profitably.'
>
> *U.K. Institute of Marketing, quoted in Wilmshurst (1978), p. 1.*

> 'The essence of the marketing way of management is to identify your prospective customer, to understand his way of life and his turn of mind, and then concentrate your productive and other resources on satisfying his needs at a profit.'
>
> *McIver (1972), p. 5*

> 'Marketing is human activity directed at satisfying needs and wants through exchange processes.'
>
> *Kotler (1976), p. 5.*

Although these definitions vary in wording, the meaning they convey is substantially the same. It is that marketing is not, as is commonly supposed, synonymous with simply 'selling'. Selling is merely the final phase of marketing. The earlier phases consist of analysing customer needs and wants and matching these with the capabilities of the firm. This allows the production of goods or services in such a way that corporate objectives are met.

An additional point of definition is the distinction between marketing directed at final consumers, and that aimed at firms which then in turn are concerned with output for final consumption. The former activity is known as *consumer marketing*. It is distinguishable because it usually deals with items of a relatively low unit price, which are sold without a great deal of contact between consumer and producer. The latter process, *industrial marketing*, is notable because markets are often concentrated in the hands of only a small numbers of buyers, unit prices commonly are much higher, and both market research and selling can be done by direct negotiation between producer and buyer.

The differences between consumer and industrial marketing are important in the study of commercial aviation. The leisure segment of the air passenger market provides an example of consumer marketing. Marketing to the business passenger segment and especially the marketing of air freight services, coincide very well with the industrial model.

Both consumer and industrial marketing need to be placed in an appropriate context for the book by looking at the application of the theory of marketing to business decision-making. This material is now included.

1.2 The Application of Marketing Theory

There is now an extensive literature setting out the principles of marketing.[1] For the basic outline needed in a book of this type, the literature can best be summarized by examining the way in which a firm might proceed if it were to implement these principles. For the sake of simplicity, we will begin by assuming that the firm is intending to introduce a single product into a single market. Later, the more realistic situation of a multi-product, multi-market model will be brought in.

For a single market, marketing theory indicates a progression through eight phases of activity, as shown in Fig. 1.1. At this point, it will be useful to list these stages, and to indicate the decisions and constraints which will face firms with respect to each of them. The reader is advised to refer to Fig. 1.1 prior to reading each section, to assist in the understanding of the links between the stages.

1.2.1 Market Investigation

As a first stage in the study of marketing, Kotler (1976, pp. 12–14) suggests that a business may employ three different philosophies. It may exhibit *production orientation*. Here, the main emphasis of corporate effort is directed to the manufacture of high-quality products. If the products are good enough, it is expected that markets will become available for them. At a later stage, the firm may show *sales orientation*, when competition forces it to give more and more attention to selling. This selling emphasis can take the form of costly expenditure on advertising, trade promotions through inducements or price cuts, or high-pressure selling by a large sales force. Finally, as a much superior form of operation, the firm can become

---

1 Besides the Wilmshurst, McIver and Kotler books cited in Section 1.1, further standard references are: Bell (1972), Boyd and Massey (1972), and Baker (1979).

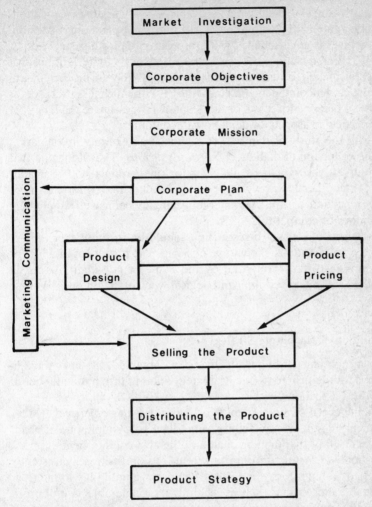

Figure 1.1 Stages in the application of a marketing model

marketing orientated. Here, its initial efforts are directed neither at product development nor at selling. Instead, after consideration of the broad market areas in which the firm might conceivably wish to participate, research is conducted to gain a thorough knowledge of the structure of these markets. This research is known as the market investigation stage of marketing. If it is successful, it will show areas where consumer wants and needs are unsatisfied, or are being satisfied less well than they might be. At the same time, it should anticipate market developments by analysing those wants and needs which may disappear, and any which may come into existence, either by a natural process, or by judicious promotion.

A standard range of techniques is available for market investigation. They include analysis of past purchases, attitude surveys amongst consumers, and the use of government, trade association and other statistics. A firm can use these techniques to derive estimates of the nature of product requirements, the quantities in which goods are likely to be demanded, and the price and income demand elasticities.[2] With much less precision, it will be able to prepare forecasts of these data which estimate the length of time that particular aspects of demand will continue.

Along with the study of the market, a crucial part of any investigation must be the collection of data on *competitor's actions*. Thus it may be that an initial survey shows a large demand for one product and a smaller potential for another. However, the latter product may offer the more promising opportunity if the main market is already being well supplied by a large number of competitors.

The end result of market investigation should be to show areas where worthwhile participation is likely to be possible. The process of looking for these openings is often formalized by the name of *gap analysis*, but in essence it is merely a sensible and logical way of beginning business planning.

1.2.2 Definition of Corporate Strategy

Once a thorough market knowledge has been obtained, the next stage in marketing is for the firm to define its strategy. This in turn has a number of distinct phases associated with it.

An initial concern of strategy must be with the firm's *objectives*. Under classical economic theory, objectives came down to a simple one of profit maximization. Only by pursuing such an objective could a firm ensure a sufficient supply of the factors of production. If its profits were consistently below those of competitors, the factors would move until they found their most profitable employment. However, today, a single objective of profit maximization is unlikely to be appropriate for any firm. Possible objectives related to the internal needs of the firm can range widely, and to a degree be conflicting. For example, a firm might have to decide between objectives related to short-term profits, and those which might require some short-term profit to be foregone in pursuit of long-term market growth. Alternatively, the greatest profits might only be available in risky markets, with the company then faced with a particularly difficult compromise between profit and stability.

Business-orientated objectives pose many problems for management today. However, it has become a feature of business activity that firms must increasingly consider *social* objectives as well. Thus objectives

2 *See* Section 2.2.

relating to the minimization of environmental nuisance, to employment (in a situation of rising structural unemployment) and to the meeting of other social goals have become important to many businesses, and, as we shall see, especially so to airlines.

Once objectives have been settled, most marketing writers go on to suggest a stage of defining the *corporate mission*. This is a simple, often one-sentence, statement of the broad area of activity with which the firm is concerned. Thus a motor-car producer might have a corporate mission to help in meeting the needs of mankind for personal mobility, or indeed a university or polytechnic a mission to assist in ensuring adequate supplies of well-trained manpower for a national economy.

With objectives and corporate mission settled, a firm is in a position to begin the third aspect of defining corporate strategy—the adoption of a corporate *plan*. Such a plan should be a synthesis of three sets of data: the nature of consumer wants and needs, the actions of competitors, and the strengths and weaknesses of the firm setting the plan. The aim of the plan must be to use market gaps which can exploit the strengths of the firm whilst reducing or eliminating its weaknesses.

Corporate strengths may come from a number of sources. For example, a firm may have a capability which allows for low-cost or high-quality production (or both), when this can only be acquired by rivals after the lapse of a period of time. An example would be a firm which has very good labour-relations. This may allow it to assimilate new technology rapidly, whereas its competitors are held back by trade union resistance to such innovation. Alternatively, the firm may have a new product which other firms may not be able to imitate quickly because of the time required for research and development and also perhaps because of patent protection given to the initial innovator.

Once a corporate strategy has been defined, a firm can move into the first phase of the application of *marketing communication*. As will be shown, one of the main functions of communication is to secure the sale of products in particular markets. However, it usually has also a longer term function as well in the promotion of the *corporate image* the firm needs as part of its strategy. If corporate image is important—and it is clear today that it can be a vital variable in any competitive market[3]—then decisions regarding image and its promotion need to be made at the same time as the strategic plan is formulated.

1.2.3 Organizing for Marketing

At an early stage of the marketing process, decisions must be made on suitable forms of organization. These must cover *internal* organization,

---

3 *See*, for example, Olins (1979).

with the definition of a corporate management structure, and the application of appropriate personnel recruitment and training policies. Decisions will also be needed on *external* organization. These will define the role to be played by outsiders in marketing and who these outsiders should be.

At many stages of marketing, a firm will have a choice between deploying its own resources or else hiring-in services. For example, at the market investigation phase, firms may rely on their own market research, or wholly or in part hire the services of consultants. With product development, they may conduct their own internal research or contract it out to a specialist organization. With selling, they have a choice between carrying out all their own selling, or using one or more of the different types of *marketing intermediary* for the execution of part of the selling function. These intermediaries can be divided into *retailers*, specializing in selling to final consumers, and *wholesalers*, who act as intermediaries between producers and retailers. The use of wholesalers and retailers raises important questions for all businesses, most notably so for airlines.

1.2.4 Designing the Product

For any firm correctly employing a marketing philosophy, the results of market investigation, gap analysis, the productive capabilities of the firm and the imposition of an appropriate organization should show clear areas where product development work is needed. The ideal of product development is therefore a phase whereby products are made of a type, and in a sufficient quantity, to allow a launch that will meet genuinely understood and researched consumer needs.

1.2.5 Pricing the Product

Decisions regarding price cannot be separated from other aspects of marketing. Indeed, product development, pricing, selling and distribution service can be assembled under a general heading of the *marketing mix*. Wherever pricing is placed, decisions must be made about the general level of prices of products, and also about any readjustments necessary to give psychologically appealing and convenient prices. We will see later how important are considerations of equity in pricing, especially for airlines where the pricing of different products must be seen to reflect costs in order to ensure fairness between different classes of consumer.

1.2.6 Selling the Product

Only at this, the sixth stage of the marketing model, do we reach the point of being concerned with selling. Selling is not a synonym for 'marketing,' but rather a culmination of the marketing process, where products planned on the basis of detailed market investigation are offered to and bought by consumers.

Selling divides into two parts. There must be *communication* with potential customers, up to the point of persuading them of the merits of a product so that they order it, and then *administration* of the order through suitable procedures.

With marketing communication, firms must first of all decide what proportion of corporate resources are to be devoted to it. All communication activity is expensive, and everything spent must be justified as being the best available use for the committed resources. For example, it may be that a firm finding itself having to spend very heavily on communication to maintain the competitiveness of its products might be better advised to use some capital for new product development. This might ensure a product range which can sell in the market place without an excessive communication cost.

Once the resource decision has been taken, management must then allocate communication expenditure between the different possible uses for it. Resources may be used for *direct representation* of the sales message to the customer. This will involve employing salesmen to travel and speak directly to customers. Alternatively, funds can be spent on *media advertising*, as large sums currently are by most manufacturers of consumer goods. The firm may find it worthwhile to invest in *public relations*, with the aim of stimulating press coverage of the firm and its products, usually as a supplement to media advertising campaigns. Finally, cash may be given to *promotions* and other *'below-the-line'*[4] expenditure.

The breakdown of the communications budget will depend on the nature of the product. For industrial marketing, the number of final buyers is often quite small and an individual purchase may involve the spending of a large capital sum. Therefore, the greater part of the budget will usually be devoted to direct representation, with advertising and public relations ensuring that buyers have a familiarity with the nature of the firm, its products and reputation. For many consumer products, however, direct communication with the final consumer is not practicable. Here, the emphasis of the communication budget must be placed on media advertising, with representation being used merely for contact with wholesalers and retailers.

1.2.7 Distributing the Product

In many industries today, product distribution often takes place in advance of sale, due to customer demands for an immediate availability of goods through point-of-sale stockholding. However, whenever distribution occurs, it must be seen as a crucial part of marketing. It gives time- and

---

4 *See* Christopher (1972).

place-utility to goods as a way of satisfying current customer wants and, through good distribution service, securing loyalty for future sales.

1.2.8 Product Strategy and Life Cycles

Until now, the discussion of marketing theory has, for reasons of simplicity, been based on the artificial premise of a firm with a single market and a single product. It is most unlikely that such a strategy will prove to be an appropriate way of meeting corporate objectives. A diversification into a range of products will be necessary for a number of reasons, among them *market stability* and *market opportunity*.

With regard to market stability, almost all markets go through difficult periods because of supply problems, competitors' actions in advertising and promotional schemes, short-term changes in consumer tastes, and the like. A firm supplying a single product into one market is at the mercy of these events. However, one offering a range of products is much better placed because of the probability that a downturn in some markets will be counterbalanced by greater-than-expected prosperity in others.

Market opportunity will be important because firms cannot enter or leave markets at will. Substantial investment will be required to enter, and disinvestment to leave. This almost certainly will mean a lapse of time between the making of a decision and its implementation. Also, a long period may be needed before the firm has developed a sufficient reputation to allow it full participation in the market. Market forecasting is an uncertain art, with no firm possessing the foresight to know in advance the exact direction and extent of market trends. Presence in a number of markets will give management an assurance that whatever direction these trends do take, it will be well placed to exploit them.

A further reason for product and market diversification is that of *synergy*—a vital marketing concept which will be especially important in our examination of airlines corporate strategies in Chapter Three. Synergy is the term used to describe a situation where a firm producing several products is able to do so more effectively than a set of firms with each firm concentrating on a single item. It comes about because of a favourable interaction between the products. For example, a producer with a high reputation for a certain product may find that this helps in launching others into the same market segment which consumes the first. Alternatively, a firm facing a peaked demand pattern could obtain a synergistic relationship by utilizing off-peak capacity to manufacture another product, without the heavy investment in plant and machinery which would be required of one starting with the latter product. Or again, a firm may find that there is a residue from its raw materials which can profitably be turned into a by-product.

A final reason for diversification is the existence of a phenomenon known as the *product life cycle*. Any new product, providing it has been properly researched and promoted, should have a considerable appeal as a result of its innovative qualities. At this '*infant*' stage it will therefore have scarcity value and will command high prices. Then, the product may move into a '*developmental*' phase when the innovating firm is favoured by a rapid increase in demand. This comes as sales promotional efforts reach full fruition and demonstration of the product in action leads to imitative buying by successive groups of consumers. Expansion in demand is normally helped by economies of scale becoming available and a learning-curve effect making production more efficient. These factors reduce unit costs and therefore enable the firm to offer lower but still profitable prices. Such prices in turn expand demand by allowing it to move progressively down-market.

The developmental phase of a successful product innovation should be one of high sales to the innovating firm, with such sales allowing it to begin to recover costs of research and development. However, high sales will have another effect. They will show the firm's competitors that a substantial market has been isolated. These competitors will then have every incentive to begin developing their own rival products. Eventually, this will move the market into a '*mature*' phase. Demand reaches its maximum as it moves as far down-market as it is capable of going. However, in contrast to the earlier stages, maturity is characterized by intense competition as imitating firms complete research, development and manufacture of their own products. This competition depresses profits to low levels which do little more than cover production costs and may even fail to do this in some cases. Finally, the stage of maturity can be expected to give way to one of '*decline*'. For any consumer durable, many people who have already bought it will find that it is still functioning effectively, with no need for a further purchase. Also, innovation of other possible ways for consumers to spend their money will be continuing and there will be progressive changes in consumer tastes which will move demand away from a product which, though once regarded as fresh and innovative, becomes old-fashioned.

The existence of product life cycles has been demonstrated in many industries—motor cars, electrical consumer goods and pocket calculators are three examples where life cycles can be seen in various stages of development at the present time. Later in the book it will be argued that the life-cycle concept can be valuable in the analysis of airline products. However, what is true for all industries is that few firms can rely on a single product for their continued prosperity. Even if such a product is selling well and producing adequate profits at the present time, the life-cycle concept offers a likelihood that such success may not continue. Indeed, the better a product is selling, the more incentive there is for imitators to cream off some of the market.

The life-cycle concept allows only one policy to the firm wishing to ensure its long-term success. The process of product development and innovation must be a never-ending one, as the firm seeks always to have a range of products at various stages of their life cycles. Thus, as an initial product moves towards maturity and eventual decline, that will be the correct moment to be introducing a new product able to take advantage of the favourable period at the beginning of the life cycle.

1.3 Marketing and Airlines

Of necessity, it is only possible to give a cursory examination of the application of marketing theory to business activity here. The interested reader is referred for more detailed discussion to the standard references on the subject quoted earlier. However, it is hoped that enough has been said to indicate that the science of marketing has advanced to the point where it provides a logically consistent framework for the conduct of business.

We can now turn to the main questions which the book tries to answer. Can this theory of marketing provide a framework with which to view *airline* activity within the contemporary civil aviation industry? If it can—and it is a basic thesis of the book that airline managements have much to gain from giving attention to the principles of marketing—what guidelines does marketing theory provide for airline policy decisions? As we go through the different sub-functions of marketing, beginning in the next chapter with the structure of the air transport market, it will become clear that the theory of marketing can indeed indicate a logical process for airline decision-making.

2 The Market for Air Transport Services

Discussion of the market for air transport services clearly will form a necessary basis for the study of marketing in an airline context. But what information do we need to provide in order to give sufficient material for such a purpose?

It is assumed that all those who are reading the book will be familiar with the main reasons why people travel, and why goods need to be moved in physical distribution operations. It is also likely that there will be a general acceptance of the existence of a potential for airline service from those who are seeking fast, convenient transport. This chapter therefore concentrates firstly on providing the reader with information on the techniques available for market investigation in aviation. It then goes on to consider the ways in which an airline's passenger and freight markets can be classified into their principal segments. In an important concluding section, we cover the question of the projection of market trends into the future. First of all, however, it is necessary to cover some basic points which will be fundamental to the chapter's overall aim of giving a familiarity with the structure of the aviation industry's markets.

2.1 Air Transport Demand—Basic Concepts

As a first consideration, our attention in the chapter must be confined to a true demand of those who actually use airline service, and those who do not do so at the moment but who might be persuaded to by the introduction of a new product or by an appropriate promotional method. Demand must also be limited to the demand of those who would be prepared to pay a price which allows firms a reasonable opportunity of carrying them or their goods profitably. This kind of limitation does, of course, have to be made for all types of marketing, but, given the emotional appeal of aviation, is of particular importance in air transport.

As well as the idea of true potential demand, it is also useful to make a distinction between the air passenger and the air freight market. Today many so-called passenger-carriers are earning more than fifteen per cent

Table 2.1. Proportion of total revenues derived from air freight, 1978
Sample of scheduled airlines

Airline	Percentage of revenue obtained from Freight, Express and Diplomatic bags	Airline	Percentage of revenue obtained from Freight, Express and Diplomatic bags
1. Aer Lingus	8·8	11. Lufthansa	18·8
2. Aerolineas Argentinas	8·4	12. Pakistan International	13·2
3. Air Canada	9·2	13. Pan American	13·7
4. Air India	18·1	14. Sabena	18·6
5. American Airlines	8·1	15. Singapore Airlines	14·6
6. British Airways	9·3	16. South African Airways	15·9
7. Finnair	8·4	17. Swissair	13·7
8. Japan Airlines	13·8	18. United	6·8
9. KLM	17·9	19. Varig	19·1
10. Korean Airlines	21·5	20. Viasa	13·9

Source: ICAO Financial Data.

of their revenue from freight (*see* Table 2.1). Depending on the costing methods used, freight may be seen as contributing an even higher proportion of airlines' hitherto meagre profits. In this book, therefore, full attention must be given to the freight side of the business. However, it will still be convenient to separate consideration of the air passenger and air freight markets. As has been noted, air passenger marketing mostly conforms to the 'consumer marketing' model whilst air freight must be seen as 'industrial marketing.'

As a final introductory point, demand analysis in any transport industry poses problems because it cannot be viewed in isolation. Rather, it has inextricable links with supply. When an airline introduces service on to a route, notable developments may follow. In the short term, tourism and industrial growth may be stimulated, with, in turn, a further boost to air transport demand. In the longer term, entire social patterns within a community may be altered as contacts, necessitating further travelling, are built up with distant places. These will often be at the expense of local community links. In such a situation, again, enhanced demand for air travel will arise purely as a result of service provision. This must lead to important philosophical questions about levels of 'true' demand. Indeed, a growing disquiet is now apparent from some commentators (for example, Adams (1971), Thomson (1974, pp. 30–2)) regarding the long-term effects of such social changes. We will return to this point later, but for the moment it is important to emphasize the link between the supply of services and the demand for them as a complicting factor in air transport demand analysis.

2.2 Techniques of Market Investigation

To begin the substance of the chapter, we must start by considering the techniques available for airlines wishing to investigate their markets. For such airlines, study of the market has two purposes. It must first of all show them the nature of present-day demand, and the reaction of consumers to products which are currently supplied. It may, by doing so, show improvements which can be made in these products to preserve or enhance their market appeal. At the same time it must consider trends in the market and possible consumer reaction to products which have not yet been introduced, but which could be in the future.

For all firms, there is a standard range of market research techniques available. All these are potentially of use to airlines, though, as one would expect, some are much easier to employ than others.

For all businesses, *desk research* is a very cheap aspect of market research. For airlines, publicly-available statistical data can reveal details of traffic flows, income levels and consumer expenditure patterns. Also, many airline trade associations are responsible for the collection of statistics which are then made available to their members.

For defining the reaction of airline customers to existing products, *consumer surveys* can be helpful. Such surveys are usually taken in-flight, when response rates are very good, as airlines have the advantage that potential respondents are available throughout a flight with perhaps little else to do except fill in a questionnaire. Providing the questionnaire is designed properly, useful data can be obtained. The only disadvantage of a form which travellers fill in themselves is that questions must be kept simple, and the expected answers very short. A possible way round this is to use interviewers to conduct the survey, but mostly this has been avoided because of the higher costs of an interview survey.

Consumer surveys can be an effective way for airlines to define reaction to existing products. With the search for data on the possible appeal of new products, however, carriers face decided disadvantages. In any industry dealing with manufactured goods, data for this purpose can be collected quite easily by investing limited amounts of money in the production of a prototype. This can then be tested by gathering together representative groups of potential consumers, who will then have a tangible item which they can use, see, taste or whatever, in giving a verdict based on actual experience. Problems remain of ensuring that any sample is representative, but the manufacturer can usually obtain worthwhile data from such experiments.

No such advantages are available to the marketer of the airline product. In-flight surveys can only reach actual, rather than potential consumers. In any case, in them, questions about possible new developments can be based merely on descriptions, either by an interviewer or in written form, as to what a new product might be like. Most product changes in air transport consist of two things—a change in price and a change in the service which is offered. A survey may indicate a warm support for a product change based on a lower price and a lower service quality. However, the traveller will be able to appreciate readily what a lower price will mean in terms of his expenditure. He may not be able to identify with the lower quality of service without actual experience of it. He will not, therefore, be able to say in advance if the lower-price/lower-quality option appears an acceptable tradeoff.

Along with the difficulties of using surveys to test reaction to new products, airlines can only employ to a limited extent a classic technique of market research, that of *test marketing*. A manufacturer of a tangible product, who feels, but is not certain, that a new product is likely to be successful, can gain additional data by mounting a campaign over only a small part of the market area he hopes eventually to penetrate. Data from this campaign can either reinforce a go-ahead decision, or prevent the costly mistake of a wide launch of a product for which market prospects are not as good as had been thought. Examples do exist of airlines using test marketing for product developments—perhaps the limited introduction made by some airlines of the three-class aeroplane concept[1] can be seen in this light—but generally it has not been possible for test marketing to form the important part of the market investigation process in aviation that it can in many other industries.

As an alternative to survey or test marketing techniques, the use of *consumer groups* may be a way of gathering information about future product requirements. For example, in the U.K., the Civil Aviation Authority has been responsible for setting up the Air Transport User's Committee to represent the views of air travellers. Also, international groupings such as the International Chamber of Commerce can and do provide a forum for committees of travellers to meet and discuss travel needs. Another approach to this problem has been tried by British Airways which, in addition, presumably, to taking note of the views of the Air Transport User's Committee, has formed its own consumer committees with the specific task of advising the airline on future market needs.[2]

Consumer committees of whatever type clearly have a role to play in defining product requirements, but in no way can they provide airlines with information as reliable as can be obtained by the manufacturer of consumer goods through his testing activities. Air travel is too emotional a subject for consumers who are representative of the entire market to be found easily, with the consequent risk that decisions of a committee may respond to the particular viewpoints of one or two of its most articulate members.

As a final approach to deciding market needs, deduction from easily available data has much to commend it. A deductive approach might have as its constituent parts the collection of extensive data on reaction to existing products, where such techniques as in-flight surveys can be useful and reliable, and then collection of data on the consumer needs which air travel can help to meet. Forecasting the nature of broad changes in these needs may often be done with some degree of confidence, in a way which is not possible when assessing customer reaction to changes in product detail. From analysis of needs, it is then possible to deduce the kinds of product which can be expected to meet the requirements of the greatest proportion of the market.

There can never be any certainty about the correctness of a product innovation until it has been actually introduced into the market-place[3] and consumer reaction to it analysed. Even here, true long-term reaction may take a considerable time to appear, and then only after all effects of the novelty value of the new product and the bravado normally attending its

1 *See* Section 5.5.3. **2** *See* British Airways (1977), p. 14.
3 *See* Civil Aviation Authority, *Annual Report*, 1972–3, pp. 30–1.

introduction have disappeared. However, enough has been said to indicate that there is a range of techniques available which can be used by airlines to obtain data on the structure of their market. It is now necessary to turn to an examination of the structure in terms of market segmentation, which the use of these techniques has shown to exist.

2.3 Air Passenger Market Segmentation

A successful market segmentation will produce a classification of a market where variations *within* each segment are significantly less than those *between* them. For each segment defined—and ideally the number of segments should be small—it will give estimates of segment size, of the product requirements which will lead to the needs of the segment being satisfied, and finally of the 'willingness to pay' of the members of the segment. This will be in terms of their price and income demand elasticities and any relevant cross-elasticities.[4] It is fortunate that, despite the very wide range of possible motivations for air travel consumers, there is now a commonly-agreed segmentation for air passenger demand into: those who are travelling on *business*; those who are using airline service for *leisure* purposes; and those who are travelling for *personal* reasons.

2.3.1 The Business Travel Market

The business traveller, along with travel by wealthy leisure passengers, was the foundation of the early years of growth of the airline industry, and he remains important today. However, the relative significance of business travel fell during the 1950s and 1960s. For the U.K., business travel is now holding steady at between a fifth and a quarter of the total market, as measured by numbers of journeys (*see* Table 2.2, Column Two).

Business travel can be defined as any journey undertaken for reasons directly related to a person's employment, and for which the employee is not paying out of his personal income. A number of facts about the business traveller stem from this definition.

---

4 The concept of demand elasticity is important to any form of market analysis, and it is suggested that those unfamiliar with it should refer to any of the standard economics texts on this subject (for example, Lipsey (1975), Perrow (1971)). To outline the concept briefly, demand elasticity is a ratio measuring the response of demand to changes in the factors believed to cause a given level of demand to arise. Of these factors, product price and income levels of consumers are usually the most important. Where the proportionate response in demand is less than the change in the causative factor, demand is said to be inelastic. If the response is greater, demand is described as elastic. Cross-elasticities are important where conditions for a given product remain constant, but where there are changes in the price or quality of a competing product, for example, with short-haul air transport, a very relevant cross-elasticity is that relating to the price and quality of competing rail services.

Table 2.2. Segmentation of the U.K. Air Travel Market
International air passenger travel:
Visits abroad by U.K. residents ⎫
Visits to U.K. by overseas residents ⎭

Year	1. Total number of trips		2. Business		3. Holiday		4. Visiting Friends and Relations		5. Other	
					Journey Purpose t h o u s a n d s					
1970	8,304	100%	1,957	23·6%	4,411	53·1%	985	11·9%	951	11·4%
1971	9,433	100%	2,047	21·7%	5,611	59·5%	1,105	11·7%	670	7·1%
1972	10,975	100%	2,174	19·8%	6,773	61·7%	1,289	11·7%	746	6·8%
1973	11,886	100%	2,424	20·4%	7,251	61·0%	1,433	12·0%	778	6·5%
1974	10,755	100%	2,623	24·4%	5,891	55·6%	1,509	14·0%	782	7·3%
1975	11,559	100%	2,567	22·2%	6,341	54·9%	1,717	14·9%	934	8·8%
1976	12,064	100%	2,859	23·7%	6,377	52·9%	1,792	14·9%	1,036	8·6%
1977	12,919	100%	3,051	23·6%	6,684	51·7%	1,984	15·4%	1,200	9·3%
1978	14,214	100%	3,192	22·4%	7,516	52·8%	2,134	15·0%	1,372	9·6%
1979	17,155	100%	3,980	23·2%	8,940	52·1%	2,802	16·3%	1,433	8·3%

Source: Department of Trade: *International Passenger Survey.*

If the traveller is not paying his own fare, with the ticket price merely being an entry on an expense account, he may, as a direct result, be willing to pay a higher price than would otherwise be the case. Also, whilst there is now evidence to suggest that many firms are monitoring travel expenditure more closely (*see* Section 7.2.2), in many companies high expenditure on travel is recognized both as a business perk, and as being indicative of corporate status. There are thus often institutional pressures leading to the purchase of premium transport products. These pressures may be increased by the fact that, to the firm, travel expenditure will be deductable against tax, so that true ticket prices are reduced. Finally, very often, business air travel will be undertaken in order to attend to a problem or objective which will render variations in travel prices irrelevant. For example, an executive travelling to deal with a situation where immense production losses are being incurred in an out-of-action factory is unlikely to be deterred from travelling by even very large fare increases.

All these arguments have been used to deduce a traditional view that business travel is price inelastic.[5] Undoubtedly this is true in most markets, where the use of expensive First Class and Normal Economy tickets is concentrated in the business segment. However, it was notable that, in the U.K. market at least, the business recession of the mid-1970s saw a decline in business travel. This was accounted for both by a slump in world trade leading to a lower level of business interaction, but also perhaps by firms under acute cash constraints beginning to see travel expenditure as an area where cut-back might be made. Effects of this have been both a reduction, in some cases, in the amounts of business travel undertaken, and, much more serious, a growing willingness on the part of firms to insist that cheaper Special Economy Fares[6] are used where possible.[7]

With regard to the age structure of the business travel market, the age range is very narrowly defined. It is concentrated in the ages from early 30s to early 50s. Before the early 30s it is unlikely that an executive will have risen to a position in his company which will make extensive travel necessary, whilst there is a tendency for the rate of trip generation to fall off near to retirement.[8] With regard to the sex structure, the business market is overwhelmingly dominated by men, being upwards of 97 per cent

5 However, it is possible to distinguish a sub-segment of 'independent business travellers,' those who run their own firms and who will therefore see expenditure on air fares to be a reduction in their income. In such cases, a higher price elasticity is to be expected.
6 *See* section 6.2.1.
7 In the U.K. indicators of these trends are the growth in membership of the Institute of Travel Managers as the professional body of those responsible for business-house travel arrangements, and the pressures from the Guild of Business Travel Agents that the government should investigate the activities of 'bucket shop' discount travel agencies, whose activities in offering cheap tickets, and the use of these tickets by business houses, were believed to be taking business away from G.B.T.A. members. *See* Department of Trade (1978).
8 *See* Welburn (1979), p. 347.

male in many countries. However, there are now signs that, with women's liberation and evolving family structures which are allowing women to spend more of their lives at work, the importance of women in business travel is increasing. A recent U.S. survey has suggested that now nearly 20 per cent of business travellers in the U.S. domestic market are women.[9]

One final importance feature of the business market is that it is highly concentrated. Whereas on the leisure side of the industry it will be uncommon to find a traveller making more than a few trips a year—many leisure travellers in fact make only one return journey for their annual holiday—the business travel market consists of relatively small numbers of people who are each making many trips.[10] This has important favourable consequences in terms of revenue for any airline which can gain its loyalty. Also significant is the fact that business air travellers are often notably up-market in their socio-economic characteristics.[11] They have high personal incomes, and often travel extensively for leisure purposes as well. An airline which can sell its services successfully to a business traveller may therefore gain revenue from additional leisure journeys.

With the question of service requirements of business travellers, we have available statements by businessmen on their travel needs[12] and surveys of the market such as the already-quoted Narodick report. However, a large part of the business travel need can also be deduced from consideration of the nature of business and the derivation of travel demand from it.

Probably the factor of most importance in business travel is that a proportion of the business market will be unable to foresee very far in advance that a need to travel is likely to arise. The 'factory out of action' emergency is a classic example of this, as is, say, a complaint regarding bad service from an overseas customer which requires someone to visit him in order to rectify matters. Both of these situations will give rise to unpredictable travel demand at short notice, with the likelihood of high costs of lost sales if a journey cannot be made quickly. However, equally there are some business travel requirements which can be planned quite well ahead. For example, when someone flies to an overseas conference or trade fair, or when air travel is used as part of an incentive scheme[13] within a company, advanced planning of travel arrangements will be possible.

---

9 *Travel Trade Gazette* (8.9.1978).

10 *See* Narodick (1978), p. 215; *Business Week* (1979). **11** Welburn (1979).

12 For example Ashton-Hill (1978), Camalich (1976).

13 With increasing attempts by governments to limit wage and salary increases for inflation-control reasons, and the high rates of taxation levied on incremental income of already highly-paid executives, incentive schemes have assumed more and more importance during the 1970s. Air travel has gained substantially from this trend. Foreign holidays provide a particularly attractive incentive and one which unlike schemes based on consumer goods, can rarely be fully satisfied. Incentive travel is currently the fastest growing part of the business travel market in the U.K.

These differences in the degree to which demand can be predicted give a number of sub-divisions to the market needs of the business travel segment. For all business travellers, the fact that someone else is paying and the status aspects involved mean that the traveller will be attracted to airlines offering a high quality of in-flight service and comfortable aircraft. However, for the subsegment where demand cannot be forecast very far ahead, or where last-minute alterations in travel plans are likely to occur, the dominating requirement will be that an airline should give the highest possible flight frequency between each point in its network. This will ensure that there should be the best probability of the passenger finding a departure near to his preferred time of travel.[14] For this subsegment, seat availability will also be vital. It will be of no comfort to the traveller with an urgent and unexpected need to fly to find that, although an airline has a service only a short time ahead, this flight is fully booked, with a long wait before a flight goes on which a seat is still available to be booked.

For the subsegment where demand can be predicted in advance, then flight frequency and seat availability will be correspondingly less important. The passenger will be concerned merely that a seat will be offered to him when he is prepared to book on a flight with a convenient arrival and departure time. This booking may be made several weeks or more before a journey, as shown by the successful attempts being mounted by a number of airlines to sell package deals to businessmen based on the twin ideas of advanced booking and the use of off-peak flights.[15]

The relative sizes of these subsegments of the business travel market is a point of great interest. Available evidence from one airline suggests that whilst 'plannable' business travel to trade fairs, conferences and incentive holidays make up only a quarter of total business journeys at the present time, the size of this subgrouping is increasing rapidly, with its overall significance likely to grow during the next few years.

2.3.2 The Leisure Travel Market

Despite the unquestioned and continuing importance of business travel to the airline industry, the dominant market segment today in terms of passenger numbers is that of leisure travel. For example, with journeys to and from the U.K., the 1970s saw a consistent pattern of around 70 per cent of air journeys made for leisure purposes (see Table 2.2, columns 3 and 4). The leisure segment is thus so large and its characteristics so different from those of the business travellers' segment that considerable space must be devoted to a discussion of it.

14 The market needs of business travellers are discussed in Pugh (1978), p. 9.
15 *See* Section 7.2.2.

Leisure travel by air may be defined as any journey undertaken by a person in time outside his working time, for purposes associated with planned decisions as to how such time should be used. It does, however, exclude journeys to and from work. It exhibits a number of features which distinguish it totally from business travel.

Of these, the most important is that the leisure traveller is almost always paying his own fare, with an inevitable reluctance to part willingly with a large part of post-tax income. The effects of this reluctance are then reinforced by the fact that many leisure air trips are undertaken as the annual family holiday. Any fare increases will have an extra significance in monetary terms because they will be multiplied by the number of people in the family group. Finally, unlike much business travel where large financial losses will be incurred if a trip is not made, leisure travel does not *have* to be undertaken. However, here it will be suggested in Section 2.8.2 that aviation has established a strong grip on the buying habits of a large part of the world's population, and consequently, an air-based holiday is something which many will give up only with extreme reluctance and after they have abandoned the consumption of many other, apparently desirable commodities. Equally, the wish to make longer journeys to more exotic locations and to take more frequent trips are factors which mean that air travel is one of the items on which increments of income are spent as people become better-off.

The fact that the consumer himself is paying for a non-essential, albeit highly-desirable, item can be put forward as an indicator that leisure demand is always likely to be price- and income-elastic. Strong support for this proposition comes from the large gains in traffic which have often followed fare reductions, especially when these have been introduced in situations of economic stability.[16] Whether or not leisure travel responds by similar falls if prices go up and/or real incomes go down is a particularly important question which we shall need to consider. However, for the moment, the fact of high elasticities for fare reductions and/or income gains must be emphasized as a characteristic of the leisure market which is of fundamental importance.

With age and sex structure, the leisure market again differs from the typical business travel market. It divides approximately equally between males and females, with a slight tendency for a balance in favour of women in older age groups because of their longer life-expectancy. With age structure, the trip generation rate amongst children is quite low, with then

---

16 An illustration of this phenomenon came with the new low APEX fares which were introduced by British Airways and Qantas in the U.K.-Australia market from January 1979. Both airlines reported a heavy demand for the new fare with, in particular, interest from those travelling by air for the first time (*see* Table 2.3). Wheatcroft (1978) pp. 16–18 gives a similar interpretation to events in the North Atlantic market during the summer of 1978.

Table 2.3. Traffic in the U.K./Australia–New Zealand Market January–May 1978 compared with January–May 1979. Total Scheduled Passengers.

	1978	*1979*	*Percentage change*
January	27,896	39,621	+40%
February	30,178	46,009	+52%
March	31,376	53,308	+70%
April	32,518	48,737	+50%
May	38,120	55,186	+45%

Source: C.A.A. Monthly Statistics.

a pronounced rise in this rate as people reach a stage in life where salaries and wages begin to be earned. For an age group of between, say, 19 and 27, trip generation is high both for holiday travel and for 'visiting friends' (V.F.) trips. Generation rates then fall sharply for families with young children (*see* Table 2.4), for reasons related both to the well-known problems of air travel with the very young, and to lower disposable incomes. Once families have grown up, trip generation rises once again, with, in particular, a peaking of travel in the rapidly-growing sub-segment of 'V.R.' or 'visiting relations' travel. This to a large extent consists of grandparents visiting grandchildren. Finally, generation rates fall as one would expect amongst the old, though we shall be discussing in Section 2.8.2 the future impact of such factors as longer life expectancy and improving pension arrangements as being likely to lead to an increase in post-retirement travel.

Another feature of the leisure air travel market is the link between air travel demand and the costs of other components of a trip. For anyone travelling on a holiday, it has been estimated that travel expenditure accounts for an average of only 37 per cent of total trip costs.[17] The remaining costs are made up of payments for accommodation, meals, entertainment, etc. A relationship is therefore likely to exist between changes in the prices for these commodities and the demand for air travel. In recent years such prices have been strongly affected by exchange-rate fluctuations. Favourable movements in exchange rates (in the sense of favouring the potential traveller) have complicated attempts to explain demand growth on particular routes. However, for anyone travelling to visit friends and relations, normally it will not be expected that they will pay for their accommodation or meals, with this being important in deciding both the cost of a trip, and also the degree to which exchange-rate fluctuations will affect demand.

With regard to service requirements of leisure travellers, as with any market with high price elasticities, price levels are likely to assume great

[17] Wheatcroft (1977) p. 6.

Table 2.4. Age and Family Structures of Leisure Passengers at The London Area Airports, 1978.

A. Age-distribution of U.K. Terminal leisure passengers at the London-area Airports in 1978

Age	Age distribution of population of England and Wales (%)	Age distribution of U.K. terminal Leisure passengers (%)
Under 2	2	0·1
2–10	14	1·1
11–15	8	3·2
16–24	13	20·1
25–29	8	13·6
30–39	12	19·4
40–49	11	16·6
50–59	12	14·8
60–64	6	5·7
65 and over	14	5·5
	100	100

B. Family structure of leisure passengers using the London-area Airports in 1978

	(%)
No children	73·3
Children (i.e. under 14)	26·8
	100

Source: C.A.A. (1980) Passengers at the London Area Airports, 1978. CAP 430.

importance. The response of demand to price reductions is indicative of price having paramount significance to a large proportion of actual and potential users. Therefore, any airline which is to meet the needs of the leisure segment successfully will concentrate on making available low prices for a given journey. In doing so, it will be helped by the fact that leisure travellers are known to have different travel requirements from businessmen, requirements which can be met at much lower costs.

These contrasts in travel needs spring from two characteristics of leisure journeys. Firstly, leisure trips are usually for a longer time than those on business. Only a minority of business trips last for more than a few days, whereas leisure journeys very commonly will involve a stay at the destination of 2, 3 or 4 weeks. Therefore, flight frequencies will probably be less important to most leisure travellers. Secondly, leisure trips are generally booked well in advance of the date of travel, or at least *can* be if airlines give an incentive to do so through the offer of a lower fare. This is shown in the data given in Table 2.5. A possible cause of advanced booking is that dates of absence are often known beforehand due to the allocation of holidays by employers. There is also a need to book accommodation, or inform relatives of arrival dates (in the case of V.F.R. travel). Finally, once a decision to travel has been made, people are normally anxious to make a booking in order to remove any uncertainty.

Table 2.5. Booking Patterns of Business and Leisure Travellers. International Terminal Passengers at the London Area Airports, 1972.

Length of time ahead booking made	% of business travellers	% of leisure travellers
Under 1 week	50	14
1 week to 1 month	38	23
2 months to 3 months	9	25
4 months to 6 months	2	15
Over 6 months	1	22

Source: C.A.A. (1975) Origins and Destinations of Passengers at United Kingdom Airports— CAP 363.

The effect of the willingness to book ahead is that airlines usually do not have to offer seat availability near to flight departure time to the leisure passenger. They can, therefore, operate at very high average seat factors without a loss of competitiveness against rival carriers (*see* Section 5.3.1). Flight frequencies, and flight departure times also will be less significant, with the concern of the leisure passenger that a flight should be offered to him with a seat available at a departure and arrival time which is reasonably convenient, when he wishes to book. Within these limits, there is usually considerable flexibility, and certainly nothing comparable to the tight peaking of business demand around the morning and evening as businessmen try and optimize the use of their time.

Despite these favourable factors affecting costs, leisure travel does present one supreme operational problem to the industry, because of its steep weekly and seasonal peaking characteristics. Leisure travel is often heavily concentrated in the early part of the weekend, and in the summer-time as the dominant holiday season.[18] For example, in the U.K. market, as shown in Table 2.6, a very much higher proportion of leisure trips are concentrated in the third quarter of the year than is the case with business travel. However, particularly if pricing policies and creative marketing are used to cream off the peaks and fill in the troughs in demand, there are several reasons why airlines should be able to meet the needs of leisure travellers efficiently at lower costs than they can meet the requirements of the business segment. Less expensive inflight servicing, higher average seat factors and, with flight frequency

---

18 Though on some leisure routes such as those in the eastern United States the peak is a winter one as passengers travel for winter vacations in warmer climates.

being unimportant, the ability to use large aeroplanes with low seat-kilometre costs are all helpful in this respect.

Table 2.6. Demand Peaking in the U.K. Air Travel Market, 1978

	Total business trips (000's)	Annual total (%)	Total leisure trips (000's)	Annual total (%)
1st quarter	858	23·1	1,691	15·8
2nd quarter	978	26·3	2,544	23·7
3rd quarter	850	22·9	4,218	39·5
4th quarter	1,023	27·6	2,237	20·9
Annual total	3,709	100·0	10,690	100·0

Source: U.K. Department of Trade, *International Passenger Survey.*

2.3.3 Personal Travel

Although the air passenger market is dominated by business and leisure travel, these two categories are not enough to segment demand completely. Most modes of transport show an additional third segment to their markets of *personal* trips. These are made by people who are travelling in their own time and paying fares with their own money, but who have tighter timing and routing constraints than those applicable to true leisure journeys. Again in most modes, the dominant form of such travel is the journey-to-work. As far as most employees are concerned this cannot be described as leisure travel, but it is paid for out of post-tax income and therefore separable from true business travel. In air transport the journey-to-work is poorly represented, with high costs the main reason for the lack of any notable development of air commuting.[19] The personal segment is therefore the smallest of the three segments of the air market. However, examples of personal travel by air are journeys brought about by urgent and unpredictable family matters such as illness or bereavement. Here, travel requirements are unlike those for leisure journeys in that they cannot be foreseen or booked in advance, but the fares are paid out of the traveller's own income. Service needs, on the other hand, are very similar to those of the business market, with flight frequency and seat availability being very important. The personal segment is therefore a difficult one for airlines. The product it requires can only be supplied at high cost, yet there have been understandable objections from consumerist organizations that people travelling under distressing personal circumstances should be

---

19 Although the large traffic flows characteristic of movements of migrant workers could be said to be another form of the journey-to-work by air, but on a seasonal rather than daily basis.

required to pay Normal Economy Fares mainly aimed at the expense-account businessman.

2.4 Passenger Market Potential

Besides data on segmentation of the passenger market, any detailed analysis dictates that we should also try to place segmentation data in a real world context by looking at the factors which affect the air travel potential of a given route. Here, at least four factors need to be invoked in providing an explanation of air travel demand.

The first of these will be the *characteristics of the origin*[20] of the route. The actual nature of the origin will, of course, vary with the size of the market area which a route is able to command. This will depend in turn on the availability of services. Long-haul operations are concentrated on a small number of airports, and potential travellers may be willing to make quite long journeys to connect with them by surface transport or 'feeder' air services. The true 'origin' may therefore extend over a whole country or even more widely. For short-haul operations, on the other hand, the market area may be quite small, as potential passengers some distance away from the originating airport will be attracted by alternative services from other airports.

Whatever the true origin, there will be a number of characteristics of it which will explain a given air transport potential. Of these, apparently the one most likely to be important is *size of population*. All other things being equal, a market area containing a large number of people should be a better air travel generator than one with only a small population. However, population totals alone are often notable for being very poorly correlated with travel demand. For example, a country such as India with a huge population generates only a small number of trips. Others with small populations—the Netherlands is a good example—are the centres of major air-travel markets.

Much better indicators of potential are *industrial structure* and *per capita incomes* of the origin. An industrial structure based mainly on primary production of agricultural and mineral raw materials will give rise to very little business travel by air. One with an emphasis on manufacturing—particularly if such activity results in extensive international and interregional trade—will be an important travel generator. Best of all will be those centres which combine manufacturing with status as international banking and commercial centres. New York, London and Tokyo illustrate this ideal structure.

Per capita incomes—obviously linked with industrial structure—will be very important in deciding leisure air-travel potential. In countries with very

20 In talking of origins and destinations it should be borne in mind, of course, that any air travel route consists of two-way flows, and that therefore both ends of a route will need analysis in terms of travel origins.

low incomes, almost all of such income is taken up in providing the necessities of life. Little remains for expenditure on luxury items such as air travel, no matter how desirable they may seem. In wealthy countries, on the other hand, large amounts of income come in the disposable category in the sense of being available for discretionary spending after necessities have been purchased. It is in countries such as these that leisure travel potential is at its greatest.

Other factors influencing leisure travel can be the *age structure* of the population, and *family structures*. Recent trends in Western countries for the average number of children per family to fall has reduced the numbers of people in the categories having very young children and therefore characterized by low leisure air-travel generation.

Finally in terms of origin characteristics and leisure travel, *ethnic links* are becoming important on many routes. As we shall see when discussing demand growth, the introduction of more low fare services and rising consumer aspirations have led to increases in V.F.R. travel for airlines fortunate enough to operate where, due to population migrations, important ethnic links exist between the two ends of a route.

As a second characteristic likely to affect travel potential, the *level of air fares* on a route will obviously be crucial, particularly for leisure journeys where price elasticities tend to be high. Air fares will to some extent be correlated with distance. It is generally true that demand potential over long-haul routes is less than that over short ones. This is because of the higher price of travel and also the reduced probability of spatial interaction taking place over long distances. However, as we shall discuss fully in Chapter Six, distance is by no means the only factor affecting fare levels. In recent years some routes have had very cheap air fares made available through the introduction of charters and/or lower scheduled fares. On others, a combination of government and airline resistance has prevented almost all low-fare innovation.

As a third route characteristic, demand for air travel will be related to the *characteristics of the destination*. Routes to major business centres, to holiday resorts and to destinations where ethnic links exist to the origin will be the ones where potential demand will be greatest.

The origin, the level of air fares and the destination characteristics will be the dominant factors deciding total travel on a route. However, to assess air transport potential, it is necessary to take into account the *characteristics of competing modes of transport*. The consumer's choice of travel mode is now an area of transport where an extensive theory is available, and the interested reader is referred to some of the many references on this subject.[21] However, deduction from this theory is well capable of supporting the observed fact, that over long-haul routes there is

21 For example: Bruton (1975); Lane, Powell and Prestwood-Smith (1971).

now no effective competition for air passenger transport. Airlines have both a speed and cost advantage over surface shipping, and aviation has achieved an almost total penetration of the long-haul passenger market.[22] Only the ability of steamship companies to offer cruise facilities has allowed them to retain at least a small proportion of the long-haul international tourism business, though even here airlines have often participated in the growth of the cruise business by flying passengers to and from seaports.

On short and medium-haul routes, the competitive situation could not be more different. Here, airlines are locked in a competitive battle with the private car, with train services and to a lesser extent with coaches and buses. Car transport has the advantage over air of giving a door-to-door journey without timetabling constraints. Also, the rapid increase in recent years in the numbers of companies giving cars as a business perk has had a corresponding impact on modal split for business journeys. Train services can be competitive because of their ability to give city-centre to city-centre transport. This is likely to be of great value to the business traveller, but it will be relevant to the whole market in that city centres are served by radial transport links which make them equally accessible from all suburban points. Airports, in contrast, are normally peripherally located and can be highly inaccessible from suburbs located on the opposite side of the city. Railways can also often continue operations in adverse weather, particularly fog, which can impose delays and diversions on airline passengers. Finally, with bus services, these do not usually provide intense competition for air transport in that they are characterized by being relatively slow in comparison with other modes, particularly where they are affected by car-induced traffic congestion. However, the basis of successful bus competition where it does occur is always the low fares which are offered, and so on some routes airlines may lose potential passengers to buses.

Surface transport competition has been one of the dominating factors in the development of civil aviation. However, as all the signs are that it will increase, rather than diminish, in importance in the future, we will defer further consideration of it until section 2.8.2, dealing with market growth prospects.

2.5 The Air Freight Market

Before going on to a consideration of the future of market potential, however, it is essential to complete the background work on market structure by looking at the freight side of the industry. The air freight market is very different from that for passengers—indeed the only common factor

22 *See* De Neufville (1976), p. 62.

between the two is that aeroplanes are used to carry the demand coming forward. With the importance of freight, we must begin by looking at these contrasts, which are concentrated in the following areas:

(*a*) Unlike passenger demand, freight is notable for the existence of pronounced *directional imbalances*. With passengers, most travellers who move outbound on a route will also return on it, unless they are emigrating or are unfortunate enough to die at their destination. Although directional problems do occur on the passenger side—for example, some routes show a peaking of outbound demand at the beginning of a holiday period, and in inbound demand at the end—most passenger routes end up approximately directionally balanced when taken over a year. On freight routes, directional *imbalance* is the commonest situation. The degree of imbalance reaches substantial proportions on some routes. For example, of all air freight traffic moving in the Europe-Australia market, about 80 per cent moves in the direction to Australia, and only 20 per cent to Europe.

(*b*) Again totally unlike passengers, who can be treated as a relatively homogeneous 'commodity', freight is totally heterogeneous. Consignment sizes can vary from a few grammes in the case of precious stones, up to something in excess of 100 tonnes. Commodity types can include goods needing special handling, such as live animals or hazardous goods, whilst there can be a large variation in consignment density.

(*c*) As we have seen, the business travel market is to some extent a concentrated one, in that it consists of a relatively small number of people making regular and frequent journeys. However, in contrast, the leisure market is a dispersed one, with the decision-making for a trip carried out by the individual or family group. The air *freight* market is the most concentrated of all the markets of the airline industry. Decision-making is in the hands of a small number of shipping and distribution managers. Concentration is increased still further by the role of the air freight forwarder.[23]

(*d*) The final respect in which the freight market differs from the passenger is the most important of all. We have seen how on long-haul routes, airlines have eliminated nearly all competition on the passenger side. Only on short and medium-haul routes is there still extensive competition between air and surface modes. With freight, competition from surface transport exists on *all* routes. For every type of cargo, unless it is highly perishable, an option exists for the shipper (or consignee) to accept a delay compared with the express delivery which air freight can provide. This delay becomes well worthwhile if the shipper in return receives a more-than-compensating reduction in freight rates. Surface transport operators have been able to maintain their competitive position by the offer of freight rates which mostly have been very much below those

23 *See* Section 7.3.1.

of airlines. At the present time, it is common on long-haul routes to find air freight rates which are more than four times those of competing surface operators. On short hauls, rate differentials may not be so high—although air freight will almost always be more expensive than surface—but air freight's competitive position is now even worse due to the rapid improvements which have taken place in the quality of surface transport. This development is covered in Section 2.6.3.

With these differences in demand characteristics between air freight and air passenger transport, market segmentation for freight assumes particular importance, and it is to this question which we now turn.

2.6 Air Freight Market Segmentation

In looking at the freight market, we are faced immediately by the problem that there is no commonly-agreed segmentation, in the way that a division of the passenger market into business, leisure and personal travel is found to be widely applicable. Recently, however, attempts at freight segmentation have been made and it would seem that there is developing a polarization around the possibility of basing segmentation on the justifications for using air freight rather than surface transport.[24] Certainly these justifications will be important in discussing marketing policies, and so we will use a three-way segmentation of the reasons for employing air freight as follows.

2.6.1 Emergency Traffic

Emergency situations where goods need to move extremely quickly have been the foundation of the air freight industry. Several types of distribution problem can be isolated where goods have to have the fastest possible transit time, with the costs incurred in providing such a transit being of secondary importance. For example, an *operating* emergency might be one where an overseas factory is out-of-action because of a shortage of a necessary component, or because of a breakdown in one of the machines making up the production line. In either of these instances, a company could use surface transport to move the componenet or spare part, and it would pay a low freight rate if it did so. However, this low rate would be of no benefit if transit times were slow. Longer journey times would have a cost—probably immense—of additional lost production which could have been saved with the use of air freight.

As an alternative, an emergency situation might be of the *marketing* kind, as when a customer becomes restive over delays by a supplier in

24 *See* Schneider (1973), pp. 26–33.

meeting an order. It may then be worthwhile for the supplier to use air transport to get the goods to the customer quickly. To fail to do so might result in the loss of the order or, in extreme situations, the loss of the customer's entire business.

Emergency situations are ones where the justification for using air freight as the fastest mode of transport is beyond dispute. With regard to the service requirements of the emergency segment, we can point to the need for the shortest possible door-to-door transit times, and a high level of departure frequency and space availability to take account of the fact that a requirement for transport for emergency reasons cannot be forseen very far in advance. Emergency air freight is also more likely than any other segment of the air transport market to show a low price elasticity. However, even here, competition between airlines may mean a degree of price sensitivity as a result of either open or covert attempts by airlines (or freight forwarders) to offer deals to those who are regularly involved in a need to ship goods under emergency conditions.

With regard to the size of the emergency segment, the lack of data on this aspect is one of the problems of planning services and pricing policy in air freight. Schneider (1973, p. 35) quotes instances of large variations in the views on the size of the urgent segment within freight managements of the same airline. A study by the U.K. Civil Aviation Authority (C.A.A., 1977b), in producing an estimate that roughly 50 per cent of present day air freight in the U.K. market is placeable in a premium service category, comes down towards the highest estimate quoted by Schneider.

2.6.2 Routine Perishable Traffic

Whatever the actual proportion of present-day air freight traffic moving under emergency conditions, it is certain first of all that air freight's penetration of the emergency segment is already high, and also that the long-term growth potential of this segment is limited. Therefore, for air freight to have a future as a major mode of freight transport, we must examine situations where the speed (and cost) of air freight will be a viable alternative for traffic moving under routine, as opposed to emergency, conditions.

Here, a very clear possibility, where air freight has already achieved considerable success, is for traffic which is perishable in that its retail selling value falls significantly after the lapse of a comparatively short time.

Perishability in a distribution sense can take on two different forms, though in each case the argument for using air freight as the fastest mode of transport will be the same. *Physical* perishability occurs in a situation where goods deteriorate quickly, with examples such as cut flowers, soft fruits and some types of sea food. For producers of these goods, two options will be open. The first will be to sell locally, which will bring very low distribution costs, but with the penalty of poor selling prices in a saturated market. The alternative will be to send the goods to distant locations. Here, much higher prices will be obtainable if the product is scarce and in demand. However, if the shipper were to use slow surface transport to reach such markets, the transit time would mean that the goods would be in an unsaleable condition by the time the destination was reached. The more feasible option is therefore to use air freight, with the extra freight costs of air transport compensated for by the higher prices obtainable.

The other perishable situation may be called *economic* perishability. It occurs not when the products themselves are perishable in a physical sense, but rather when market conditions are prone to change extremely quickly. This can lead to problems of obsolescence, if goods do not arrive at a market at the correct time. The classic example of such a product is newspapers, where failure to reach the market during the period of currency of a paper results in large amounts of production becoming quite useless. However, problems of highly volatile markets can affect a wide range of goods. These include fashion clothing, pop records, and the peculiar kinds of consumer items which can become 'crazes' for a short time. For each of these, product life cycles can be so short that they pose real problems to entrepreneurs attempting to exploit markets in the earlier stages of the cycle where demand is increasing, competition still limited, and prices therefore high. The use of slow surface transport may mean delays in reaching markets where demand conditions are ideal, and, worse still, goods finally reaching such markets when demand has passed its peak. Then the market will be saturated since other producers, recognizing the opportunity, will have had sufficient time for the production and distribution of competing products. Again, the best option is to use air freight, thus allowing goods which have been produced to be sent to any market in the world in a matter of days, and ensuring that all markets can be exploited in their prime condition of rising demand and a shortfall in supply (*see* Fig. 2.1).

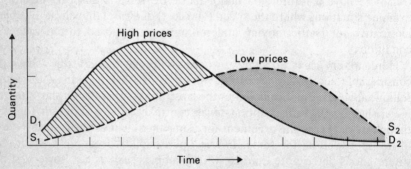

Figure 2.1 Demand and supply patterns with economically perishable goods. $D_1 \rightarrow D_2$ = demand through time; $S_1 \rightarrow S_2$ = supply through time

The question of service requirements and demand elasticities with perishable goods is an interesting one. Using the deductive approach, the nature of demand is such that speed and reliability of transit are likely to be of prime importance. With price elasticity, there is every reason to expect inelastic demand in the short run. Goods have been produced which are totally reliant on air freight for their successful marketing, though even here cross-elasticity effects of prices asked by other airlines may mean a degree of price responsiveness in some cases. However, in the long run, steep increases in air freight rates may cancel out the extra profits to be earned by selling in distant rather than in local markets, so it would probably be wrong to expect that demand will be unresponsive to price in the longer term. Equally, the introduction of lower airline rates may mean more local production being geared to long-haul distribution, with a consequent increase in air freight traffic.

2.6.3 Routine Non-Perishable Traffic

Despite the validity of both the emergency and the routine perishable categories, it is logical to expect that the greatest proportion of traffic moving in international distribution will be neither emergency nor perishable. Therefore, arguments must be formulated which can persuade shipping and distribution management to make use of air transport for their routine, non-perishable traffic. The development of these arguments has proved to be a great challenge in the marketing of air freight.

For a minority of goods, genuine price competition between air and surface transport is possible. This is because of the different methods of charging employed by air and surface operators. Surface carriers mainly base their rates on a volumetric principle and airlines on weight. These differences can mean that for goods in the middle ranges of density, there can in fact be a pricing advantage for air freight.

Instances of price competition have been unimportant in air freight marketing until now. Much more common have been the situations where air freight has been more expensive than surface transport in terms of a comparison of freight rates. It has then been the task of sales management to demonstrate that the better quality of air freight can more than make up for the higher direct costs.

For some goods, this is not difficult. Very high value cargoes, such as jewellery and banknotes, will always go by air because of the extra time they will be at risk during a surface transit. However, for all goods below those of extreme high value, the advantages of air freight can only be shown by a comparison of a large number of variables.

Of these, a traditional starting point has been the *environment for carriage* offered by air compared with surface. Protagonists of the advantages of air freight[25] have argued that its environment offers better

---

25 For example, Jackson and Brackenridge (1971), Slater (1974) Coltmann (1976).

handling and carriage conditions. This, coupled with the shorter lengths of time for which goods are at risk will mean that packaging can be minimal by air. The result will be savings in the cost of packaging materials, in the cost of the packaging operation, and in freight charges. Also, insurance premiums will be lower, whilst reductions in damage and pilferage rates will curb the incidence of customer dissatisfaction at goods arriving in a damaged condition, or failing to arrive at all. Those disagreeing with such a view would, however, point to the difficulties inherent in air freight handling, many of which have yet to be overcome,[26] and also to the improvements in the quality of surface transport in recent years following the adoption of the principles of containerization and roll-on/roll-off (*see* pp. 35–40).

Whatever the truth of the argument regarding environment for carriage, a decision to use air freight or surface transport will seldom depend on it. Almost always, the crucial advantage claimed for air freight will be that it can *reduce warehousing and inventory costs*. This argument is so important that we shall need to spend considerable time on it, with a first requirement being to clarify the meaning of the term 'inventory'.[27]

As a definition, it can be stated that inventory is 'a stock of goods held between the location of production and the location of the final consumer'. It is therefore representative of a gap in time between the goods being produced and the customer taking delivery of them. To some extent inventory holding is inevitable in manufacturing industries, in that there is always likely to be transit inventory en route between producer and consumer. However, by far the greater part of the inventory held by most companies is in static rather than transit form, with two main reasons explaining the need for it. For any company working with a range of products—and this would include the majority of companies today—inventory holding is necessary for *production* reasons. A firm manufacturing more than one item on a production line will generally find it cheaper to run the line on one product for as long as possible, and then to use inventory built-up to meet customer demand for this product until its turn on the line comes round again. The alternative of repeatedly changing the line to ensure a continuous availability of each product would be most unlikely to be an acceptable option. However, from the point of view of air freight, the *production* reason for inventory is outweighed in importance by the *marketing* justification.

For some products—principally those of an extreme luxury nature, or industrial goods which are required infrequently and which absorb large capital sums when they are bought—inventory holding is not necessary.

26 *See* Section 5.6.
27 A full discussion of the concepts of inventory management can be found in Murphy (1978), pp. 168–78, and in Howard (1973).

For these goods, it is possible for all the processes of assembly of raw materials, manufacture and distribution to be carried out after an order has been placed. However, such items are rare. Much more common is a situation where a customer regards a wait of weeks or months after ordering as being unacceptable. For household grocery items and similar goods, the only adequate service level is that they should be instantly available 'off the shelf'. For other products, such as electrical consumer goods, most customers will be happy to place an order, and then take delivery of the goods—preferably direct to their homes—within, say, a week. However, even in the case where some lapse of time between ordering and receipt will be tolerated, it will not be regarded as being adequate service for a company to manufacture after taking the order. Therefore, to remain competitive, most firms must hold an inventory of their goods, ready manufactured, to be supplied to their customers once orders have been placed. It is this fact above all others which gives air freight a competitive opportunity with routine non-perishable traffic, as the expenses of inventory holding are amongst the highest—and fastest rising—costs of manufacturing industry.

Inventory costs divided into two. *Inventory carrying costs* are those of physically holding stock: the warehousing needed, the possible deterioration in goods, the risk of pilferage and of obsolesence as market conditions change. *Inventory capital costs* are those associated with the fact that any inventory is representative of time between money being invested in the production of the goods and a return being obtained through their sale. There is, therefore, a cost of interest on the capital tied up. This is only avoidable in times of very rapid inflation when the resale price of inventory is increasing at a rate which cancels out interest payments.

The combination of carrying and capital costs means that inventory-associated expenses may make up 8 to 10 per cent or even more of the costs of doing business for a company. The minimization of inventory costs whilst maintaining an appropriate customer service level must be one of the major objectives of distribution policy. But how can the use of air freight help in the achievement of such an objective?

Let us take the example of a European company attempting to open up a new export market in a distant location—perhaps high value electrical consumer goods in Australia would be a case in point. In trying to do so, it is first of all certain that the company will face intense competition. A market which is attractive for one company's products will be equally so to its rivals. Therefore, for everyone, distribution service levels are likely to be of paramount importance in ensuring a successful penetration.

In developing the market, our firm will have a number of possibilities open to it. The first will be to begin advertising and selling in the market—or to appoint sales agents to do so—which should lead to the first orders being taken. These orders can then be communicated to the

European headquarters, and, after order-processing, the goods made ready for transport. For such transport, the cheapest option in terms of direct costs will be to send the goods by surface to the destination. However, the disadvantage of this is that a period of months will elapse before the customer is able to take delivery. It is most unlikely that he will regard this as a satisfactory service level, unless the goods in question are of quite outstandingly better value-for-money than those offered by other firms. Much more probable would be a loss of potential business to competitors, with probably a need after a very short time to withdraw from the market entirely.

To avoid such problems as these, the firm can consider as an alternative holding local inventory in the overseas market. This will mean investment in a warehouse or warehouses. In our Australian example, perhaps a warehouse in Sydney and one in Perth might be appropriate. This policy will entail hiring local labour, and most important, will mean shipping out substantial amounts of the company's products in advance of orders being obtained, to provide stock for the warehouses. However, if all these things can be accomplished, two advantages will accrue. The company can continue to serve the market using surface transport with its low freight rates, and objections from customers regarding poor service levels can be eliminated. Instead of orders being communicated to Europe upon receipt, they will be sent to the warehouses, with only a need for local surface transport following order-processing and dispatch. This will mean delivery to the customer within perhaps five days of ordering, a service level likely to be competitive with that offered by local producers.

Despite these advantages, the air freight industry can argue that such a situation will still be substantially less than the optimum, as a number of disadvantages too will be present. The policy will make penetrating a market a slow and risky business. A period of years could elapse between a decision to enter the market and operations in it actually being commenced. Such delays would result from the time taken to obtain warehouse capacity, recruit and train labour and ship out stock. By the time operations did start, such is the rate of change in consumer tastes, real income levels, the extent of competition and foreign currency values that the market conditions which had prompted the decision to enter could have changed totally. Even if they had not done so, the uncertainties attending any marketing decision mean that sales may not come up to expectations, because of a misreading of likely competitive conditions. The overall result could be that after a substantial investment of corporate resources, the venture is a failure, with a further large increment of cost still to be incurred in disinvestment as withdrawal from the market takes place.

The air freight industry has as one of its selling points that it provides an alternative distribution philosophy to the one outlined above. A system based on air freight need not involve local stockholding in the market-place. Instead, when an order has been received in the overseas country, it can be communicated to the headquarters of the company involved—in Europe in our example—rather than to a local warehouse. To avoid the problems of long lead times which the use of surface transport in such a situation entails, air freight rather than surface transport is then used. Air freight can enable goods to be sent anywhere in the world in a matter of a few days. Customers can then take delivery in what they are likely to regard as an acceptable time after placing an order, without the company needing to hold local inventory.

A distribution system based on air freight does, of course, bring with it the penalty that transport costs will be significantly higher—often by a factor of four or five times—than would be obtainable if surface transport were to be used. However, the air freight industry would argue that it gives a number of compensating advantages, which may be more than enough to cancel out the penalty of higher freight rates. A system of air freight distribution will have as a very significant gain that, if managed properly, it should be highly flexible. Markets can be entered and abandoned quickly, without long delays or large capital commitment. Indeed, extensive test marketing should be possible, allowing the company to experiment and find those markets to which its products are best suited. At the same time, inventory costs should be reduced by the centralization of inventory holding. Instead of operating a large number of small warehouses in each of its market areas, a company can serve all its world markets from a single centralized warehouse. This should mean that economies of scale in warehouse operations will be available, as a large warehouse will normally show a lower cost per tonne of throughput than a small one. Also, total quantities of inventory can be lowered. A proportion of inventory will always be held to ensure a continuation of an acceptable customer service level in the face of likely but unforecastable fluctuations in sales, with what is known as *safety inventory*[28] held against situations when sales are higher than expected. For any company basing its distribution on surface trans-port, this safety inventory must be held in all markets. An increase in sales may occur anywhere, with a need for stock cover against that eventuality. However, with the centralized inventory holding of an air freight-based system, it becomes a reasonable assumption to make that, in the different markets served by the company, some will show higher-than-forecast sales, whilst others will be lower-than-forecast. In this way, sales variations will, to some extent, cancel one another out. If they do, safety inventory can be reduced compared with a surface-based system.

These arguments for the existence of a routine non-perishable segment of the air freight market are undoubtedly valid, and we shall discuss fully in

28 For a discussion of the concept of safety inventory, *see* de Raismes (1975).

Chapter 7 the methods for exploiting them. However, in putting forward the view that such a segment does exist, it is equally necessary to indicate the qualifications which need to be made. In fact, the benefits which air freight can bring are confined to a relatively small number of distribution situations. In particular, these benefits will be affected by the *value-to-weight ratio* of the goods question, and the *extent of the speed and service advantage* held by air freight compared with surface transport.

Value-to-weight ratio is important because many of the advantages claimed by air freight will only apply to goods of a high value. For all valuable cargoes, the significance of the air freight rate will be reduced by the fact that transport costs will make up a lower proportion of the final selling price. Cost savings by air freight in such areas as packaging and insurance are likely to be greater. Finally, and most importantly, the inventory capital costs where air freight can make a particular contribution will obviously be affected by value-to-weight ratio.

Speed and service advantages are crucial to the whole argument for the use of air freight for routine non-perishable traffic. Such advantages are a function not only of air freight services, but also of the quality of competing surface modes and it is here that improvements have begun to appear. On long-haul routes, the last ten years have been notable for the adoption of the principle of *containerization* by surface transport operators.[29] This has not altered the fact that there are still large discrepancies in the line-haul speeds of air and surface transport, though typically container ships do cruise somewhat faster than the conventional dry cargo ships they have replaced. However, containerization has meant an improvement in the quality of surface transport operations with, in particular, greater reliability due to a shortening of vessel port turnround times. There have also been notable gains in environment-for-carriage due to the ease of container handling and the protection which containers provide. The effect of these changes has been that, although air freight still has a speed advantage over surface transport on long-haul routes, the difference is not as great as it once was, whilst in terms of reliability of service and environment-for-carriage, there may be little to choose between them in many situations.

Despite the significance of deep-sea containerization for the competitive position of the air freight industry, it is developments on short-haul routes which are posing the greatest threat. On overland journeys the improvements in rail freight services and the growth of door-to-door trucking are both constraining air freight growth. However, it is on sectors involving over-sea movements that surface transport developments have had such an impact on air freight's formerly strong speed and service advantage. Here, the principle used has been that of *roll-on/roll-off*. Ferries have been introduced which allow pre-loaded road vehicles to be driven on and off, greatly reducing in-port delays. Today, for short hauls such as those from Britain to Western Europe, the effect of 'ro-ro' has been very marked. On any occasion where road transport can give a door-to-door journey, it is capable of a transit time which is very little different from that of air freight, bearing in mind airport access journeys and delays at airports before and after carriage. Even when a door-to-door movement is not possible due to a need for groupage of small loads, any longer transit time by road may be more than compensated for by lower freight rates. Many airlines have reported disappointing growth rates for short-haul air freight in recent years. These have been a reflection of narrowing speed and service differentials between air and surface transport.

The question of the future of short haul freight is a matter for considerable debate at the moment. However, it is hoped that sufficient has been said in this section to indicate the validity of the concept of a routine non-perishable segment of the air freight market, even if it may be that this segment is mainly concentrated around goods with a high value-to-weight ratio and over routes where air freight has a large speed and service advantage over its competitors.

The question of service requirements and demand elasticities for the routine non-perishable segment is a particularly important one, which has implications both for regulatory policies and for the design of the freight product.[30] One can say intuitively that price elasticities will be considerably higher than for either emergency or perishable segments, due to the option to use cheaper surface transport. Cross-elasticity effects of prices charged by competing airlines are also likely to be significant. Service requirements will depend very much on the nature of the distribution system of the company concerned. Where a company is holding local inventory in the overseas market, it may be that a considerable amount of preplanning and forecasting of when shipment will take place is possible—in return for lower freight rates. If, however, the company is opting for the low inventory costs which can be obtained by eliminating all local stockholding, it will need to ensure a transit time which will match the customer's view of a reasonable period between placing an order and receipt of goods. Space availability will therefore be important, to allow a prompt dispatch once an order has been received. Transit time reliability will be another aspect of customer satisfaction. However, within these two constraints, the exact requirement of the routine non-perishable shipper for speed of transit depends on a number of factors. It is theoretically quite wrong to pay out extra in freight rates to secure the fastest possible transit time, if the customer would be prepared to continue dealing with the company without withdrawing any orders if such times were lengthened. Indeed, the

30 The question of demand elasticities for air cargo is discussed fully in Sletmo (1973).

customer might prefer longer transit times if they meant that his purchase price were lower (under c.i.f. trading) or his transport bill less (under f.o.b.).

2.7 Freight Market Potential

Just as with the passenger market (Section 2.4) it is worthwhile to review briefly the indicators which can be used to show the potential for air freight which is likely to be present on a given route.

With the characteristics of origin and destination, these will be especially important in deciding the directional balance on a route. An area producing high-value goods, or having a consumer demand for large quantities of such goods, is likely to lead to a high market potential in one direction. However, it is possible that a country with a consumer demand for valuable goods may produce very few of them, with output instead concentrated in primary products. If this is the case, potential may be lower in the reverse direction with very real operational and marketing problems.

The other main deciding factor in freight market potential will be that of *route distance* and the *characteristics of the different modes of transport*. We have already seen how air passenger transport faces considerable competition on short-haul routes, with this competition deciding air market potential. With air freight, the nature and extent of competition will be of decisive importance on all routes, both long and short-haul. Air freight has a particularly high potential relative to total demand on routes such as those to interior Africa where primitive infrastructure can mean that surface transit times can stretch into months or even years. In contrast, short hauls such as those between Britain and Europe and in the United States domestic market are almost certain to have their air freight development held back by the excellence of the surface transport links now available, with, in the case of Europe, these links likely to become even more competitive were a Channel Tunnel ever to be built.

2.8 The Future of Demand

Interesting though analysis of the present state of demand is to the marketing manager, it is the question of future demand levels which will be of still greater significance. The future of demand will decide whether a new product is worthwhile, bearing in mind that it may take several years before a return on an initial investment is obtained. Equally, forecasts of the future will affect a decision as to whether or not money should be invested to improve existing products. These products may be in a declining market with a need for them to be abandoned now and investment channelled into more worthwhile areas.

In this section, we look briefly at the standard techniques available for demand forecasting in aviation and the shortcomings that these techniques have. In a concluding part, a qualitative discussion is included which considers some of the main trends in growth patterns.

2.8.1 Demand Forecasting Techniques

Demand forecasting is, of course, central to planning in any form of economic activity. For airlines, this is especially the case. Fleet planning decisions will often be taken 4 or 5 years before aircraft actually come into a carrier's fleet, whilst, once they are there, their service life may be 15 to 17 years or more. If it is intended that the aircraft should remain with the airline throughout this time, an investment appraisal of aircraft needs may therefore stand or fall on estimates of demand extending twenty years ahead.

Unfortunately, despite its importance, forecasting in aviation is affected by fundamental difficulties. As we have seen, air transport demand responds to a wide range of variables including the levels of air fares, incomes of potential travellers, structure of the population and trends in social and business interaction. All these are affected by uncertainties which are important in deciding future demand, but which often cannot be forseen even days or weeks ahead, let alone periods of many years. We will return to this point later, but we begin our discussion by looking at the families of techniques which have been used in air transport demand forecasting.

These techniques range from those which have as their characteristics limited data and computing requirements but a crudeness which reduced their intellectual appeal, up to those involving massive data collection and computational exercises in the cause of producing arguably better results. To most techniques in the former category we can give the generic name of *growth factor* methods.

All growth factor techniques have in common the attempt to derive a time-series of past traffic data covering a period of years prior to the forecasting base. They then rely on an assumption that, if a trend of growth (or decline) can be extrapolated from these past years, it can be used to project future growth. For example, if the past five years have shown an average annual growth of 5 per cent, the growth factor technique would be based on the idea that such a trend might be expected to continue into the future, though presumably with it being modified subjectively by taking into account any indication that conditions in the future are likely to be different from those which prevailed during the period from which the forecasting time-series has been derived.[31]

31 An alternative to a simple extrapolation of past trends is the use of a theoretical curve, rather than a straight line to project future demand. An example of this is the use of the Gompertz curve where it is postulated that a product is currently at a stage of rapid growth, but where a more mature phase is expected to be reached at some time in the future.

Any growth factor forecast brings with it the advantage that it can normally be provided quickly without the need for a great deal of time to be spent in data collection and processing. However, such an advantage must be placed against two very real disadvantages. Firstly, with any such forecast, there is always a risk that one or two exceptional years near to the base of the forecast may have an undue influence. For example, with a base forecasting year of 1980, very high traffic totals in 1978 and 1979 would have two possible interpretations. They could be regarded as indicating an acceleration in the long-term trend, with a need to revise demand forecasts upwards as a result. Alternatively, they could be taken merely as random variations around the trend, with the likelihood of future years showing variations below it. As a possible way of reducing this problem, a number of curve-smoothing techniques are available, such as those based on linear regression of time series data or on the use of moving averages,[32] but such techniques have a statistical, rather than a real-world justification.

The second objection to growth factor forecasting is the conceptual one that it is not behaviourally based. It is concerned with an analysis of *what* happens rather than *why*. It has been this criticism which has been the dominant factor in attempts made in recent years to broaden the basis of forecasting to bring in behavioural aspects which will explain a given demand, rather than merely analyse the level of demand itself.

Of the techniques designed to do this, two broad families can be distinguished. The first is *category analysis*, whereby forecasting is attempted by dividing up the population of the market area into a number of categories—often a large number—according to socioeconomic characteristics. For each category, questionnaire and other research is then conducted to isolate air travel trends and in particular a 'propensity to travel' in terms of the average number of air trips made during a year made by the members of each group. The forecasting phase consists of predicting for the required period the demographic, social and economic variables on which the original categorization has been based. This allows a forecast of the numbers of people appearing in each category through the forecasting period, with the consequent ability, through the propensity to travel, to calculate total trip generation for each category and, by combining the category totals, for the whole market.

The use of category analysis may well provide a more comprehensive analysis than is possible using one of the growth factor techniques, though of course, this does only come at the penalty of a very sizeable increase in data collection and computation costs. However, category analysis also suffers from a serious conceptual weakness. In its pure form it involves making the assumption that propensities to travel based on past travel

32 Allen (1966), pp. 134–8.

patterns will continue to be an accurate representation of the future. There are at least two reasons why this is unlikely to be the case. Firstly, the price of air travel may change relative to the prices of other commodities, with the result that propensities to travel within a given group may also change. Secondly, and with a similar result, consumer preferences may evolve with people becoming willing to spend more (or, of course, less) of their disposable income on air travel. If either of these possibilities is thought at all likely to occur, there will be a need to change propensities to travel through time, but with little more than hunch or guesswork on which to base the degree of these changes.

The alternative approach to category analysis in demand forecasting is to use some form of *multiple regression analysis*. This directly relates changes in demand to those factors which are believed to cause such changes to arise. The actual statistical working of multiple regression is rather complex[33] but its principles are quite straightforward. For air transport demand forecasting, time series data are built up which allow an examination of changes in a dependent variable (air transport demand) and in a number of independent variables. A postulation is made of a likely correlation between changes in the independent variables and the dependent one. In any multiple regression analysis in aviation forecasting, the two most significant independent variables will always be the price of air travel and the incomes of potential travellers.[34] If, on completing the analysis of past trends, it becomes possible to explain a high proportion of the variations in the dependent variable by changes in the independent ones, predicting the independent variables into the future will allow a demand forecast to be produced.

Multiple regression analysis has as its advantage over category analysis that the data collection and analysis requirement is of a more manageable size. Most of the data will normally be available from published sources, rather than extremely costly social surveys being needed. Conceptual criticisms are that to an even greater extent than category analysis it relies on an assumption that statistical trends isolated from past data will continue to apply into the future. Almost certainly they will not. Also, the validity of the technique statistically depends on there being no, or at least very little, correlation between the independent variables. If such correlation is present the effect is to produce superficially highly appealing—but in fact totally spurious—results.

Arguments about the relative merits of growth factor, category analysis and multiple regression analysis are, of course, important, but it is very necessary that the air transport economist should not become excessively absorbed in discussion of different statistical techniques, at the expense of

33 A full description of these techniques is to be found in Taneja (1976) and (1978).
34 *See* Green (1978).

losing sight of the nature of the industry in which he works and the purpose for which a demand forecast will be used.

Consideration of the nature of the industry allows us to bring in one fundamental fact which applies to any forecasting technique, irrespective of its statistical sophistication. The history of air transport is full of discrete events—such as wars, civil disturbances, fuel shortages and price increases, natural disasters etc.—which in the very truest sense are not amenable to precise forecasting. Also, many of the variables such as income levels and air travel prices which are produced as input into multi-variate statistical models are in themselves subject to forecasting errors which will have an impact on any result which is eventually produced.

After a great deal of thought on this subject, there would now seem to be a developing consensus in the industry that accurate demand forecasting beyond a short time ahead is simply not possible. Instead, a much more appropriate policy is that planning should be based on the assumption that demand forecasts will almost certainly be wrong over the long term. The need is instead for flexibility, to enable a course of action to be changed as the true level of demand begins to make itself apparent.[35]

Where demand forecasting is essential—and for many planning decisions of course it is[36]—the most successful forecasts are not likely to be made by those with the greatest mastery of sophisticated statistical techniques, but rather by those with a genuine understanding and feel for the likely nature of future trends in the aviation industry. It is in pursuit of such a philosophy that we now conclude this chapter with a qualitative discussion of some of the factors which may affect in some way future levels of demand.

2.8.2 Factors Affecting Future Demand Levels

Future demand for air travel will be influenced by three variables: the price of air tickets, the size of the potential market in terms of demographic and economic characteristics and, given the inextricable links between supply and demand in transport, the extent and quality of provision of airline and airport services.

1. The Price of Air Travel

For any product, prediction of the influence of prices on demand requires consideration of a number of aspects. *Resource availability and costs* will form a background to any trend in total costs. Then, *efficiency in resource*

35 de Neufville (1976), Ch. 3, gives an outline of such a philosophy, with the chapter appropriately entitled 'Guessing at the Future.' R. Shaw (1979) also emphasizes the need to modify statistical rigidity with qualitative judgement on future trends.
36 *See* Wheatcroft (1977), p. 366.

utilization will decide the way in which resource costs are translated into product costs. Such efficiency will be a function both of *production technology* and *management efficiency* in controlling the production process. The detail of the *type of product* will be crucial in deciding unit costs, especially if firms decide to take large quantities of resources to make premium products. Unit costs will then be affected by the *rate of return* expected by entrepreneurs as they translate costs into the prices which they will charge. Finally, in assessing the significance of price, there is, of course, no such thing as an absolute price. Prices are fixed only in relation to market demand. Therefore, in trying to estimate future demand, we must be concerned with *demand elasticities*.

As a way of approaching the question of the future of air transport costs, it is first of all instructive to examine past trends. Here, the record of the aviation industry has been one of consistently falling costs over a prolonged period. Table 2.7 presents data for unit costs of the scheduled sector of the industry during the post-war period. These costs are in monetary values and are therefore in no way corrected for inflation. They reveal a notable fact: that the airline industry's average unit costs were lower in 1978 at the end of the period under discussion than they were more than thirty years before. If allowance is made for the fall in the value of money during this time, then the fall in costs in real terms becomes very large indeed.

Within the overall trend of falling costs, several subdivisions are possible.

Table 2.7. Average Unit Costs: Scheduled Airlines Reporting to the International Civil Aviation Organisation, 1947–78. U.S. cents per available tonne-kilometre

Year	Costs	Percentage change compared with previous year	Year	Costs	Percentage change compared with previous year
1947	31·7		1963	19.2	− 5·0
1948	30·7	− 3·3	1964	18·2	− 5·2
1949	27·0	−13·7	1965	17·5	− 3·9
1950	25·0	− 8·0	1966	17·1	− 2·3
1951	25·2	+ 0·8	1967	16·2	− 5·3
1952	25·4	+ 0·9	1968	15·6	− 3·7
1953	24·8	− 2·4	1969	15·4	− 1·3
1954	24·0	− 3·2	1970	16·2	+ 5·2
1955	23·7	− 2·2	1971	16·5	+ 1·9
1956	24·0	+ 1·2	1972	17·6	+ 6·7
1957	23·6	− 1·7	1973	18·1	+ 2·8
1958	23·1	− 2·2	1974	22·8	+26·0
1959	23·2	+ 0·4	1975	24·9	+ 9·2
1960	22·9	− 1·3	1976	25·2	+ 1·2
1961	21·4	− 6·6	1977	27·5	+ 9·1
1962	20·2	− 5·7	1978	30·3	+10·2

Source: ICAO Annual Reports.

From 1947 until 1959, cost levels were erratic, but with a tendency towards lowering costs and already a large reduction by 1959. From 1959 until 1969, the industry entered a period in which average unit costs fell in every single year. By 1969, costs were at less than half the level of twenty years before in monetary terms, with a much greater fall in real terms. From 1969 onwards, costs began to rise, a trend which has continued up to the present time. However, only in one year—1974—has the rise in the airline industry's costs exceeded that of the general rise in retail prices. In all other years, the rise in costs has been below that of most other prices, with the consequence that air transport has continued to become cheaper in comparison with other products.

With this pattern, two questions are of vital importance. Firstly, why have trends towards falling costs been such a feature of the industry in the postwar period? Secondly, will these trends continue into the future?

With the explanations of falling cost levels, a number of factors can be invoked. For example, many industries are observed to experience reducing costs as they move from an infant to a mature stage, with one of the reasons being the full utilization of investment. A certain minimum investment is always necessary for production to begin at all, and costs can be expected to fall as output builds up to ensure that this minimum investment is fully employed. In aviation, such investment has been in areas such as maintenance facilities, airport handling equipment and reservation systems, and it was to be expected that some cost reductions would appear as a result of full utilization.

As a second explanation, *technological innovation* is of paramount importance. Postwar aviation has seen a pace of technical change[37] and innovation which has been equalled in few other industries. Piston-engined technology has been succeeded by turbo-prop and then jet propulsion, first on long-haul routes and then on short hauls as well. Finally, turbo-jet technology has been superseded by the high-bypass-ratio turbo-fan engines powering the modern generation of wide-bodied aeroplanes.

Changing technology has led to improvements in passenger comfort and other aspects of service provision. However, in the context of operating costs, its impact has been revolutionary. The changeover from piston to turboprop and jet propulsion has given the industry savings in the fuel consumption of engines, with the current generation of high-bypass-ratio turbo-fans being especially fuel efficient. Technology has reduced maintenance costs, with all turbine-powered aircraft having direct maintenance costs below those of piston-engined planes, and showing advantages because of the lower frequency with which maintenance is required. Also the increasing range-capability of aircraft has allowed for a reduction of the costs associated with intermediate stops. However, of most importance in

---

37 *See* Miller and Sawers (1968) for a full discussion of these changes.

Table 2.8. Aircraft Operating Costs reported to C.A.B.—1978—U.S. Dollars

Flight Operations	747	DC-10-40	DC-10-10	L.1011	A300	707-320C	727-200	737-200	FH227	DHC-6
Crew	468·8	435·3	433·5	432·8	428·0	463·0	321·7	358·33	130·5	127·9
Fuel and Oil	1322·4	919·62	869·7	932·6	683·3	728·3	533·4	336·71	118·4	36·9
Insurance	22·7	14·9	15·5	12·8	14·9	2·6	7·0	2·6	2·00	2·6
Other	0·4	1·6	0·3	0·6	0	0	0·2	0·1	0·4	0·0
Sub-total	1814·3	1371·4	1319·0	1378·7	1126·2	1193·9	862·4	697·7	251·3	167·4
Maintenance—Flight Equip.										
Airframe/Other	205·6	118·6	130·7	175·1	106·3	87·8	61·9	72·2	84·9	28·0
Engine	261·3	141·0	230·6	188·9	46·6	76·5	44·8	48·2	70·5	17·2
Burden	308·5	95·4	181·9	285·4	87·6	151·6	94·9	93·6	91·3	16·8
Sub-total	775·3	355·0	543·2	649·4	240·5	315·9	201·7	214·1	246·8	61·95
Depreciation & Rentals	490·3	703·78	348·3	497·0	287·26	159·9	160·36	84·6	5·58	34·01
Total Direct Exp/block hr.	3079·9	2430·1	2210·5	2525·1	1654·0	1669·7	1224·5	996·34	503·67	263·3
Average stage (miles)	1794	768	1348	950	882	1122	533	302	112	107
Average seats	374·3	236	254·5	268·7	230·8	154·8	132	101·9	44·0	19·0
Average b-b speed	453	371	487	473	446	474	357	369	197	150
Fuel/U.S. gal.	39·13	38·96	38·43	38·28	37·36	37·92	38·53	38·57	41·19	43·81
Total direct/aircraft mile $	6·90	6·62	5·14	6·36	4·57	4·07	3·46	3·38	3·31	1·89
Total direct/available seat mile c	1·845	2·806	2·018	2·37	1·98	2·665	2·62	3·322	7·63	9·95

Source: Civil Aeronautics Board.

unit cost reduction has been the increasing size and productivity of aircraft. Many of the costs associated with aircraft operation do not rise in proportion with aircraft size. For instance as shown in Table 2.8, the costs of crew time in the examples of different-sized aircraft do not vary in proportion to the seating capacity. Therefore lower seat-kilometre costs will be obtainable from the larger aircraft. The post-war period has seen the size of aircraft increase from the 20 to 30 seats typical of the DC 3/4 era, to the 250 seats or more placed in the wide-bodied planes. With calculations[38] suggesting that a doubling of aircraft size may reduce available seat-kilometre costs by around 15 per cent, the impact of increasing aircraft size on aircraft operating costs has clearly been substantial. Increasing aircraft speeds—again a feature of the post-war period— have also been important in improving aircraft productivity.

With any discussion of aviation costs, *fuel prices* will always assume great significance. The international oil market, on which aviation depends, has exhibited a number of important changes in the post-war period. Before the early 1970s, oil output generally expanded quickly, at a rate which was more than enough to keep pace with the rapid growth in demand (*see* Table 2.9). An excess of supply over demand is, of course, an indicator of a likelihood of a low market price, whilst an additional factor in favour of this with oil was the absence of any significant cartelization of the market by the producing countries. The overall result was that oil prices were low and falling throughout the 1950s and 1960s (*see* Wilkinson (1976), p. 227). Consequently, the proportion of airline expenses made up by fuel costs remained steady at only about ten per cent of total costs.

The 1970s have seen a complete change. A large part of the oil market *has* been cartelized through the activities of the Organization of Petroleum

Table 2.9. World Oil Consumption 1945–76. (Excluding U.S.S.R., Eastern Europe and China.)

Year	Oil consumption (millions of barrels daily)
1945	6·9
1950	10·1
1955	14·6
1960	19·2
1965	27·0
1970	41·0
1973	48·4
1976	48·2

Source: McFadzean (1978) p. 73.

38 Wheatcroft (1977), Wilkinson (1977).

Exporting Countries, whilst many of the producing nations have become progressively more concerned with the threat of exhaustion of supplies. The effect of these changes has been to cause a growing interest in the conservation of reserves on the part of the producing countries, together with a determination by them to secure the maximum amount of revenue from all oil released. Also, to meet ever-growing demand, oil companies have been forced to begin the exploitation of more remote and expensive sources such as those of Alaska and the North Sea, whilst instabilities in exchange rates have lent a further uncertainty.

Oil prices can be invoked in a number of ways to explain the pattern of costs in Table 2.7. The period of low costs during the 1950s and 1960s can be partly attributed to low and often falling prices of aviation fuel. The one year—1974—when aviation costs have risen in real terms can be seen as a response to the quadrupling of fuel prices which took place around that time. The return of comparative price stability for oil in the 1975–7 period was again reflected in steadying industry unit costs, although the shortages and price increases of 1979 served as a salutary reminder of how finely balanced is the question of the industry's fuel supplies.

There are two additional factors which need to be mentioned in describing the past pattern of costs, with the question of *subsidy* the first of these. Government subsidization has been a feature of aviation throughout the post-war period—indeed, throughout the industry's history (*see* de Neufville, 1976, pp. 146–50). Subsidies have been paid in two forms. *Direct* subsidies have often been given to airlines, as where a government writes off the losses of a state-owned airline, or gives such an airline an exemption from paying taxes. In many cases, governments have made available cheap loans to airlines, in such a way as to have a direct impact on costs. *Indirect* subsidies have been even more common. For example, governments in many countries have provided funds for airport development.[39] Also, air traffic control and air navigation services have often been operated at charges which are well below the cost of provision, as is indicated by the continuing losses being sustained by the Eurocontrol system for European ATC.

The last factor which needs to be discussed in explaining past cost levels is that of *labour*. Despite appearances to the contrary brought about by their capital requirements, almost all airlines are markedly labour-intensive in their structure of input costs. Thus it will be changes in labour prices which will have the greatest single impact on unit costs. A part of the decline in airline costs during the 1950s and 1960s can be put down to the general stability in labour costs in most countries of the world during that time. Also, technological innovation and expanding output allowed for a

---

39 The United States gives such funds under the Airport Development Aid Programme (A.D.A.P.).

progressive improvement in the productivity of such labour as was employed. However, the period of rapid increases in fuel prices between 1973 and 1975 was also a time of rising labour costs, whilst there was a slowdown in traffic growth which prevented airlines from using improving productivity as a way of holding back the effects of higher input prices on unit costs. Most certainly, therefore, trends in labour costs may be included as an explanatory factor in the analysis of past patterns of unit costs.

For consideration of the future of airline demand, it will not, of course, be past costs which are important, but rather future ones. To what extent, therefore, can it be expected that tendencies towards falling costs in real terms will continue? Or will entirely new trends begin to emerge?

With the question of technology, there is still a considerable amount to be gained in terms of further cost reductions. For example, most contemporary short- and medium-haul air transport is carried on with aircraft in the Boeing 727, Boeing 737, McDonnel-Douglas DC-9 and British Aerospace 1-11 families. These aircraft use engine technology (the Pratt and Whitney JT-8D series and the Rolls-Royce Spey) dating from the late 1950s in its initial design. The advent of the planned 757,767 and A310 families in the period from 1982 onward (*see* Sweetman (1979)) will bring high by-pass turbo-fan engine technology to medium-sized short/medium-haul markets. In addition to further improvements in engine availability, manufacturers are now actively looking at the possibility of stretching their wide-bodied types, with Boeing considering a stretch of the 747–200 and McDonnel-Douglas a variety of stretches of the DC-10. If these new large aircraft are eventually developed, they will give the industry the opportunity to gain further aircraft-size economies. Finally, and in the longer term, there are aerodynamic and structural weight improvements to be considered, with such concepts as the greater use of carbon fibre materials in aircraft structures.

Despite the certainty of technology providing further cost reductions, it is probably wrong to exaggerate the importance which these will have. The main reductions in operating costs have come with the changeover from piston-engined aircraft to jets. Table 2.10 presents data from 1967, the last year that piston-engined, turbo-prop and jet types were all being operated in substantial numbers by the U.S. trunk airlines. (The use of purely U.S. statistics is necessary because the American industry provides the only publicly-available source of aircraft operating cost data. However, this does not affect the wider validity of the conclusions.)

The relevant comparison in the Table is that between the 707–320C and 727–100 as jet-powered aircraft and the DC-6 and DC-7 as piston-engined planes. The comparison shows that seat-mile costs for the jets were very much below those of the aircraft they were replacing, with, in the case of the 707 compared with the DC-7, the reduction being of the order of 120 per cent.

Table 2.10. Aircraft Operating Costs Reported by U.S. Trunk Airlines to Civil Aeronautics Board, 1967. U.S. Dollars per block hour (Passenger Services)

	707-320C	727-100	L-188 (Electra)	V-700 (Viscount)	DC-6	DC-7/7B
Flying Operations						
Crew	116·91	124·28	104·07	98·37	101·95	97·35
Fuel and oil	172·12	130·53	66·69	43·74	66·31	78·50
Insurance	14·36	11·43	3·61	0·66	0·57	1·69
Other flight operations costs	0·43	0·30	0·34	0·17	0·22	0·0
Sub-total	303·81	266·54	174·71	142·93	169·05	177·54
Maintenance—flight equipment						
Airframe and other	28·04	47·00	57·65	37·43	38·44	44·07
Engine	35·77	60·60	48·13	9·18	32·69	65·82
Burden of maintenance overheads	30·23	59·29	53·31	53·43	64·37	74·01
Sub-total	94·03	166·89	159·09	100·67	135·50	183·91
Depreciation and rentals	136·39	114·38	52·08	29·19	2·51	4·00
Total direct expense per block hour ($)	534·23	547·8	385·88	272·79	307·06	365·45
Average stage (miles)	775	505	203	187	171	215
Average seats in aircraft	124·1	96·5	82·1	46	67·6	77
Average block-to-block speed	383	369	233	191	180	197
Cost of fuel (c per U.S. gal)	9·068	9·574	9·622	10·19	14·977	13·65
Total direct cost per aircraft mile ($)	1·44	1·54	1·73	1·50	1·96	1·98
Total direct cost per available ton-mile (c)	6·707	12·144	17·722	32·0	24·78	21·306
Total direct cost per available seat-mile (c)	1·166	1·597	2·102	3·273	2·903	2·574

Source: CAB Aircraft Operating Cost and Performance Reports.

The changeover from narrow-bodied to wide-bodied jets which has taken place during the 1970s has brought further reductions in available operating costs. For example, in the data given in Table 2.8, the comparison between the wide-bodied B747 and the narrow-bodied 707–320C shows the former giving an operating cost reduction of around 40 per cent. However, in this case the reductions have been made up to a considerable degree by means of increased aircraft size, and many thin routes have not had the traffic potential to allow for the profitable exploitation of wide-bodied economies.

In the future, there is widespread agreement[40] that we shall see no more of the 'overnight' cost reductions which jets and then wide-bodied aircraft brought. Instead, the reductions which technology can offer—which in any case will be smaller than those of the halcyon days of the 1960s—will be spread over periods of years as relatively small advances in different areas are introduced.

If an argument can be produced that the future is less promising than the past as far as cost savings from technological innovation are concerned, then a similar, but even stronger case can be made out for the future of oil prices. As has been noted, the 1970s saw a transformation in the world oil market. A continuing increase in demand was met only by exploitation of remote and expensive sources of supply. The growing realization of the need to secure an adequate return from oil before supplies are exhausted contributed to a cartelization of the large part of the market through the Organization of Petroleum Exporting Countries. These developments alone will be sufficient to ensure that most certainly there will not be any reduction in the price of fuel in the future, with the most likely result being further sharp price increases in real terms.

In the longer term, however, even more serious possibilities begin to appear. Until now, the aviation industry at least has been fortunate that the opening up of new oil fields has allowed the supply of oil to keep pace with expanding demand. Such a situation cannot continue for ever. As time goes by there will be increasing problems from the exhaustion of established oil-fields. If world demand for oil continues, a day must eventually come when supply and demand become permanently out-of-balance as 'natural' demand comes into conflict with a falling supply. In such a situation, a new market equilibrium will only be found by very substantial price increases which could make those of the 1970s pale into comparative insignificance.

No one in the aviation industry presumably would dispute that such a day will eventually arrive, unless in the meantime some really viable alternative fuel should become available. However, there is the greatest disagreement as to the likely time ahead that it will happen. Optimists[41]

---

40 *See*, for example, Barfield (1977), p. 16.   **41** For example, McFadzean (1978).

point to the fact that similar scare stories have been about since the 1950s. Predictions that disaster is looming because the world only has a few years' supply at forecast consumption rates and known reserves have always been proved wrong by the discovery and exploitation of new fields. Such a situation can be held to prevail today. New fields such as Britain's North Sea—and the technology developed for them—offer possibilities of extracting what are believed to be immense deposits of oil in ideal geological structures on the continental shelves around our land masses. Also, developing technology will allow for a fuller exploitation of the reserves which are discovered. The pessimistic viewpoint, on the other hand, is now suggesting the period as soon as the middle 1990s as the time when significant fuel shortages will begin to arise. Even before then, large price increases will occur due to a growing divergence between supply and demand as a result of production cutbacks by the OPEC countries,[42] and periods of political instability in major producing countries.

Whenever the time of shortage of oil does arrive, the position of the aviation industry in securing adequate supplies may not be entirely hopeless. Air transport uses a cut of the crude oil barrel for which there is only one major competitor—domestic central heating. It is also possible technically for oil companies to vary the cracking process so that the oil which is available is refined to produce a greater proportion of light fuels rather than heavier diesel and motor fuels. However, what is certain is that if aviation is to secure a large proportion of such fuel as is available, it will only do so by paying prices which are higher than can be obtained by the producing countries and the oil companies in selling to competing users. Therefore, the time of oil shortage will be one of sharply rising aviation fuel prices in real terms.

An alternative possibility to a continued reliance on natural crude oil supplies is, of course, to look to different fuels where supply shortages are not likely to occur. There are very large deposits of oil shales and coal around the world which can be processed in such a way as to augment the world's supplies of oil. However, the costs of such extraction will only be worthwhile if natural oil prices reach a high level, and so coal and shale do not offer more than a partial solution to the industry's eventual problem of chronically-high fuel prices. It may therefore be that the time may be approaching when the costs of research into different methods of aviation propulsion may be worthwhile. Here, the use of hydrogen is likely to be considered most seriously. Hydrogen is available in limitless supply, burns efficiently and without the pollution problems of conventional fossil fuels. However, it too brings problems with the low temperatures at which it must be stored and handled, and because of its low density.

As an overall conclusion to a discussion of fuel prices and their influence on the costs of air transport, it can be said with certainty that, whilst fuel prices

42 *See* Bailey (1977).

have been a major factor in the reduction of operating costs in the past, their effect from now on will be precisely the opposite. In the future, fuel prices will rise a great deal in real terms. The high proportion of airline costs now made up by fuel (Table 2.11) will mean that fuel will have a substantial impact on airline unit costs.

Table 2.11. Proportion of Airline Costs made up by Labour and Fuel expenses 1978–79. Sample of Scheduled Airlines

Airline	Percentage of total costs made up by labour expenses	Percentage of total costs made up by fuel expenses
1. Air Canada	39	20
2. Air New Zealand	34	15
3. British Airways	34	18
4. Eastern	40	24
5. Finnair	29	17
6. Pan American	38	19

Source: Airline Annual Reports.

With the question of subsidization of the airline industry, again the outlook is unpromising from the carrier's viewpoint. During the 1970s, a trend grew up for governments to become unwilling to accept the correctness of subsidies for such things as airport and air traffic control provision, or of subsidization of the workings of unprofitable airlines.[43] Reasons given for this have included the need to keep down taxation and to limit government spending for macro-economic reasons. Also, it is seen as unfair that taxation revenue obtained from most members of a population should be used to subsidize aviation which in most countries is still only used by a minority. Whatever the validity of such arguments, the effect of them has been clear-cut. Airport and air navigation charges are amongst the fastest rising cost items for all airlines. Only the comparatively small proportion of total costs made up by them has so far reduced the impact of the increases on unit cost levels. However, this impact will rise as such charges assume a greater relative importance. This will be particularly so if airport operators see congestion pricing as a way of attempting to alleviate the worst excesses of airport capacity shortages[44] whilst raising further revenue.

Finally with labour and its future impact on cost levels, it is first of all to the industry's advantage that it is unlikely to have difficulties with the supply of labour. Aviation has always been an attractive industry within which to work, whilst the problem of structural unemployment will mean that a substantial pool of labour will be available to the industry. However,

---

43 *See* Boyd-Carpenter (1975).   **44** *See* Little and McCleod (1972).

problems are likely to arise with both the quality and the price of labour which will have an impact on future costs.

With quality, many airlines are now facing up to the certainty of shortages of skilled labour during the next few years, particularly with engineers. The combination of the peak in retirement as the post-war generation of recruits reaches retiring age and the expansion in fleet size anticipated by almost all airlines[45] are placing acute pressures on staff recruitment and training. Qualified and experienced personnel can of course only be produced after many years. The result of the shortages which are going to occur will be to force up the price of skilled labour as airlines vie with one another to recruit such staff as are available.

However, even with the question of unskilled labour, the outlook is by no means hopeful. Airports have always proved suitable places for the development of intensive trade unionism. This has been due to the large numbers of people working in close proximity and the power possessed by many groups within airlines to shut down operations. The future is likely to see a further strengthening of the bargaining power of labour with the twin effects of rising wage rates and also—increasingly important—pressure by unions for further recruitment as traffic increases. This will reduce the value of the option that airlines have always had in the past to balance rising wage rates with improving labour productivity.

The combination of future trends in the areas of technology, fuel, user charges for airport and air navigation facilities and labour costs permit only a pessimistic conclusion to be drawn on airline unit costs. There are few grounds for expecting past favourable trends in costs to continue, with a much greater likelihood of aviation costs rising as fast or even faster than the general trend in retail prices.

Rising cost levels overall, therefore, are likely to mean that even more attention will need to be given in the future to the detail of *product design* as a way of taking the broad trend of costs available to the industry and translating these into specific products and prices paid by customers. Here, at least, there are grounds for optimism. We shall see in Section 9.1.1 that the post-war period has been notable for the development of new air transport products, particularly those based on the planeload charter and the exploitation of cheaply-available seats on scheduled services. The most important way in which the aviation industry will be able to reduce the impact of rising operating costs on demand will be to ensure that such costs as are incurred are used for the kinds of product which most nearly match consumer needs. If this can be done successfully a further exploitation of potential demand in the leisure segment of the market may still be possible, despite the certainty that the lowering of

---

45 Of all the large number of aircraft ordered in recent years, only approximately 30 per cent are expected to replace pre-existing capacity. The remainder are for capacity expansion.

operating costs will not be available as it has been in the past to assist such a process.

2. Trends in Air Travel Market Potential

Future costs and therefore prices of air travel clearly will be one set of factors influencing demand. However, demand will also be strongly affected by trends in the marketplace, with these divisible into two. Firstly, there will be trends in absolute demand in terms of the numbers of potential travellers and their ideal travel patterns. Secondly, there is the much more difficult area of the relationship between this potential demand and the services and prices which airlines will make available. This latter point will bring us into discussion of price elasticities for air transport, in each of the major demand segments of business, leisure and personal travellers. It is an important conceptual criticism that past attempts at analysis have seldom examined demand by market segment, despite the sound theoretical reasons for expecting business and leisure travel to have different demand characteristics.

A. Business Travel Demand

With the future of business travel demand, clearly there is likely to be a correlation between such demand and the growth of world trade. The chief factors which will cause an increase in air travel costs—particularly rising fuel prices—will also have an effect on activity in the world economy. Increasing fuel prices could thus have an impact both on the costs and on the market potential of the aviation industry, with both these aspects needing to be the subject of airline concern for the future.

Even within general trends in costs and prices, there are grounds for expecting a slowdown in the rate of increase of business travel relative to the rate of economic growth. This is because of improvements in communications technology.

Aviation has by no means been alone in making substantial technological progress during the post-war period, with the communications industry also being notable in this respect. Reliable long-distance telephone links, the development of Telex services and now the technology available for automated document transmission and audio-visual telephone communication are all important here. There is now the suggestion that the currently high levels of business travel by air are no more than a transient phase before a communications revolution obviates the need for a significant proportion of it.

As another factor relating to business travel demand, we have seen how business travel has commonly been regarded as a perk by executives and an indicator of corporate status. However, there are now signs that the increasing hassles associated with air travel, particularly with respect to airport handling, are reducing this aspect of the appeal of business travel, or at least ensuring that, if it does exist in anything like its old form, it soon disappears as travellers become fully experienced.

There are, of course, counterbalancing arguments which can be made to a viewpoint that the future will see a slower growth in business travel. To many executives, there can be no substitute for face-to-face discussions; and communications technology, however good, provides no opportunities for the offer of business-related entertainment. For east–west communications over long distances, time-zone differences mean that the periods available for contact will be very short without foreign travel. Finally, whatever current trends may indicate, travel is likely to remain an important aspect of job satisfaction for many people.

As an overall conclusion, a reasonable view would be that the immediate future will not see any decline in the actual numbers of business travellers. Indeed current airline marketing efforts to generate new business travel[46] are likely to lead to a further expansion in demand. However, the advances in communications technology and the decreasing appeal of air travel may eventually depress growth rates below the levels which might otherwise have been expected from past patterns of business travel growth compared with world trade. An additional factor here may also be that an increasing proportion of business travellers may use air taxi and executive aircraft, and thereby come outside the traditional areas of scheduled airline activity.

B. Leisure Travel Demand

The future of leisure potential is, if anything, even more uncertain than that of business travel. Many factors can be put forward suggesting a likelihood of continuing strong growth in the leisure segment. For example, increasing leisure time and longer holidays have been a feature of almost all industrialized countries in the post-war period. This trend will be continued by the industrial impact of micro-processors. Also, lengthening life expectancies, improving health and earlier retirement are making the post-retirement period both longer and more active for many. This, in combination with improved pension arrangements and the development of the 'visiting relations' subsegment of demand, are suggesting the post-retirement period as an increasingly promising one from the point of view of airline marketing. Again, changing family and social structures in many countries during the 1960s and 70s have meant a pronounced fall in the birth-rate. This is reducing to a minimum those in the categories of parents with very young children and therefore in consequence a low trip generation rate.

Despite the significance of these social and demographic trends, a full consideration of the future of leisure demand must focus on the questions

---

46 *See* Section 7.2.2.

of the relationships between leisure demand, income levels of consumers and the price of air travel. All the evidence so far available confirms the theoretical view discussed earlier that demand for air travel from leisure consumers is highly income-elastic. Several estimates[47] suggest that this elasticity may be around 2·0. Therefore, should economic growth continue to give expanding personal incomes, air travel is one of the items on which such increments of income will be spent. It is becoming clear, too, that once people have sampled the pleasures of an air-based holiday, they are most anxious to continue them, and that therefore a high income elasticity is not so noticeable for the situation of falling real incomes. It does seem that consumers will forgo many other items before abandoning their annual air holiday, once an initial price reduction or income gain has brought them into the market. For example, in the U.K. during the recession in business travel of 1975 the demand for leisure air travel actually increased (Table 2.2), an increase only partly explained by the problems which had been experienced in the previous year. This is an encouraging aspect for future discussion of leisure air travel demand relative to income levels, and the fact that in most countries of the world the majority of the population do not[48,49] travel by air is indicative of a very large market potential which rising income levels should make available to the airline industry, and which it should then retain to a large degree even in the event of subsequent recession.[50] There are many areas of the world where it is reasonable to anticipate rising real incomes over the next few years. These include countries with substantial natural resource deposits and also the countries of South-East Asia with their huge resources of labour and entrepreneurial talent. Both these situations will give rise to large new air travel markets.

There are only three factors which can be put forward as indicating a limit to potential leisure travel demand by air. The first of these is the problem of tourism saturation of leisure facilities. Many people begin the practice of air holidays to reach exotic, out-of-the way destinations, and perhaps also because air travel brings with it social status gains. It is a chronic problem of the tourism industry that improving the accessibility of a location by airport and road investment may bring in such crowds of visitors that all are eventually denied the opportunities for enjoyment that they are seeking. If this happens it may then be that the tourism location

47 Wheatcroft (1978), Table 4A.
48 As one example, it has been calculated that in a country as economically developed as France, 93 per cent of the population currently do not make an air trip during an average year.
49 *See* R. Shaw (1979).
50 However, even here, there may be an effect of people coming to spend more on home-based entertainments, as these can be enjoyed without the problems and expense of travel. *See* Waddington (1978).

enters a decline. This may be happening now as far as European visitors to Spain are concerned. However, whilst tourism saturation of an area may have important consequences for its economy, it is unlikely in itself to affect the total amount of leisure air travel undertaken. There is a clear trend for tourists always to move to new and more desirable locations. Indeed at the time of writing the relative decline in Southern Europe is being matched by the growth of North America as a holiday destination.

A factor which it has been suggested will affect the future of travel demand in visiting-relations markets is that inevitably such markets are transient. The main VR markets of recent years have been those which have sprung up following the substantial population migrations of the twentieth century, and especially those of the post-World-War-II period. Now, however, many governments are trying to control immigration because of the social and political consequences which it brings. In markets where this control has been achieved, VR travel is coming increasingly to consist of ageing parents visiting their children and grandchildren. The implication is that, as the years go by, travel potential will fall. There are already signs of stagnation in the first of the main air transport VFR markets—that of Irish emigrants to the U.S.A. It seems a reasonable assumption that a similar trend will eventually appear in the longer-established markets such as those between the U.K. and Canada and Australia. However, in the latter two cases at least, current attempts to develop the home tourism industry may mean that holidaymakers will counterbalance any decline in visiting-friends-and-relations traffic.

With the specific question of the future of the holiday market, *accommodation* is likely to be a constraint in some areas. The market for holiday air travel only exists as a result of sufficient accommodation being available in tourism destinations to cater for expanding numbers of visitors. There have already been suggestions from the British Tourist Authority[51] that a shortfall in investment in budget-class accommodation may inhibit tourism growth. It is also known that countries which climatically might be suitable for tourism development are being prevented from achieving their potential by a lack of suitable tourism hotels. However, structural unemployment is now a problem, and tourism is a comparatively labour-intensive activity. It is therefore likely that requests for investment funds by the tourism industry will be comparatively successful in most Western countries at least. Even so, there may be periods when the growth of travel demand and the provision of accommodation become temporarily out-of-step.

Finally with the question of future potential of leisure air travel, we must come on to the most important constaint of all—the likely relationship between leisure travel demand and contemporary air travel prices. We

51 *See Travel Trade Gazette*, 4 May 1979.

have already seen in the last section that the future trend in air travel costs is likely to be quite different from the past, with these costs rising as fast—or even faster—than the general trend in retail prices. This makes the question of the price elasticity of demand for leisure travel one of the crucial deciding factors in the future of market potential.

Investigations of price elasticities do, of course, present fundamental analytical problems, and there has been very large range in the elasticity estimates produced.[52] Indeed, as has been noted, many of the past studies of elasticities[53] are of little use in that they fail to make the basic distinction of separate calculations for the business and leisure segments of the market. However, if there is a consensus to be drawn from the extensive amount of work undertaken in this area in recent years, it is that a good measure of price responsiveness can be isolated with leisure air travel demand (*see* Taplin, 1980). If this is true, it will mean that future air travel prices may have a significant effect in constraining demand growth in countries where incomes do not increase quickly enough to counterbalance rising prices.

There are, of course, arguments which can be put forward against such a view. In particular, all air transport demand studies have inevitably been based on past data. It is a widely-made criticism that the post-war period has seen an under-supply into the market-place of the kinds of low-cost/low-priced services which can best meet the needs of the leisure traveller. Equally, we will note in Section 4.3 that one of the consequences of the trend towards reduced regulation during the 1970s has been that airlines have gained and used an increasing freedom to innovate with new product types. The result has been that substantial falls in air fares to leisure travellers have occurred, in return for their acceptance of product types such as Skytrain, charter and APEX. It is likely that this process of product innovation will continue, reducing the impact of any overall trend towards higher operating costs. If it does, it may make air travel more of a bargain in the eyes of the consumer, with therefore an increased willingness to purchase. Or again, many consumer products in their life cycle go through a period of substantial price elasticity early in their development, when their possession is regarded as a pure luxury. Later, however, when the product is widely consumed, it is remarkable to note the number of once-luxuries which are now regarded as being necessities by the majority of Western households. For example, it is now unlikely that even substantial price rises will affect the total demand for televisions or vacuum cleaners, although such price rises may give rise to movements within the market as consumers switch from high-quality to lower-quality products.

It is this latter point which gives us the key to a balanced judgement on the effect of prices on the future of leisure travel demand. Air travel is in

---

52 *See* De Neufville (1976), p. 49.   **53** For example, Mutti and Murai (1977).

the process of achieving such a grip on the buying habits of some sectors of the world's population that only very large price rises indeed—probably well beyond the general level of inflation—will have the effect of reducing substantially the total number of leisure air journeys undertaken. More probable is a situation where moderate price increases in real terms will cause readjustments within the market, in that they will lead to a greater emphasis on the use of more basic air travel products. This fact will be very important in the many economies of the Western World, where the 1980s now seem to offer the likelihood of only a slow growth in real incomes.

3. The Provision of Air Transport Services

Future air travel prices and market potential will decide maximum possible demand for the airline industry. It is hoped that enough has been said to emphasize that a large demand will continue to be available in spite of cost and price increases. However, of course, as in any transport industry, supply and demand are intimately linked. Actual future demand will not be decided by maximum possible demand, but rather by the combination of this demand and the supply which is offered.

In most industries, of course, the problem of a shortfall in meeting demand does not exist. If demand potential is there, entrepreneurs can be expected to recognize the opportunities for profit, and to build up production until supply and demand are in equilibrium. In aviation, such considerations only apply to the aircraft manufacturing and airline sectors of the industry. Increasingly they do not apply to the sectors concerned with the provision of air traffic control facilities, or of airports.

With air traffic control, there must be doubts as to the ability of the ATC systems in some of the world's busiest aviation markets to cope with forecast increases in air traffic. These doubts spring from the technical complexity of doing so, with advances such as computerization only likely to alleviate partially the problems of handling air traffic in tightly congested situations. Also there are problems in co-operation in what inevitably needs to be internationally-based decision-making. Finally, at the time of writing there is growing militancy of ATC officers in some countries with the realization by them of the immense industrial power which they have. All these factors may limit the effectiveness of ATC systems in the future.

With airports, it is very much the case that the future will be very different from the past. The industry can by no means be certain that airport capacity will be provided in sufficient amounts to enable it to operate at the scale which it might choose were it to be free of airport constraints. The land requirements of airports; the continuance, though at a lower level, of airport noise nuisance; and the fact that the industry's traffic base is now so large that even quite small percentage increases in traffic can be expected to give huge requirements in the physical expansion of airport sites; these may all combine to give a serious shortfall in airport capacity. At worst, such shortages could become a permanent feature, seriously limiting growth potential. Even at best, it is likely that there will be problems of airport development lagging behind capacity needs, with short-term penalties of congestion and increased operating costs.

2.8.3 Conclusion on the Future of the Market

An overall conclusion as to the future of market growth must be that we have now reached an important stage in the development of the aviation industry's markets. Several trends would indicate a large market potential for the future, especially of leisure travel. These trends include the consumer appeal of air travel, increased leisure time, longer and more prosperous retirement periods and the development of aircraft technology and airline products capable of making mass travel a reality. However, equally, there are now threats to this potential especially in the longer term. Resource constraints particularly relating to fuel will mean cost pressures on the industry such as it has never faced before. These may also have a depressive effect on the world economy as a whole and slow down growth in real incomes in some countries. (However, this trend will be counterbalanced to some extent by faster growth of incomes in countries fortunate enough to have indigenous natural resources.) Industrial militancy, pressure on air traffic control systems and the long-term threat of widespread shortages of airport capacity may all mean that the industry faces difficulties in offering the kinds of quality of product and prices which will fully allow for the exploitation of market potential. Finally, tourism saturation may come to affect many tourism-receiving areas.

The author's view is that, despite the short-term pressures and threats, we can expect a strong pattern of growth to persist through at least the next twenty years, though with occasional ups and downs through fluctuations in the world economy. Beyond the end of the century, however, the prospects become more uncertain. It could be that we shall then be moving into a world dominated by the twin factors of advanced electronic technology[54] and chronic and growing resources shortages. If this happened, it would mean a transformation in the world economy which could not fail to have repercussions on the airline industry and its markets. Such long-term possibilities cannot be disregarded even now, bearing in mind the operating lives of, say, airport facilities and the new aircraft families which are now being planned.

In this chapter we have now considered the structure of the air transport industry's markets, both at the present time and in the future. This, therefore, completes the study of the first stage of the application of the marketing model to the aviation industry.

---

54 See Gershuny (1978) for a discussion of this post-industrial society.

3 Airline Objectives and Corporate Strategies

In Chapter 1, we saw that, following investigation of the market, the next phase in the application of marketing theory to business was for the firm to define its objectives and the corporate strategy to be pursued in order to ensure that these objectives are met. In this chapter, therefore, we shall continue to apply the theory to the airline industry by looking at some of the principles which should be considered by airlines in the formulation of objectives and in the definition of strategy. We shall also need to bring in material covering the structure of the air transport business, and the wider economic and social implications of airline activity, as both these aspects should be important in decisions regarding strategies.

As we go through this material, it will become clear to those who are reading the book from the point of view of a purely domestic carrier, that their airline may not have to consider the same range of effects as an international airline. However, it is still hoped that the chapter will be seen as providing useful background information. Indeed, recent trends for formerly domestic airlines to seek an international role—the United States and Australian examples are very good illustrations—mean that there are fewer and fewer carriers which can operate without considering the international implications of their activities.

In the chapter we begin by looking briefly at the structure of civil aviation in system terms. Then more detailed material is included specifically on the structure of the airline sector of the industry. Moving on from this, we look at the implications of airline activity for other members of the system, and at the broad range of possible objectives open to airlines. In a final section, we consider the different families of strategy available to airline managements. If the chapter is successful, it will then leave the reader with at least an initial feel for the complexities of correct strategy definition in aviation.

3.1 The Civil Aviation System

As Fig. 3.1 shows, civil aviation comprises at least five interconnected

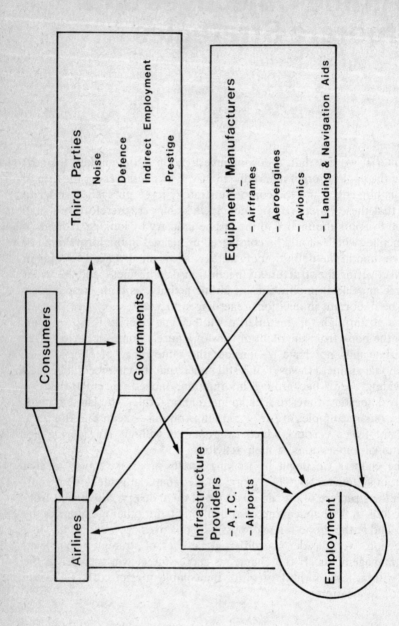

Figure 3.1 The Civil Aviation System

groups of individuals and organizations, each with a vital interest in the workings of the industry.[1] We must first of all look at these groups:

1. Airlines

The principle interest of this book is with airlines. However, it must be emphasized that we must involve ourselves also with the consequences of the activities of airlines for others in the civil aviation system.

2. Airports and Providers of Air Traffic Control Facilities

Unlike some transport undertakings—for example, railways—airlines have confined themselves to the running of vehicles. For sound reasons, airport facilities have mostly been the responsibility of national or local government. The operation of the airlines' 'track'—controlled airspace—has again been accepted as a government task with a strong element of intergovernmental co-operation. It is quite wrong for airlines to formulate marketing policies which ignore the implications of such policies for the airports and A.T.C. This is because the lead times for new investment by airlines are usually comparatively short, whereas for air traffic control, and especially airport operators, lead times will extend to periods of several years or even decades before plans can be brought to fruition.

3. Equipment Manufacturers

Today, production of equipment for the airline industry is one of the world's leading manufacturing industries. The producers of airframes and aeroengines and their subcontractors, the engineering and construction firms involved in airport development and the electronics and avionics producers concerned with air traffic control and air navigation together make up a formidable grouping, the fortunes of which are entirely dependent on aviation.

4. Consumers

Consumers of air transport clearly have an interest in the activities of the industry. They include both air passengers and the shippers of air freight. Also, in terms of the views to be represented, attention should be given to *potential* consumers. These people have a desire to use airline services, and are willing to pay a reasonable price in order to do so. However, the correct type of product has yet to be made available for them.

5. Third Parties

It has been stated that 'transport is the pre-eminent example of an external cost industry'.[2] Air transport is no exception to this general rule. Aviation

1 *See* Ellison and Stafford (1974) for a discussion of these interrelationships.
2 Thomson (1974), p. 91.

can have an effect, both good and bad, on large numbers of people and organizations which may have no direct concern with it, and which we shall therefore refer to as Third Parties. Aircraft noise nuisance has been an example of such an indirect effect since the advent of jet propulsion in the 1950s. Other indirect effects can include those on a country's balance of payments, and employment implications stemming from the spending of incomes by employees of airlines, infrastructure providers and equipment manufacturers. A country's inhabitants may find their national security enhanced by aviation, whilst some nations apparently feel an important gain in prestige can come from it.

Given the interplay of forces at work, it is naïve to expect that the correct setting of airline marketing objectives will be either simple or straightforward. This point can be made even clearer by looking at the structure of the airline sector of the industry more fully, and considering in more detail the economic and social implications which result from its activities.

3.2 Structure of the Airline Industry

Describing the structure of any industry is a difficult problem. One has to decide on the measures which provide the most appropriate summary, from a large number of possible indicators. However, a good deal of data on an industry can usually be derived from consideration of total output, regional variations in output, and output and financial performance of participating firms.

3.2.1 The Patterns of Growth

In total output, air transport still exhibits some of the characteristics of an infant industry. It is still less than eighty years since the first aeroplane flew, and less than forty since the widespread inception of modern commercial air services in the period following the Second World War. In common with most industries at an early stage of development, aviation has shown rapid *growth*, with output increasing by nearly twenty times during the past twentyfive years, as shown in Table 3.1. Again indicative of an early development phase, expansion has been highly *erratic* through time.

In addition to erratic growth through time, such growth has been *uneven in its geographical distribution*. The earliest market to show substantial development was that of the United States. Still, over 40 per cent of all scheduled tonne-kilometres are performed by U.S.-based airlines, as shown in Table 3.2. However, in recent years, patterns of growth have begun to change. There has been slower growth in the long-established markets of the U.S. and to a lesser extent, Europe. Areas of fast expansion have been the grouping of countries in Asia and the Pacific, and those of

Table 3.1. Growth in Output of the Civil Aviation Industry Operations of IATA Member Airlines

Passengers carried on scheduled services	
Year	millions
1950	22
1955	68
1960	106
1965	177
1970	312
1975	436

Source: International Air Transport Association, *World Air Transport Statistics.*

the Middle East. This has resulted in the proportion of the world market held by airlines from these countries increasing. The market share of European nations has remained more or less constant and the United States has begun to experience a decline in the proportion of industry output which it holds.

3.2.2 Industry Participants

The structure of the airline industry regarding its participating airlines is one of intense *concentration*. More than 40 per cent of total output is provided by only eighteen airlines, as shown in Table 3.3. Of these airlines, nine are accounted for by the *United States trunk airlines*, which, with two others (Continental Airlines and Western Airlines), form a distinct industry grouping. These carriers are all privately-owned and therefore presumably rely on profitability for their continued existence. As a further grouping, the *U.S. regional carriers* can be distinguished, although one of these, USAir, is in fact one of the world's largest airlines and bigger then some of the trunks. The regional carriers are again independently owned, though even here the beginnings of governmental involvement can be seen with the subsidies which are still paid to some of them for maintaining 'social' services on unremunerative routes.

Such state involvement becomes more pronounced with the next grouping of *national airlines of countries other than the U.S.A.* Outside the United States there has been a tendency for scheduled air services to become concentrated within one airline, recognized as a national flag-carrier. Such airlines are almost all either wholly-owned by governments, or have a majority state shareholding. Indeed, on examination of Table 3.4, it is difficult to find names of world airlines which are not included in it. Such airlines as Swissair (25 per cent state ownership) and the Brazilian carrier V.A.R.I.G. (no direct government shareholding) provide rare examples of national carriers without a majority state interest.

Table 3.2. Regional percentage distribution of total tonne-kilometres performed on scheduled services, 1970–1979. (The figures shown for each region include all scheduled operations of airlines of ICAO Contracting States registered in the region)

Years	ICAO World	North America*	Europe	Asia and Pacific	Latin America and Caribbean	Middle East	Africa
All services							
1970	100	50·0	35·0	7·8	3·8	1·5	1·9
1971	100	48·0	36·0	8·1	4·1	1·7	2·1
1972	100	47·6	35·9	8·4	4·4	1·7	2·0
1973	100	46·2	36·1	9·8	4·0	1·9	2·0
1974	100	44·1	36·4	10·7	4·4	2·1	2·3
1975	100	41·6	36·8	12·1	4·7	2·3	2·5
1976	100	41·1	36·5	12·4	4·8	2·7	2·5
1977	100	40·8	35·7	13·0	5·0	3·0	2·5
1978	100	41·0	35·0	13·5	4·9	3·1	2·5
1979	100	40·4	34·6	14·3	5·2	3·0	2·5
International							
1970	100	31·3	44·2	11·2	6·1	3·4	3·8
1971	100	29·7	44·7	11·6	5·9	4·0	4·1
1972	100	29·1	44·7	12·6	5·7	4·0	3·8
1973	100	26·6	44·9	15·0	5·7	4·0	3·8
1974	100	24·4	44·3	16·4	6·4	4·3	4·2
1975	100	22·1	43·5	18·7	6·6	4·6	4·5
1976	100	21·2	43·0	19·6	6·4	5·3	4·5
1977	100	20·8	42·7	19·9	6·6	5·7	4·3
1978	100	20·5	42·4	20·6	6·6	5·6	4·3
1979	100	20·0	41·7	21·6	6·8	5·5	4·3
Domestic							
1970	100	62·3	28·9	5·6	2·3	0·2	0·7
1971	100	60·5	30·3	5·8	2·5	0·2	0·7
1972	100	61·4	29·7	5·4	2·5	0·3	0·7
1973	100	60·9	29·4	5·9	2·7	0·3	0·8
1974	100	59·2	30·2	6·4	3·0	0·3	0·9
1975	100	57·0	31·6	6·9	3·2	0·4	0·9
1976	100	57·3	31·2	6·5	3·5	0·6	0·9
1977	100	58·1	29·6	7·1	3·6	0·7	0·9
1978	100	59·2	28·4	7·2	3·5	0·8	0·9
1979	100	58·8	28·5	7·3	3·8	0·7	0·9

*Canada and United States only
Source: International Civil Aviation Organisation, *Annual Report* 1980.

With regard to a category of *other non-United States scheduled airlines*, it is notable only for the fact of emphasizing the extent to which industry development in particular countries has been concentrated in the hands of a single state-owned carrier. In some countries, a definite policy has been adopted of allowing a limited entry to a second scheduled airline on

Table 3.3. I.A.T.A. Member Airlines carrying more than 5m passengers, 1978

Airline	Passengers carried ($\times 10^3$)
1. United	41,292
2. Eastern	37,853
3. American	28,193
4. T.W.A.	19,895
5. British Airways	15,706
6. Iberia	13,598
7. Japan Airlines	12,303
8. Lufthansa	11,710
9. Braniff	11,551
10. Air Canada	11,038
11. Air France	10,056
12. Pan-American	8,803
13. Scandinavian Airlines	7,937
14. National	6,983
15. Alitalia	6,856
16. Saudia	6,268
17. Swissair	5,687
18. Mexicana	5,289
Total for 18 airlines	261,018

Source: I.A.T.A.: *World Air Transport Statistics.*

long-haul routes, C.P. Air (Canada), U.T.A. (France) and British Caledonian (U.K.) are examples of airlines which have benefitted from such a policy. However, with these exceptions, such additional entry as has been allowed has been restricted mostly to domestic and short-haul international operations.

Charter[3] airlines make up another grouping. Market participation has been granted to carriers for purely charter services by the United States, where the so-called Supplemental Airlines have developed on a mixture of civil charters and military contract work. Charter service has also been permitted in Europe, where a large number of charter airlines now operate. These are either subsidiaries of established scheduled airlines (for example British Airtours of British Airways and Condor of Lufthansa), or privately-owned independents. The independents often, in turn, have links with the major inclusive-tour holiday companies.

The final section of the industry can be classified as the *local service-/commuter/general aviation* sector. Again, this sector has seen its greatest

---

3 The largely artificial distinction between scheduled and charter operations is dealt with in Section 4.1.1.

Table 3.4. Major Scheduled Airlines with fifty per cent or more State Ownership

Airline	Proportion of state ownership (%)	Airline	Proportion of state ownership (%)
1. Aer Lingus	100	21. Thai International	100
2. Aero Mexico	100	22. Trans-Australian	100
3. Aerolineas Argentinas	100	23. Tunis Air	100
4. Air Algerie	100	24. THY-Turkey	99·9
5. Air India	100	25. Alitalia	99·0
6. Air Jamaica	100	26. Air France	98·93
7. Air New Zealand	100	27. Iberia	98·68
8. Alia	100	28. VASP	98·21
9. British Airways	100	29. El Al	98·0
10. Egyptair	100	30. Phillipines Airlines	92·0
11. Garuda	100	31. Sabena	90·0
12. Gulfair	100	32. Royal Air Maroc	89·84
13. Indian Airlines	100	33. Tunis Air	85·0
14. Kuwait Airways	100	34. Finnair	79·1
15. Olympic Airways	100	35. KLM	75·5
16. Qantas	100	36. Lufthansa	74·31
17. Saudia	100	37. Pakistan International	64·6
18. Singapore Airlines	100	38. Air Canada	50·0
19. South African Airways	100		
20. Tap-Air Portugal	100		

Source: Interavia, November 1980.

development in the United States, where services to small communities, and such general aviation activities as air taxi, corporate flying and pleasure flying, have all seen extensive development. However, now there are signs of fast growth in this sector in other regions as well, particularly Europe.

3.2.3 Industry Financial Performance

In terms of financial performance, aviation is notable for being one of the world's most unprofitable industries. Even in its best years—for example, the late 1960s—the scheduled sector has earned a net return of only around 4·5 per cent, whilst there have been periods—such as during 1974 and 1975—of very marginal financial performance, as shown in Table 3.5. Such financial performance, too, has by no means been uniform across the industry. Table 3.6—admittedly probably distorted because of differing accounting and taxation policies—shows that even in 1977, a comparatively good year by the industry's own depressing standards, some airlines still incurred heavy losses.

In the charter sector, where government regulation has sometimes allowed a reasonable freedom of entry and exit, profitability has again been poor. However, with ownership of charter carriers mostly in private hands, low profits have found their expression in acute instability. Bankruptcies such as that of Court Line Ltd. in the United Kingdom in 1974 have provided well-publicized illustrations of a tendency towards instability in the charter sector. This instability might have been greater still but for the support which some airlines have received from military contract work.

With such a financial performance, the micro-economic theory referred to earlier suggests that the industry should no longer exist. Factors of production should have moved away from it towards more lucrative employment. Exactly why industry profitability should have been so low is therefore an interesting subject for speculation.

As an initial consideration, air transport is, of course, by no means unique amongst industries undergoing rapid development in returning low profits. As noted earlier, many products do go through a cycle of an initial period of high profits where comparatively few firms have entered the market and where the product still has novelty value. Then a second stage follows, as many firms enter, attracted by the early profits. During this stage, profits may be forced down to low levels by the intense competition. Indeed, the further existence of the industry may only be sustained through investment capital attracted by the promise of future prosperity in an expanding market. Finally, a mature stage is reached. Here, growth in demand slows or even stagnates. The pressure of entry is reduced, and existing participants may come together either by merger or market collusion to reduce the extent of competition. Under such oligopolistic

Table 3.5. Operating Result of Scheduled Airlines of I.C.A.O. Contracting States 1974–79

	Operating revenue ($ \times 10^6$)	Operating expenses ($ \times 10^6$)	Operating profit ($ \times 10^6$)	(%)
1974	33,100	32,300	800	2·4
1975	38,300	37,600	700	1·9
1976	43,400	41,250	2,150	5·0
1977	50,350	47,700	2,650	5·2
1978	58,769	55,669	3,100	5·3
1979	70,500	69,800	700	1·0

Source: ICAO Bulletin, June 1980.

Table 3.6. Profitability Variations between Industry Participants, 1977. Sample of Scheduled Airlines

Airline	Revenues (U.S. $ millions)	Net result (U.S. $ millions)	% profitability (Net result as % of total revenue)
1. Aer Lingus (Eire)	122	11·3	9·3
2. Air India (India)	342	30·4	8·9
3. Air New Zealand (New Zealand)	227	5·4	1·9
4. Alia (Jordan)	91	0·7	0·8
5. American (U.S.A.)	2,277	82·0	3·6
6. Austrian (Austria)	150	1·2	0·8
7. Braniff (U.S.A.)	786	38·6	4·9
8. British Airways (U.K.)	2,093	32·6	1·6
9. British Caledonian (U.K.)	244	10·4	4·3
10. Japan Airlines (Japan)	1,660	31·7	1·9
11. KLM (Netherlands)	1,059	62·6	5·9
12. Lufthansa (West Germany)	1,690	17·1	1·0
13. Pakistan International (Pakistan)	269	11·5	4·3
14. Sabena (Belgium)	531	−28·0	−5·2
15. SAS (Scandinavia)	801	14·2	1·7
16. South African Airways (S. Africa)	404	−0·9	−0·2
17. THY (Turkey)	143	−17·8	−12·4
18. Trans-World Airlines (U.S.A.)	2,220	65·8	3·0
19. U.T.A. (France)	505	6·8	1·3
20. United (U.S.A.)	2,944	102·1	3·5

Source: ICAO Financial Data.

conditions, profits rise to more normal levels. Other industries have certainly shown this pattern in the past, though cynics would say that if the model is applicable to the airline business, its period of initial prosperity was brief indeed!

A second possible argument comes from the view that airlines can be sustained on a rate of earnings significantly lower than that which needs to be achieved in almost all other industries. This is because of the nature of their investment. They usually concentrate more than 90 per cent of their capital in vehicles, and pay out very little in fixed costs for terminals and track. These are mostly paid for as variable costs through the charges levied by airport operators and air traffic control agencies. The situation is different for, say, railways or indeed almost any manufacturing industry. Here, large amounts must be invested in fixed facilities which have few alternative uses and where scrap values will be negligible. A lender of capital will therefore face losses should a business fail. With airlines, however, investment is mainly in aircraft, which are produced in a standardized form by a small number of manufacturers. For the more popular types, resale may be very easy, and even profitable when demand for capacity is buoyant. Investment risks are therefore lower, and it may be that the industry will be able to attract investment on a long-term basis with a relatively low rate-of-return.

The arguments of 'infant industry' and 'low investment risk' may be put forward as theoretical viewpoints on poor airline profits. However, there are other explanations of low profitability which rely less on theory and more on the practicalities of the airline business. For example, it is known that many airlines do not operate to objectives based purely on profitability. For such carriers, high profits would not necessarily be regarded as indicating a satisfactory performance.[4] Also, scheduled airlines[5] have argued that they have been placed in a position where profits have been impossible on a sustained basis. This is because of the inequity of competition between highly-regulated scheduled airlines and the much-less-regulated charter sector. Finally, there have been many criticisms, particularly from academic economists,[6] that regulation has been responsible for low profits. Regulation reduces the areas available for competition. The result, so this argument suggests, is that airlines have tended to compete to an excessive extent in those aspects where the regulator has allowed competition to continue. This in turn has increased costs. It has therefore added to a general tendency for high costs in the industry, with these costs rising inexorably to swallow up almost all the guaranteed revenue that regulation has provided. This argument will be considered again in Section 4.2.2.

4 *See* Cabral (1978).   5 *See*, for example, Masefield (1977).
6 *See* Douglas and Miller (1974).

3.3 Aviation and the Economy

As was noted in Section 3.1, air transport can have important consequences for a national economy. In this section, it is our aim to amplify these economic effects with discussion of the impact of aviation on employment, economic development and the national balance of payments. Some of these effects will be most apparent for airlines which operate international services. However, even purely domestic airlines can be the cause of broadly-based consequences in an economy.

3.3.1 Aviation and Employment

The question of employment emerged during the 1970s as one of the fundamental issues of economic planning in the Western World. Depressed conditions in the world economy, technological innovation which allowed machinery to replace labour—something which is now proceeding quickly with the refinement of micro-processors—and the development of intense price-competition from the cheap-labour countries of South-East Asia, all combined to mean levels of unemployment unprecedented in the post-war period. Many forecasts are available which suggest that this high unemployment is by no means a transient phase. It is likely to persist—or worsen—in the future.

In this environment, the fact that aviation provides large amounts of employment must be the first of its important economic effects. In terms of direct airline employment, aviation remains relatively labour intensive in its input cost structures. Airlines are therefore large employers, with an estimated 2 to $2\frac{1}{2}$ million workers employed directly by the world's airlines. However, as was suggested in Section 3.1, indirect employment is also important. Jobs in infrastructure provision and equipment manufacture are of great consequence in many countries. The equipment category, especially, provides a vital component of the industrial structure of the United States and several European countries.

If a broad definition of indirect employment is taken, the significance of air transport becomes greater still, for aviation has been a catalyst of tourism. Tourism is now one of the world's most important economic activities,[7] with the promise that it will become the largest item in world trade before the end of the century. Employment in the tourism industry is known to be immense, with approximately $1\frac{1}{2}$ million jobs tourism-related in the United Kingdom alone.[8] Also, air transport has been important in developing trade and commercial links, with consequent employment gains resulting from increasing international trade. It has also a role in

---

7 *See* Boyd-Carpenter (1974), p. 181.   **8** Greater London Council (1978), p. 4.

promoting regional accessibility in remote areas, thereby spreading employment throughout an economy.

3.3.2 Aviation and the Balance of Payments

International aviation affects the balance-of-payments position of all countries. Positive aspects include air fares, with travel by a foreigner using the home airline meaning that the prices of the ticket becomes a favourable item in the trade balance, and the gains resulting from tourism. However, a balance-of-payments deficit will result from fares paid to foreign airlines and from the cash which is spent at overseas destinations by international travellers. Also important in balance-of-payments terms is the purchase of aviation equipment, where the U.S.A. has a large balance-of-payments surplus and almost every other country a deficit. With aviation fuel, the escalation in fuel prices during the 1970s has meant that the industry has been responsible for a growing negative trade contribution in all countries which are not self-sufficient in oil supplies.

Balance-of-payments effects of air transport are often so complex that a single event can produce both a positive and a negative impact. For example, in the summer of 1978, the United Kingdom share of traffic on the North Atlantic increased at the expense of United States airlines. Passengers carried by British Airways on this route were up by over 40 per cent compared with 1977 and the Laker Airways Ltd. Skytrain also made a successful initial impact. However, closer inspection of the low-fare regime which brought about the changes showed that generated traffic had come largely from the U.K. There was an increase of around 40 per cent in the numbers of travellers from the U.K. to the States, but only of 6 per cent in Americans visiting Britain. Therefore, although the new fares were hailed as a success from the British viewpoint, a detailed analysis might well have shown a negative overall impact on the U.K. economy.

3.4 Social Implications of Air Transport

Just as aviation has a wide economic impact, it brings with it important social effects as well. The implications for society of air transport come from the competition for resources which its existence implies and because of the social costs which result from its operations.

3.4.1 Resources for Air Transport

Aviation causes a competition for resources which can have broadly-based consequences in society. For example, high consumption of aviation fuel may cause increased prices in other markets such as that for domestic heating oils. Or again, for any airline dependent on state governments for investment funding, use of investment cash for airline finance means that it is not available for use elsewhere. Indeed, if it is used for the import of foreign aircraft, it is in a sense lost entirely to the national economy. Finally, and quite apart from the loss of amenity aspects dealt with below, aviation is a competitor for scarce land resources because of the size of modern airports. These tend to be located near to cities where land is a scarce commodity in the truest sense. Use of land for airports means that it is not available for the alternative of agricultural or industrial production or for residential/amenity development.

The fact that aviation is a voracious resource-consumer has been one of the factors which has led to a growing interest in recent years in the efficiency of resource utilization by airlines. We look in Chapter 8 at some of the attempts which have been made to measure such efficiency.

3.4.2 Social Costs of Aviation

Air transport brings with it many costs which are not borne by those causing them to be incurred, and which are therefore regarded by the economist as being 'social' costs. These may be in monetary form, as where an airline makes use of a loss-making airport which is in turn subsidized by local or national taxation. They may also be intangible, as for example with the widespread nuisance caused by the noise of jet aircraft. An especial feature of this latter cost is that it does not fall uniformly on all members of a society. It is very heavily concentrated on those living close to airports, who have a particular right to feel aggrieved should the nuisance arise after they have moved into an area.[9]

3.5 The Setting of Airline Corporate Objectives

The background material so far included on the structure and effects of the aviation industry will be important now in looking at the setting of corporate objectives for airlines. In doing this, it is first of all necessary to emphasize that standard books on corporate strategy[10] stress the point that even internally within the firm there are likely to be conflicts between different objectives, and that any overall decision will be a compromise. However, it is a feature of aviation that many airlines, besides having to contend with these internal conflicts, must expect that a very important interplay will develop between internal objectives and the external envi-

9 *See* Stratford (1975) for a full discussion of the problems of airport noise nuisance.
10 For example, Ansoff (1965), Hussey (1971).

ronment. We must therefore look at both the possible internal objectives for airlines, and also those which are likely to be affected by external factors.

3.5.1 Objectives and Internal Conflicts within the Firm

Despite the 'rules' of classic micro-economic theory, no firm should expect to pursue a set of entirely complementary, consistent objectives. As was noted in Section 1.2, an example of where a conflict is likely to occur is over the question of maximizing short-term profits, or sacrificing a proportion of profit in order to promote long-term market growth. Or again, the making of maximum short-term profit may coincide with a need to penetrate unstable markets, with therefore a risk of instability in the long term. A compromise may therefore be needed between profits and the perceived need for stability in order to protect investments.

Whatever the nature of the internal conflicts, all firms should eventually reach decisions on a set of objectives. These objectives ideally will be in written form to provide guidelines for market planning and efficiency measurement. For any privately-owned airline, objectives will presumably be based on long-term financial success, though even here wider social and political objectives may intervene. However, for a state-owned airline —and we have seen how important state ownership is in the airline business—then non-profit objectives may come to dominate a carrier's operations entirely. It is to these possible non-profit objectives which we now turn. We shall find that there are as many as nine areas where a compromise regarding profit maximizing behaviour may be needed.

3.5.2 Objectives and the External Environment

1. Maximization of Market Share

Despite the vital nature of profit for the continued existence of privately-owned airlines, and the fact that many state-owned airlines are given written objectives requiring acceptable profit levels, there are few airlines which can pursue profitability irrespective of market share considerations. Maximizination of market share must therefore be the first of the alternative objectives which must be included.

Very often, of course, an objective of market share maximization is entirely compatible with one of profit maximization. However, in many situations, an airline which pursues profit at the expense of market share—for example, by concentrating its efforts only on serving high-yielding business travellers—does so at its peril. For state-owned airlines, high market shares may be part of the written or implied objectives set by government. However, even for independent airlines, market shares assume particular importance because of the total control exercised by governments over market entry (*see* Section 4.2.1). Any carrier which does not meet national balance-of-payments and foreign-exchange requirements by obtaining a good share of the market runs the risk that the government will licence new carriers to compete with it, or even withdraw its route licences altogether. It may be that recent United States government decisions to allow increased international market participation to the domestic trunk carriers spring partly from a dissatisfaction with the performance in market-share terms of the pre-existing United States flag airlines. Particular comments have been made regarding Pan American World Airways' low market shares on routes such as those to the Netherlands.[11]

2. Satisfaction of Consumer Needs

To any marketing manager, an objective of maximizing market share will automatically be achieved by the satisfaction of consumer needs, and of course the two objectives are very closely related. However, there are sound reasons for treating them separately, as the question of consumer-need satisfaction has become a political as well as a marketing factor in the industry's operations. There are strong emotional aspects to the demand for air travel. Many people feel that they have a right to low-cost vacation travel, and to visit friends and relations in distant countries at prices they can afford. Consequently, the consumerist movement of recent years has affected the airline business probably more than any other industry. An airline which fails to ensure that all actual and potential demand segments are provided with services which match their requirements again runs the risk of new entry being allowed. One may guess that the enthusiasm with which the United Kingdom Civil Aviation Authority supported the Laker Skytrain concept between 1972 and 1977 (*see* Section 4.3.1) resulted partly from the fact that a segment of potential demand for a low-cost 'no-frills' service was believed to exist. This had not been satisfied by the carriers which had been allowed entry on the London–New York route prior to the Laker application. Other examples of governments placing pressure on airlines for political reasons to ensure the full satisfaction of demand have been numerous in recent years. The Australian situation of a large potential for ethnic travel between Australia and the countries of origin of migrants is a particularly good illustration.

3. Efficient Resource Utilization

The fact that air transport competes with other activities for resources, and that in aviation there are only limited amounts of the competition which might ensure the efficient use of resources, has meant that some countries

11 *See Air Transport World*, November 1977.

have now begun to set a requirement of efficiency for their airlines. Today, no airline, no matter how well protected from competition, can contemplate operating without consideration of the use made of scarce resources such as fuel.

4. Promotion of Commercial and Industrial Development

The extent to which promotion of commercial and industrial development will be expected to come as a consequence of an airline's activities will vary with the nature of the operations of the airline concerned. However, for all international scheduled airlines, the provision of passenger and air freight services which stimulate international trade will presumably be regarded as important. For domestic carriers, particularly in countries such as Canada with large undeveloped areas, the promotion of regional accessibility may be the dominant role expected of a carrier. This role may be emphasized by the granting of subsidies and a strict regulation of competition.

5. Employment

It would presumably be anathema to the classical economist to suggest that one of the functions of economic activity is simply to provide employment. However, today, in Western economies at least, this aspect of airline operations cannot be ignored. It may not manifest itself in written objectives. However, its significance would not be in doubt if, for instance, an airline pursued a profit maximizing objective in such a way that a large number of staff redundancies became necessary. In many European countries workers are often seen as voters. Airlines in such countries are finding that an important constraint on profit-maximizing behaviour is the need—or inevitability—of maintaining high employment levels.

6. Tourism Development

For many countries, tourism development is the *raison d'être* of aviation. There are few nations today without some interest in the tourism industry. For countries in the Third World without indigenous raw materials, tourism offers one of the few hopes of eventual progress to a developed economy. Tourism promotion objectives for airlines can often be in conflict with those of profit maximization. Examples come with pressures on airlines to mount large amounts of capacity at peak holiday seasons, capacity which is poorly utilized for the rest of the year. There is also a growing tendency for governments and tourism development agencies to insist that airlines introduce low fares which may—or may not—be cost-related.

With the growth of tourism, the actual or implied importance of tourism development in airline operating objectives is likely to increase still further. The tourism boom of the late 1970s resulted in investment in hotels and other infrastructure, and a sharp rise in the numbers employed in tourism dependent industries. Soon it may be difficult in some countries for an airline aiming at profitability to raise its fares even where increases are fully justified from the airline's corporate interest. If such fare increases placed the country's tourism at a disadvantage, pressures against them could be expected from all sections of the tourism industry.[12]

7. Support for a Home Aerospace Industry

The relationship between airlines and home equipment manufacturers has always been a difficult one. The economic importance of aerospace production has been noted, with such production largely concentrated in the United States and Europe. The point at issue in discussing airline operations is whether or not it should be seen as an objective for them to support home-based equipment manufacturers.

In many situations, of course, the problem does not arise, because the products of the home aerospace industry are perceived by airlines as being the best available for their purpose. Aerospace in turn is therefore able to benefit from longer production runs for its aircraft, with a wider distribution of development and tooling costs. The home airlines also provide a shop window—and a gesture of confidence—to promote overseas sales. These sales may be further encouraged by the use of aircraft type as a product differentiating characteristic (*see* Section 7.2.2). This will place pressure on competing airlines to make purchases.

This state of affairs has almost always prevailed in the United States, whose airlines have usually been happy to use American-manufactured equipment. However, in Britain and France, the national airlines have repeatedly come into conflict with governments over fleet planning policies. In the U.K. in particular, such conflicts provide a continuing theme in the history of the industry. For example, in 1967 British European Airways stated its wish to re-equip with Boeing 727 and 737 aircraft, but permission was refused by the U.K. government. The airline was instead required to purchase units of a developed version of the Hawker-Siddeley Trident. The argument arose again in 1977 and 1978 with British Airways asking for, and eventually gaining, agreement for the purchase of Boeing 737s and 757s. This was in the face of opposition from the U.K. airframe industry which had offered 1-11-600s and the A 310 of the European Airbus Consortium, of which British Aerospace had by this time become a member. In the case of the 757/A 310 decision, the political position had become even more complex. The state-owned engine manufacturer, Rolls Royce, had an interest in British Airways being a launching customer for the 757, which will be offered by Boeing with a cutback version of the Rolls-Royce RB-211 engine.

12 Such interference with airline commercial decisions is appearing already with, for example, recent opposition to fare increases by its national airline from the Barbadian government.

The conflicts over airline fleet planning policies provide an illustration of the problems which arise when airline objectives become entwined with objectives aimed at securing the maximum benefits to a national economy from aviation operations. The airlines involved have argued that the British products have not met their needs as well as those from abroad in terms of either costs or customer appeal. They are competing in international markets and have stated that, to do so, they must have equipment which is as good as that of their rivals. In addition, an argument which has been particularly relevant to the most recent debate has been that in the future some international markets are likely to be more competitive than they have been in the past (*see* Section 4.3.1). Consequently, there will be less opportunity for airlines with high operating costs to use the blanket of regulation to protect their position. The aerospace industry, on the other hand, has pointed to the fact of the insistence of the U.K. state-owned airlines on designs which suit their own precise needs as a being a factor rendering its products less saleable to the rest of the world. The handicap of lack of home airline support does render such sales much less likely anyway. Also, aerospace interests, and the trade unions within them in particular, have emphasized the employment and balance-of-payments implications of foreign equipment purchases.

Aerospace support has had a markedly complicating effect on airline operating objectives. Such arguments are likely to continue in the future in even more exaggerated form as structural unemployment increases.

8. Defence

Civil and military aviation have, of course, always had close links. The question of civil aviation providing a back-up to military capability is still relevant to many airlines and defence considerations can therefore complicate the setting of airline objectives. A viable civil airline can be important in maintaining functioning aviation infrastructure, in providing a pool of trained pilots, and in offering airlift capacity in the event of a national emergency. Indeed, there are few countries in the world today which retain sufficient airlift capability in purely military aircraft without relying on the national airline as a back-up. A case of a very close relationship between civil and military aviation has been that of the United States Supplemental Airlines. These have existed on a mixture of military contract work, particularly at the time of U.S. involvement in Vietnam, and civil charters. From this one may guess that they provide an especially valuable addition to defence capability. At least some of the apparent American determination to protect them from attempts by scheduled airlines during the early 1970s to introduce charter-competitive fares may have come from a wish to ensure their continued viability for defence reasons.

9. Minimization of Social Costs

In theory, any airline which operated purely to a corporate criterium of profit maximization could not be expected to take adequate account of social costs. By definition such costs as noise and loss of amenity do not affect the airline, but rather the community. However, today few airlines can pursue profit maximization without taking into account social constraints as a further aspect of formulating objectives. Powerful and influential anti-noise lobbies are organized at many major airports, whilst questions such as airport expansion are now so deeply political that it is impossible for any carrier to be able to plan with confidence that such expansion will be allowed. The only answer is, of course, for airlines to take full account of social costs in their corporate decision-making by such measures as the earliest possible introduction of quieter aircraft, to ensure community acceptance of their activities. Indeed in the long term this may be the only way in which the industry will be successful in attracting sufficient resources to it.

We have listed nine possible objectives for airline operation which may be in addition to or in conflict with one of profit maximization. The list is indicative of how complicated any attempt to apply the marketing model of Chapter 1 to the airline industry is going to be. It is by no means argued, of course, that all the objectives will need to be present in the written operating objectives of all airlines. What has been shown is that there is virtually no airline in the world which can aim at pursuit of its own internal objectives without in written or tacit form bringing consideration of *some* of the other possible external ones. Indeed, there will be some airlines for whom the pressures of these additional objectives will be such as to make the traditional one of profit-making comparatively low down on any list of corporate priorities.

3.6 Airline Corporate Strategies

If we can now make the assumption that an airline's corporate objectives have been set, what alternative strategies are open to management in pursuit of them?

It is here that a marketing framework can be especially valuable. Our initial emphasis on market analysis allows a proposition to be made that today there are four broad families of strategy which are open to airlines. These stem directly from the structure of the market. We shall be arguing that most airlines today can select from strategies aimed at the exploitation of the business passenger market, the leisure passenger market, the air freight market, or a 'total' solution of a strategy based in varying degrees on all these markets. At the same time, we shall suggest that the product life cycle is becoming a very real concept in air transport and that airlines must constantly be reviewing their strategies in the light of it. It will also be made clear that government regulation of the industry provides an all-pervading constraint which modifies the application of the marketing model in its pure form.

We now begin this work by looking at each of the possible strategies in turn.

3.6.1 The Business Market Strategy

We have seen in Chapter 2 that the business travel segment makes up a substantial proportion of the passenger market, and it is possible to find examples of airlines which seem to be basing their corporate strategy on the exploitation of it.[13]

A business market strategy will bring airlines very important advantages. They will be dealing with a market where demand is relatively price-inelastic, despite possible trends towards a higher elasticity in recent years. They will therefore be able to charge high prices without the risk that these will reduce substantially the quantity of demand coming forward. A further advantage of the business market is that it has only very limited seasonal variations in demand. Christmas and other public holiday periods are times of low demand, whilst in some markets there is a slight fall-off at the peak of the holiday season. Otherwise, an airline specializing in catering for the business market will benefit from a very regular seasonal demand pattern.

Despite these positive points, a concentration on the business market does have important disadvantages which mean that few major airlines are able to pursue it to the exclusion of consideration of all other segments. In terms of passenger numbers, business travel now constitutes only the minor segment of the air travel market, with the leisure market exceeding it in aggregate size. Also, we looked in the last chapter at the sound reasons which can be put forward for suggesting that the growth for the future of business travel are less promising than those for the leisure market. Both these features mean that a business travel strategy is unlikely to be appropriate for any airline having maximization of share of the total market as one of its dominating objectives. Also, whilst the business market is normally price-inelastic and therefore willing to pay high fares, any airline which is to achieve a successful penetration of it will have to plan for the very costly products necessary to secure the custom of the business traveller. The business segment has as its requirements the provision of a wide route network with good interconnections and a high level of flight frequency. It also needs a good seat accessibility through the provision of a large amount of capacity relative to demand. Until now, airlines have been able to compete for the business traveller without incurring excessive costs because of government regulation. This has held down the extent of competition, particularly through the operation of

---

13 In the U.K., the regional carrier Air Anglia would seem to have been an example of such an airline. It is believed that over 90 per cent of its traffic was derived from the business segment prior to its merger with British Island Airways in 1979. In the U.S. domestic market, the regional carrier USAir has recently been stated to be deriving more than 80 per cent of its traffic from business travellers. See *Aviation Week and Space Technology*, 21.7.80.

capacity-controlling clauses in bi-lateral agreements.[14] However, there are signs that regulation will be reduced in some markets in the future. This may mean airlines becoming involved in more and more competition for the business traveller, a competition which will only be carried on at a cost of expensive service provision. Indeed it may be that only on thin feeder routes where market potential is insufficient to attract competing airlines will an exclusive concentration on the business market without excessive production costs be possible. Certainly such a situation would seem to typify the Air Anglia case noted earlier. This airline was carrying out a successful business market strategy, but only on feeder routes where a combination of lack of market potential and regulatory intervention limited the amount of direct competition. Where such competition is in existence, it brings pressure on airlines to increase their flight frequencies or improve seat availability near to flight departure time (with a consequence of lower load factors), with the carrier coming to rely a great deal on the inelasticity of demand to allow the charging of fares which will cover the resulting high production costs.

The last disadvantage of a strategy based exclusively on the business market is that, although business travel does not show large seasonal variations, it does show acute daily and weekly peaking. Thus on any dominantly business route, especially a short-haul one, demand is likely to peak strongly early and late in the day. There will be pronounced mid-day and late-evening troughs. Also, daily totals during the Monday to Friday period may be several times the numbers of passengers coming forward on Saturdays and Sundays. An airline concentrating on the business market will therefore find itself with a great deal of poorly utilized off-peak capacity which will have a further effect on costs.

The business market strategy has an intuitive appeal for all airlines. However, it is only likely to be appropriate for a carrier wishing to and able to shelter behind government regulation as a limiting factor on competition, or one which limits the strategy to being applied to short-haul feeder routes with sufficient traffic to fill its own services, but not enough to encourage market entry by competitors.

3.6.2. The Leisure Market Strategy

As an alternative to a concentration on the business travel market, it is possible for an airline to opt for exploitation of the leisure market as its long-term strategy. Such a policy will bring advantages and disadvantages which are almost the opposite of those for the business segment.

The leisure airline will be exploiting the largest segment of the total market, and one where long-term growth prospects are generally agreed to

14 *See* Section 4.2.1.

be significantly better than those for business travel. In addition, full exploitation will be possible using products which can be offered comparatively cheaply. As we saw in Section 2.3.2, leisure travel requirements are generally known well in advance. This makes flight frequencies, seat availability near to flight departure time, and exact flight timings of lesser importance. Leisure demand, too, tends to be in concentrated form, on routes to holiday resorts and where substantial ethnic traffic is available. These factors mean that an airline may be able to exploit the leisure market using large aircraft with low seat–kilometre operating costs, and will be in a position to use these at high average seat factors without jeopardizing the quality of service expected by customers.

Despite these advantages, a total concentration on the leisure market does also bring real problems. The leisure-oreintated airline avoids daily peaking in demand, with it often being possible to secure a high utilization of aircraft and station and ground facilities by operating flights throughout the day and often through the night as well. Night time customers are merely offered a discount in return for accepting an inconvenient arrival or departure time. However, the leisure airline will suffer from weekly and seasonal demand peaking. With weekly peaking, social patterns in the taking of holidays, and the preference of the hotel industry for the low administrative expenses of weekend to weekend bookings, dictate peaking in travel demand on Fridays and Saturdays. There is a corresponding trough earlier in the week. With seasonal peaking, it is nearly always the case that leisure demand will peak during only a few months of the year, as with the winter demand for holiday traffic between the north-east United States and Florida, and the summer peaking of the European inclusive holiday business. Only to a limited extent is it usually possible to use such palliatives as pricing policy to stabilize demand patterns.

The second disadvantage of a strategy aimed exclusively at the leisure market is that this market tends to be unstable. Many of the world's tourism areas are from time to time liable to be affected by extremes of weather or other natural disasters such as earthquakes. When these occur, the short-term effects on a particular market can be catastrophic, as with the decline of tourism traffic to Yugoslavia in the summer of 1979 following earthquakes earlier in the year. Also, besides an instability in meteorological and seismic conditions, political instability is a feature of many tourism destinations. Again, markets are liable to collapse almost overnight following civil disorder or wars such as affected Cyprus at the height of the holiday season in the summer of 1974. Also, instability in the leisure travel market can come from its high income-elasticity. An airline relying on the leisure market will have to incur costs in providing for a given quantity of production. These costs will not be readily avoidable in the short-run should any forecast increase in demand fail to come forward as a recession closes in on the economy of the traffic generating area.

The final point regarding exclusive reliance on the leisure market is probably the most important of all, and will become of even more marked significance if we are moving to an era of looser government regulation. This point is that a large part of the leisure market is known to be price-sensitive. Advantage will accrue to any airline able to offer the lowest prices in a given market, provided it can demonstrate its ability to operate safely. Many important factors in airline strategy spring from this fact. An airline concentrating on the leisure market will gain the advantage of being able to meet market needs with very low production costs, but will face the penalty that yields per passenger carried will be low. Equally, yields are likely to be unpredictable in any market where a degree of price competition prevails. When one airline in the market cuts its prices, there will be a strong pressure on all others to do so. Otherwise, these carriers may be faced with traffic losses, without the ability to vary their costs in the short-run.

There are, of course, arguments to say that this form of price competition is less dangerous than the kind of quality competition for business traffic referred to in the last section. This is because any lowering of prices under competitive pressures will open up new markets due to a high price elasticity. However, such arguments cannot be allowed to hide the dangers to airlines of becoming involved in excessive price competition for leisure traffic. Competitive pressures are always likely to mean a tendency towards price cutting, whilst the opposite process of price rises in response to increases in costs will be rendered difficult as a result of the same pressures. In the past, tight regulation of prices has prevented such trends from occurring in practice in the scheduled sector of the industry, though their effects have been visible in less-regulated charter markets. However, with the present clear trends towards deregulation of at least some scheduled service markets, the questions of price instability and very low yields should become increasingly important considerations for many airlines in deciding upon appropriate strategies with respect to the leisure market.

3.6.3 The Freight Market Strategy

Given the considerable and growing importance of freight, it is possible for an airline to adopt a strategy of concentrating its activities on the air freight market. Today, Flying Tigers Inc. is an American freight carrier heavily involved in scheduled services. Easier regulation of air freight charters in Europe during the last few years has led to the growth of a number of freight charter airlines. An example is the Luxembourg-based carrier Cargolux.

An airline specializing purely in freight carriage will have the opportunity to participate in a still comparatively small but expanding part of the industry. Long-term growth rates are likely to be good in all markets away

from very short-haul routes affected by surface transport co
Also, specialization in the freight market allows an airline to
product which is exclusively orientated towards freight cus...
which thus avoids the compromises which may be needed when attem...
are made to provide for the carriage of both passengers and freight.

Despite the undoubted viability of all-freight strategy, it brings disadvantages compared with an option of attempting joint carriage of passengers and freight. In particular, the all-freight airline is denied the advantages of using lower-hold space of aircraft carrying passengers on their
main decks, or of using main deck space for a mixture of passenger and
freight capacity in the so-called 'combi' configuration. Such space can give
joint passenger/freight airlines advantages in terms of improved flight
frequencies for freight customers. Also, although the allocation of costs is
an intractable question when passenger and freight capacity are jointly
supplied, they will probably have freight capacity available at lower costs
than when it is offered in a pure freighter aircraft.

3.6.4 The Total Market Strategy

The business market, leisure and freight market strategies can all be shown to
exist in a theoretical sense. In practice it is certainly possible to find airlines
which either by strategic planning or evolution have seemed to adopt one of
the three as the basis for their operations. Many regional and feeder carriers in
Europe and North American mainly aim their operations at the business
market. Carriers such as Laker Airways and Britannia Airways in the U.K.
plus many charter and supplemental airlines in other countries appear to base
their corporate strategy on exploitation of the leisure market, whilst we have
already noted the exclusive specialization of some carriers in the air freight
business. However, there is a fourth strategy which is both theoretically
appealing and which also matches the polices being pursued by many of the
world's largest airlines at the present time: the attempt to adopt a total market
solution by providing services for the business, leisure and freight segments.
Such a strategy gives the greatest opportunities to airlines, but also the
difficulties of designing products which meet, at acceptable costs, the often
conflicting requirements of the different segments.

The total market solution has a number of important advantages
attached to it. For any airline having as an objective the maximization of
shares of the overall market, the total market solution clearly gives the best
opportunities for this. Such a solution also offers the chance to overcome
some of the problems accruing from the contrasting demand patterns of
the different segments. For example, an airline involved in both the
business and leisure passenger markets can use aircraft on its dominantly
business routes on weekdays and then switch them—admittedly probably
with problems of seating configuration changes—to weekend charter work

for the peak in leisure travel. As another possibility, the pattern of demand for freight movement peaks strongly at night. The Boeing Company has been active in promoting *'Quick Change' (Q.C.)* versions of its short-haul jets so that these can be used as passenger aircraft during the day and then reconfigured for freight work during the night. Whilst the Q.C. principle has not developed as fast as some forecasts initially predicted, what most certainly has been successful has been the idea of *convertible* aircraft where the switch from passenger to freight configuration takes longer than for the Q.C., but where a changeover to freight usage following the end of a peak period for passenger demand may be a very attractive option to the 'total' airline. The total airline is also in a position to exploit capacity for the carriage of freight in the lower holds of passenger aircraft. This should give benefits to its freight customers and, through lower fares, to its passenger customers as well. Finally, the total airline has the greatest possibilities for stability in its present scale of operations, and of being in a position to exploit quickly any favourable movements in the market, given that such movements usually cannot be predicted very far in advance.

The total-market airline also has to face up to a number of problems. There is no possibility of limited commitment with such a strategy. A business market airline might, if it so chose, be able to restrict itself to a relatively small network between major business centres, especially if its routes made up a viable interconnecting network. The leisure carrier might be successful with a network covering only a small number of dominantly leisure routes. However, the total-market airline will need an investment of resources over a wide network covering routes with both business and leisure potential and, probably, short-haul and long-haul routes as well. This scale of services will commit it to a large investment in aircraft and other equipment, and will confine total-market operations to carriers with a substantial financial base. It will also mean that because of the route network and the—admittedly probably limited—scale economy advantages enjoyed by established air-lines, it will be difficult for an airline to move to a total-market strategy without the acceptance of loss-making—or the imposition of regulatory protection—for an initial period. It may well be, therefore, that, if government anti-monopoly legislation were to allow it, merger might become an established part of the strategy of an airline wishing to move towards a total-market philosophy.

The other problem that the total-market airline must face is that it is setting itself a very difficult product-design task. It gains because of the existence of synergy between its different products. However, as a penalty, it must ensure that its attempts to cater for price-elastic leisure travellers do not jeopardize the quality of service it is offering to its business passengers, and that there is not an excessive dilution[15] of its business

15 *See* Section 6.2.2.

travel revenue. Or again, although the ability to carry freight in the lower hold of passenger aircraft is another good example of total-market synergy, the airline must devise a policy which will deal with the problems of late-arriving passengers, whose effect is to load the aircraft beyond its weight-limited payload. If, as has usually been the case in the past, airlines always answer this situation by off-loading freight from the lower holds, it will have the short-term advantage of increased passenger revenue. In the longer term, however, it can open the way to competition from all-freight airlines. These carriers, although they will be unable to match the total-market airline in departure frequency, may gain the loyalty of shippers and freight forwarders because of a greater certainty that, once freight has been accepted for a flight, it will not be off-loaded.

This section has outlined the main strategies available to airlines, with the adoption of a strategy leading by a logical process to decisions on the market segments for which services will be provided and the routes which will be operated. However, there is one constraint which now needs to be brought in—that of government regulation of the industry. Regulation may decisively affect the ability of an airline to implement its chosen strategy. Equally, it has meant that some airlines, which by their actions have seemed to be implementing a consistent strategy aimed at a particular market segment, may have been doing no more than exploiting a distortion of the regulatory system.

4 The Role of the Regulator

A thorough knowledge of the role of government regulation as a constraint on marketing is essential for anyone who is to understand the application of marketing to the airline business. In this chapter, therefore, we must deal with regulation as it affects marketing. However, it is also necessary to provide the background material on the reasons which can be put forward to explain the importance of regulation in aviation. This will then contribute to the chapter's most important aim, to give the reader an insight into what some of the consequences of regulation have been for airline marketing, and also allow him to formulate an opinion on what the future importance of regulation is likely to be.

We shall begin this work by considering the question of the nature of aviation regulation.

4.1 What is 'Regulation'?

4.1.1 The Nature of Regulation

Regulation in air transport can be defined as *'the attempt by governments or their agents to ensure that certain objectives are met which might not be met under the operation of free market forces.'* In other words, regulation is government intervention in the working of the industry.

Such intervention remains one of the most controversial of the many policy issues facing aviation at the present time. However, the effects of it in providing a constraint on marketing are not in doubt. During the post-war period, regulation has limited airlines' *market entry and exit* policies, with entry and exit usually dependent on government agreement. It has controlled the *type of service* provided, as it has decided whether an airline has been able to engage in either so-called 'scheduled' or 'charter' operations, and also, in the case of scheduled airlines, the quality of cabin service which might be offered. In many situations, government control has affected *capacity and frequency* in a given market. Finally, it has impinged on *pricing* as a marketing decision. Regulation has frequently been imposed with the aim of eliminating all price-competition.

With the all-embracing nature of regulation in the industry, two questions immediately require to be answered. Firstly, *why* has regulation been imposed to such an extent? Secondly, *how* has it been imposed, in terms of the institutional forms which it has taken?

The next two sections are devoted to these questions.

4.1.2 Why is Air Transport a Regulated Industry?

We are not concerned in this chapter with whether or not regulation is a 'good thing', but merely with government controls as they affect marketing. However, it will be helpful to begin by giving at least some of the explanations of why regulation in its various forms has been imposed.[1]

Of these reasons, the easiest with which to deal is that of *safety*. Air transport has always been regarded as having unique safety problems because of the nature of its vehicle.[2] Therefore regulation of markets to ensure that entry is restricted to those firms which can demonstrate their ability to operate aircraft safely has been, and remains, non-controversial.[3] More difficult has been the opinion[4] that a high degree of competition is in itself dangerous, due to tendencies to cut corners with respect to safety in strongly competitive conditions. This latter viewpoint has been rejected to a large extent in recent years, with the idea that regulation of entry and monitoring of performance once entry has been granted are sufficient to maintain safety standards when coupled with airlines' strong commercial self-interest in safe operation.[5] However, current trends towards de-regulation are reviving concern about the link between competitive pressures and safety.

With purely economic, as opposed to safety, regulation, the first of the major arguments is that control must be exercised to *protect scheduled services*. The exact definition of the nature of a scheduled service has proved difficult. However, most would agree that such a service is one which is operated according to a published timetable, irrespective of short-run variations in demand. It must also have a reasonable flight frequency, with sufficient capacity available relative to demand to ensure a good probability of a seat being offered near to departure time.

It has been a traditional argument in favour of regulation to say that scheduled services are essential to any air transport systems which adequately meets consumer needs, and that free competition will result in such services being undermined. In the absence of controls, it is likely that all markets will be well served at peak times, when many carriers will be able

---

1 A full outline of the arguments for and against airline regulation can be found in *Civil Aviation Authority* (1978), pp 6–11.
2 *See* Keith-Lucas (1973), p 483.   3 *See* Ramsden (1976).
4 Edwards (1969), pp 1–2.   5 *See* Cooper and Maynard (1971).

to see opportunities for worthwhile participation. However, at off-peaks, service may be discontinued, with in consequence no true scheduled provision and a degree of inconvenience to all those wishing to travel outside the peaks. With regulation, however, a small number of carriers can be designated to provide scheduled services. These can then be protected from competition during the peak periods, on the understanding that they will in turn offer regular, reliable, year-round service. They probably will be willing to do this because the high returns earned during demand peaks will allow them overall profitability.

The question of offering protection to scheduled services has proved one of the most difficult in the regulation debate. Support for it has amounted to a decision to limit the growth of charter operations which are capable of producing air transport capacity extremely cheaply. If it is regarded as a major regulatory objective to ensure the continuation of scheduled services, then the justification for such intervention is probably well-founded. In some markets where charters have been permitted, these do indeed seem to have had an impact on the viability of scheduled services.[6] However, the difficulty arises because only business passengers and those travelling on urgent family matters really need the convenience of a scheduled product. The segment of the market consisting of leisure travellers and holidaymakers is well-suited by charter service. This offers them less convenience but low costs and low prices, things of great importance to a segment where price elasticities are high. A decision to regulate air transport in order to protect scheduled services is therefore a value judgement that the interests of one section of the travelling public should be placed before those of another.[7]

The next reason for regulatory intervention springs from the argument[8] that the nature of the airline industry is such that free competition is likely to prove unworkable or at least to bring consequences which may be substantially against the consumer's interest. This view comes from the *particular economic characteristics* which air transport is supposed to possess. For example, barriers to new entrants are quite low in aviation, given cheaply-available second-hand aircraft. Also, airlines can begin services without large investment in track and terminal facilities, Finally, product differentiation on the part of competing carriers is held to be difficult in any other way except in terms of price. This factor gives great power to a price-cutting airline, with the likelihood of destructive rate-wars occurring. This likelihood will be strengthened by the fact that airline costs

6 For example, British Airways has withdrawn scheduled services from the U.K. to many Southern European holiday resorts during the last few years, because of the impossibility of retaining them in the face of intense charter competition. *See* British Airways (1977).

7 The problems of maintaining scheduled services in freely competitive conditions are discussed by Reed (1978).

8 Put forward notably by Wheatcroft (1964), pp. 55–7, and O'Connor (1978), pp. 6–7.

are largely fixed in the short run. There is thus a strong incentive for airline managements to reduce prices and remain competitive, in order that they should obtain all the revenue they can, to help to cover costs which will be incurred anyway.

These characteristics in combination, it is argued, may result in an explosion of market entry and then successive rounds of price-cutting in a freely-competitive market, as airlines fight for advantage. In the short-term, a high level of entry and price-cutting will work in the consumer's interest because of the lower fares it will produce. However, in the longer term, this might not be the case, because it might eventually cause airline bankruptcies. These will have particularly serious consequences because air transport is based on cash being paid in advance for a service which would not then become available to a large number of potential passengers. A passenger who is the victim of a bankrupt airline will suffer considerable inconvenience if he is forced to take a later flight by another airline even if he is successful eventually in regaining his money. The bankruptcies may also give rise in turn to difficulties within the industry in raising investment capital. They may mean that the carriers surviving a series of bankruptcies, either directly or by a process of merger, will be in an excellent position to exploit monopoly power within the market. The final result of free competition then would not be the low prices which initially become available, but instead the high prices and poor services typical of monopoly.

There is clearly some truth in the 'economic characteristics' argument. Indeed, at the time of writing there are a number of air transport markets which are showing at least some of the features which proponents of this view would have expected to appear. However, opponents of it would point to the range of opportunities which are now open to airlines for product differentiation,[9] and to examples of air transport markets which have been comparatively loosely regulated, but where no signs of excessive instability have appeared, at least in recent years.

Further arguments for air transport regulation can be related to *route network* considerations. A wide route network has often been regarded as an important aspect of airline operations, bringing as it does advantages of convenience to travellers and maintenance of regional accessibility. It has been suggested[10] that regulated conditions are likely to ensure the maintenance of a wide route network better than free competition will. On any route with limited market potential, a typical regulated situation will be to grant market entry to only one or two carriers. These airlines will be able to enjoy reasonable traffic levels and to exploit such scale economies as are available. However, without regulation, it may be that initially a large number of carriers will enter the market, with no sifting process in

9 *See*, for example, Kamp (1976), pp. 22–4.   **10** For example, by Draper (1978).

operation. This will have the result of forcing up costs as carriers duplicate such investments as those in ground handling facilities. It will also cause the available traffic to be spread thinly between all the operators on a route. The possible overall result then is that no carrier will be able to maintain a viable operation, and that the route will not be served. Again, most would accept a degree of validity in such a viewpoint, but a countervailing one exists. The free market advocate would suggest that if excessive entry did occur, it would soon be corrected. Those carriers who were least able to maintain profitable operations in the competitive market—those with the highest costs—would abandon it and leave it to the most efficient airlines. The consumer would in turn benefit from the stimulus of competition.

A further, slightly different aspect of the route network issue is that related to *the maintenance of social services*. The concern of the previous paragraph has been with routes where profitable operations are possible, even if it may be necessary to impose regulation in order to ensure this. However, it has been suggested that regulation can be a way of maintaining an air service on thin routes where profits are unlikely even for efficient airlines. This is because, if market entry is restricted on dense routes, it will allow airlines which are granted entry to them to earn abnormally high profits. In return, regulators may be able to insist that such airlines also operate some unprofitable routes, on a basis of cross-subsidization.

Whilst such views are valid in any situation where such a total control of entry can be maintained, economists in recent years have strongly criticized the principle of cross-subsidization in transport.[11] They have argued instead that the potentially profitable routes should be operated competitively. Any 'social' routes where, as a political judgement, services are deemed necessary are then to be maintained by subsidies out of taxation to cover losses. This latter principle is illustrated by the extensive subsidies which are still paid to the United States local service airlines for services to small communities.

Social services arguments can also be brought into a more general argument that regulation of air transport is essential because of the *quasi-public utility* nature of the industry. We have already looked briefly at the significance of air transport in promoting regional accessibility within a country, in providing the essential communications for international trade and commerce, and, through air freight, the physical means by which an increasing amount of trade is accomplished. Because of these factors, it does have definite public utility aspects to its existence. Just as it would seem to be wasteful to allow a high degree of competition over, say, electricity or water supplies, so advocates of this view suggest that competition should be controlled in air transport. However, a balanced

11 *See*, for example, Ponsonby (1969).

judgement would probably be that, on dense mature routes at least, the public utility element to the industry's operations should not be exaggerated, with no definite grounds for the limitation of competition springing from it.

The arguments regarding safety, scheduled service protection, industry stability, route network, maintenance of social services, and public utility, can be related to all air transport networks, both international and domestic. However, there is a final group of arguments which relate purely to *international* services.

Since the signature of the Paris Agreement of 1919, the principle has been accepted of states having sovereign rights over the airspace above their territory. The result has been that international air services take place under tight protectionism. There has been none of the freedom which has characterized the growth of international maritime operations with flags of convenience and other indicators of much freer market entry. The effects of this protectionism have come out in forms of regulation which apply only to international services.

We have seen in Section 3.2.1 that aviation still exhibits some of the features of an infant industry. One of the manifestations of this is the existence of substantial differences in efficiency and competitive ability between industry participants. Given the wide social and economic impact of air transport, a country with a relatively weak national airline has a powerful list of factors which are likely to lead it to a view that regulation is very necessary to protect its national interests. Free competition against mature carriers with lower costs and a more marketable product may result in heavy losses to the infant carrier. It may give a fall in market share to very low levels with a consequent balance-of-payments impact. It may also carry the risk that the foreign carriers who dominate the market will—reasonably—act in their own interests rather than the wider economic interests of the country concerned. Examples of this would be a failure by such carriers to mount sufficient capacity for peak-season tourism traffic, or the suspension of services at the first hint of political instability.

Considerations such as these have led to a chain of events which have resulted in blanket regulation of international services. Weak nations have tended to regulate competition, and also, often, directly or indirectly, to subsidize their carrier's operations. In turn, airlines from more powerful countries have begun to argue that they face unfair competition with both subsidization and edicts such as governments placing pressure on their citizens to use the national airline contributing to this. The result has almost always been an acceptance that regulated competition is the best compromise to be achieved under the circumstances, with perhaps a further argument then appearing that regulation must act as a way of preventing abuse of the limited competition which will prevail. Indeed, the regulatory stance adopted by the U.K. Civil Aviation Authority has had the latter point as one of its most important features.

4.2 The Impact of Regulation of Airline Marketing

4.2.1 Institutions of Regulation

Given that domestic air services are under the control of one government, and that international services will involve the need to compromise between the views of two or more, it is to be expected that the institutional forms of regulation will vary substantially between domestic and international operations.

In most countries, regulation of domestic services has been carried out by a government department, or an agency of government. Thus, for example, in the United States, regulation has been the responsibility of a government agency, the Civil Aeronautics Board. The C.A.B. was set up under the Civil Aeronautics Act of 1938, with its role amended under the Federal Aviation Act of 1958. In the U.K., regulation of domestic services is now carried out by the Civil Aviation Authority. It took over this task under the terms of the 1971 Civil Aviation Act from the pre-existing Air Transport Licensing Board.

In almost all states, domestic services have been very tightly regulated indeed. Until recently, this has been most notably the case in the U.S.A., where the C.A.B. has been required to exercise control over all interstate operations. This has taken the form of rigid regulation of market entry and exit, and limits on pricing so that all price competition has been eliminated. In the U.K., similar regulation has been exercised.[12] In other countries—India is an example—regulation has been taken to the extent of confining entry to domestic markets to a single airline.

In some cases, regulation of domestic services has now come to be seen as cumbersome, slow and unnecessary. Indeed, in the U.S.A., the Airline Deregulation Act of 1978 is now providing a marketing environment of unprecedented liberality. However, before coming to look at these developments in more detail, we must examine the much more complex area of past regulation of international air services.

In international markets, regulation is based on increasingly anachronistic service distinctions, and the granting of traffic rights under strictly controlled conditions of international bargaining. Since the Second World War, regulation has depended on a distinction between 'scheduled' and 'charter' services, with scheduled operations having features of regular frequencies and a published timetable, although no precise definition of a 'scheduled service' has ever been widely adopted.[13]

Following a series of international meetings held between 1945 and 1947, scheduled services have come to be regulated by a network of

---

12 *See* Gwilliam and Mackie (1975), Ch. 15.
13 Doganis (1973) gives a full outline of the system of regulation for international air services.

bi-lateral agreements between governments. These agreements (or similar, but less formal memoranda of understanding) cover all scheduled international air services. Almost all of them have certain points in common.

Each embodies the principle of *controlled market entry* on to routes. Entry is restricted to nominated carriers—often a single carrier from each country. Each also precisely defines the *traffic rights* to be exercised by each carrier. In particular control is exercised over so-called 'Fifth Freedom' rights.[14] Most controversial of all, bi-lateral agreements have largely prevented *price competition*. Instead, the airlines concerned have been required to meet together and agree between themselves the fares and cargo rates they will charge. These are then implemented subject to government approval. In recognition of the complex, interrelated nature of international fares and rates, it has been accepted that a multi-lateral forum where large numbers of airlines could meet together to agree fares was the best arrangement. This forum has been the International Air Transport Association (I.A.T.A.). As final provisions of bi-laterals, most now incorporate some agreement on *capacity levels*, with equal amounts of capacity to be offered by the nominated airlines. Some bi-laterals take the elimination of competition to its ultimate degree by an insistence that the carriers should operate a *pooling agreement* whereby at the end of each year revenues are shared out according to a pre-existing formula.

The all-embracing nature of bi-lateral agreements means that marketing in scheduled airlines' international services has been carried out in an environment of government regulation which is tighter than that facing any other major world industry. During the late 1970s, however, the first signs appeared of possible changes in this bi-lateral framework, something with which we shall deal shortly. However, before doing so, it is essential to cover the regulation of charter services.

Charter (or 'non-scheduled') services have always been regulated in a different way from scheduled operations. In Europe, some charter services have come within the scope of multi-lateral agreements covering purely charter operations. In other markets, instead of tight agreements covering operating rights, capacity and pricing, charters have been regulated by a system of unilateral control. Each state has decided its own rules for market entry for both its own and foreign charter airlines. The result has been wide differences in charter regulation from country to country. Many

---

14 Traffic rights in bi-lateral agreements are defined under the 'Freedoms of the Air.' The Fifth Freedom is particularly controversial in that it involves the right of an airline to pick up revenue traffic in a foreign country, and set it down in another foreign state. It can thus be argued that Fifth-Freedom traffic is business in which an airline has no 'natural' right to participate. Much the same considerations apply to traffic carried under the Sixth Freedom whereby it is picked up in a foreign country, transhipped over the airline's home base, and then moved on to another foreign state, thus taking traffic away from airlines providing direct services. *See* Wassenbergh (1970) for further discussion of this aspect.

nations—for example, India, Brazil and South Africa—permit very little, if any, entry by charter airlines. Others have given such entry, usually in response to consumerist pressures for the low fares which charters can provide, or for reasons relating to tourism development. However, these countries have often confined entry to carriers providing a particular form of charter service. Thus intra-European charters are most commonly operated under the *inclusive tour* principle. This allows non-scheduled services to be made available only to those willing to buy a package of return flight and accommodation (though the I.T. conception has in fact been more and more undermined in recent years by the offer of 'packages,' with cheap or non-existent accommodation). On the North Atlantic, there was initially a rapid growth of non-scheduled operations of the *affinity group* type whereby the U.S. government in particular offered extensive opportunities for its Supplemental Airlines to develop charters for special groups.[15] Later, the widespread abuse of affinity group rules led to their replacement by the less discriminatory *advanced booking charters*.

The relationship between scheduled and charter services has provided a continuing theme of controversy in the regulation of international air transport. The scheduled airlines have, reasonably enough, complained that they have been subjected to unfair competition. They have been tightly regulated whilst the charter airlines have been allowed much more freedom, especially over price levels.[16] However, counterbalancing arguments have been the undoubted appeal of low-cost charter services to the price-conscious leisure segment of the passenger market,[17] and the fact that, for whatever reason, scheduled airlines have sometimes been slow in adjusting their own product range to encompass the needs of this segment. In most cases the adjustment has come first on those routes where extensive opportunities have been permitted to charter airlines.

We shall return shortly to the question of the competitive relationship between scheduled and charter services. However, enough has been said so far to indicate that the airline industry throughout its history has been characterized by tight regulation, with such regulation inevitably constraining airline marketing policies.

4.2.2 Consequences of Regulation

But exactly what has been the nature of the impact of regulation? It is necessary in this section to consider some of its possible effects, from a marketing viewpoint. As we shall see, a balanced view falls between the extreme opinions of the defenders of regulation and the critics who emphasize the inefficiencies which it has undoubtedly brought.

As a first point, in a marketing sense it can be perfectly right for management to support the imposition of regulatory control over an industry

15 *See* Smithies (1973).   16 *See* Doganis (1973).   17 *See* Section 9.1.1.

if it feels that such regulation will be to its advantage in meeting its corporate objectives. Therefore, in many cases, the support for regulation which has come from a large part of the airline industry may have been entirely correct. However, in supporting it, marketing management has brought upon itself two important consequences. Firstly, competitive opportunities against rival airlines have been sharply reduced. Secondly, managements have lost their freedom to respond quickly to changing market conditions, as regulation has been based on the twin processes of inter-airline and inter-governmental negotiation and compromise. There is now a growing feeling that such inflexibility has brought many problems which can only be avoided in the future by less rigid controls.

However, it must also be emphasized that regulation has brought consequences to the post-war airline industry which most people would regard as 'good.' Probably most important of all, it has provided a stable basis for the progress of the industry from its earliest stages to its current level of development. It is perhaps too easily forgotten in today's climate that, for example, the Civil Aeronautics Board was formed in 1938 to regulate a U.S. domestic industry which was still financially marginal. It had only just begun to take delivery of equipment in the shape of the DC-3, which gave it any hope of long-term financial viability.[18] It was also in the process of recovering from a series of scandals over the award of government air mail contracts.[19] Only the imposition of tight regulation at that time allowed for the subsequent development of the industry. With international regulation, the setting up of the system of bi-lateral agreements immediately following World War II provided the necessary means of compromise between the economic strength of the U.S. and the war-ruin of most of Europe. Bi-laterals and the regulatory framework they have imposed have continued to provide a pragmatic basis for air services to operate between countries where the airlines from one are in a fundamentally superior competitive position.

Another significant consequence of regulation may be that it has allowed airlines to meet the needs of the segment of their market consisting of business travellers and those flying on urgent personal matters. This segment requires frequent services at a high standard of comfort and convenience with the question of ticket price of relatively less importance. Regulation has meant a consistency of services. It has promoted a comparative simplicity of fares with easy interline arrangements as a result of all airlines working with a single, commonly-agreed tariff. It has encouraged good flight schedules and seat accessibility near to flight departure time. Good schedules have sprung from the widespread existence of revenue-pooling agreements which, theoretically at least, allow airlines to schedule flights at off-peak times without fear of losing revenue

18 See Brooks (1967), pp. 168–71. **19** *See* Davies (1972), Ch. 8.

to their competitors. Seat access has resulted from the tendency of airlines to put large amounts of capacity into markets. This capacity has been paid for by the high fares charged to business and personal travellers.

For this market segment, reduced regulation may mean an increase in tariff complexity, more difficulties in interlining, a worsening of airport services and a reduction in levels of seat accessibility. These consequences will flow naturally from a situation where airlines compete more and co-operate less, and also because of a phenomenon which Dr. Alfred Kahn—one of the arch de-regulators of the late 1970s—has called the 'tyranny of small decisions.'[20]

Despite these arguments in favour of tight regulation, the airline executive with a true marketing instinct cannot fail to be unhappy with some of the other—less satisfactory—consequences which it has brought. Indeed a cynic might suggest that a diagnostic feature of possession of such an instinct would be an unease with some of the consequences of regulation.

As a first point, regulation has meant that a large amount of airline marketing resources has been spent in co-operative discussions with other airlines, rather than, as one might argue that it should have been used, in planning, developing and selling the products to allow an improved competitive position. For example, the tariff negotiations within I.A.T.A. have become long-drawn out and often inconclusive affairs during the 1970s, whereby hundreds of airline executives have spent many weeks each year in attempts to reach a compromise over the tariff structure. Also, with the all-pervading practice of pooling, large amounts of executive time are spent in such co-operative discussions.

One accepts all the points commonly made in favour of pooling—the argument already made about scheduling, the pragmatic necessity for pooling on many routes as a result of government insistence and the argument that it does not entirely eliminate competition. Airlines still compete to ensure that the end-year split of revenue can be agreed in their favour. Yet one's unease with such a philosophy remains.[21] The pragmatic arguments may well be dominant where, say, a mature carrier is competing with an emergent airline from a newly-independent country. It is, however, inappropriate to apply the same arguments to competition between two totally mature carriers in an intra-European context. Indeed, not the

---

20 Briefly, in an air transport context, this theory states that under deregulated conditions with a widespread availability of cut-price services, a businessman will use such services whenever he can and will gain a large consumer surplus as a result. However, in doing so, there will be no way for him to know that thus he may be undermining the viability of scheduled services with a high seat-accessibility. The result will be that such services will not be available on the comparatively small number of occasions when they are needed. *See* Kahn (1969), Vol. 2, and Reed (1978).

21 *See* Straszheim (1975), p. 272.

least important of the consequences of the current move towards deregulation is the improvement in morale which it is bringing to airline marketing staff. They are finding that, for the first time in their careers, it is worthwhile expending time and effort on product development without the certainty of the past that any radical proposals would be compromised out of any meaningful existence in discussion with other airlines at I.A.T.A. Traffic Conferences, or in pool negotiations.

As a further criticism, it is a very commonly-held view that regulation has led to *wasteful competition*.[22] This is because it may not have had the effect of significantly reducing the extent to which airlines compete. Most airlines are working towards corporate objectives which can only be achieved by success against their rivals. Therefore, all that has happened under regulation has been that competitive effort has been concentrated in those areas such as cabin service, promotional expenditure and especially frequency and capacity provision where competition has remained possible. The revenue which regulated prices have ensured has been used to pay for ever more costly non-price competition. In some markets, the effect has been to force up revenue seat-kilometre costs through a combination of quality competition and very low average seat factors. This has especially been the case in the U.S. domestic industry, where seat factors during the early 1970s were very widely below 50 per cent.[23] In many other markets, very low seat factors have mostly been avoided, but only by the imposition of yet more regulation—the capacity-controlling clauses typical of most modern bi-lateral agreements.[24]

The question of wasteful competition leads to a broader view that regulation has caused an *under-supply of low-cost/low-price services*. As was noted in Section 2.3, the post-war period has been notable for a progressive change in the structure of the air travel market. The dominating market segment now consists of price- and income-elastic leisure travellers. There have been many criticisms that scheduled carriers have failed to respond as far as they should have done to this change. They have tried to continue to supply a high-cost, high-priced product, relying on the protection of regulation to guard them against the activities of competitors aiming to alter the product mix in the direction of fewer frills but lower prices. Protagonists of this view point to the popularity of the charter product in the markets where it has been permitted to develop, and the fact that, in such markets, scheduled airlines have been forced by the competition to introduce low prices of their own accord. Opponents of it amongst scheduled airlines have claimed that many of the low-fare innovations which have been made would have come anyway without the

---

22 *See*, for example, Cooper and Maynard (1971) and Douglas and Miller (1974).
23 *See* Spater (1973).
24 Shovelton (1979) puts forward a view that these clauses are essential on international routes if excessive and wasteful capacity provision is to be prevented.

impetus of charter competition. In some markets—notably the North Atlantic—scheduled airlines have been held back by regulatory intervention from low-fare innovation.[25] Whatever the truth of the matter, the existence of this argument has been a potent factor in contributing to a view that economic regulation of air transport has seen the development of an inefficient scheduled airline industry, which has failed in its task of providing the consumer with adequate choice.[26] Whether or not one accepts such a position, these arguments have been important in the developments which took place in the regulatory system during the middle and late 1970s. These suggest that in some markets at least, the future role of regulation will be very different.

4.3 The Deregulation Debate and Future Forms of Regulation

4.3.1 Developments in Regulation, 1975–1980

The United States has proved a catalyst for radical changes in regulatory philosophy during the late 1970s, both in its domestic services and also internationally. Until recently, U.S. policy has been characterized by its conservative approach in a number of areas. As has been noted, U.S. domestic services were controlled very tightly indeed before the mid-1970s. On the North Atlantic—where many of the most radical developments of recent years have come—attitudes were restrictionist in several ways. Thus the American government resisted the idea of Advanced Booking Charters and the scheduled service APEX low fares. Both these ideas were supported by the Civil Aviation Authority in the U.K., and the APEX fare by British Airways as well. Whilst it would be wrong to ascribe the developments of recent years to the actions of a single government, it has been the fundamental change in U.S. policy which has been important in deciding both the timing and extent of change. It is therefore necessary to begin by looking at the transformation which has come over the U.S. market in recent years.

The mid-1970s were a period of considerable trauma in world aviation. Rising fuel prices and depressed traffic levels resulted in unprecedented losses by many airlines. The U.S. carriers shared fully in such loss-making, with one at least, Pan American, coming near to the edge of bankruptcy. Such poor performance led to a rise of criticism regarding the inefficiencies which were supposed to exist in the regulated U.S. air transport industry. At the same time, a developing political force of consumerism and a bandwagon of 'get government out of our hair' began to find manifestation in pressure for reducing political intervention in the working of the

25 *See* Hammarskjold (1978).   26 *See* Cooper and Maynard (1971).

economy. The airline industry, given both its intrinsic importance and its emotional appeal to many people, was always likely to be a prime target for the deregulator's attentions.

In the U.S. domestic industry these trends have come together in a fast-moving series of events which have totally altered the regulatory environment of the industry. The election of President Carter in November 1976 was followed by the appointment of Dr. Alfred Kahn, a noted free-market economist, as Chairman of the Civil Aeronautics Board. Kahn, in a stay at the C.A.B. of only 18 months, proceeded to oversee an immediate relaxation in the way in which existing regulatory legislation was applied. A revolutionary Airline De-regulation Act was then put through Congress, and was signed by the President in October 1978. The result of this Act has been a loosening of controls over market entry, more flexibility to vary price levels independent of regulatory intervention, a total deregulation of air cargo services and the promise that by the end of 1983 the C.A.B. itself will have disappeared. Interstate domestic services will then be free of almost all economic regulation.

At the time of writing (Spring, 1980), it is still too early to say what the long-term effects of the U.S. domestic deregulation will be. However, from the point of view of airline marketing, the significance of the change cannot be exaggerated. We now have airlines in the U.S. domestic industry formulating marketing policies with the promise of a large degree of freedom to implement them.

As far as international services are concerned, the changes have been inevitably more fragmented and less consistent, but very real policy developments have occurred in parallel with the U.S. domestic situation. Many of these can be traced back to the decision made in June 1976 by the U.K. government to insist on a re-negotiation of the Bermuda Agreement, the bi-lateral covering air services between Britain and the U.S.A., although the new Bermuda 2 agreement has probably had more importance as a catalyst, speeding developments which would have occurred anyway.

By a supreme irony, the British position in asking for a renegotiation was that a need existed for tighter regulation. The old Bermuda Agreement had given rise to an inefficient system which worked against U.K. interests.[27] Britain therefore hoped for a reduction in U.S. Fifth Freedom rights over London, the adoption of capacity controls as part of the bi-lateral, and the acceptance by the U.S. of a principle of single designation of one carrier from each country on each route. This was in contrast to the previous situation where two U.S. carriers—Pan Am and T.W.A.—had often competed with one British one—British Airways—in such a way that all carriers were unprofitable and the U.K. could obtain only a relatively low share of the total market.

27 See Shovelton (1978).

The new Bermuda Agreement was signed after an all-night negotiating session near to the deadline, on 23rd June 1977. Whilst in it the UK by no means achieved the reductions in American rights which it was seeking, U.S. competitive opportunities were reduced. However, far from providing a new regulatory framework, in the aftermath of Bermuda 2 has come a series of events which have shaken the old regulatory system for international services to its foundations.

Following the signature of the agreement, the next major development came with the introduction of the Laker Airways Skytrain in September 1977. Laker Airways Ltd., a U.K. independent airline, had been trying for five years to introduce a low-fare, no-reservation service from London to New York. The opportunity to introduce the service finally arose when, after an important court victory achieved by Laker in December 1976, the U.K. position in the Bermuda 2 renegotiation changed to one of outright support for him. The correctness of the airline starting the service was finally accepted by the U.S., although, as it later turned out, only at a cost of substantial concessions by the U.K. on other aspects. When the Laker service began, amidst considerable publicity, there were already signs that it was bringing with it implications which were likely to be far-reaching.

Initially, whilst Skytrain was permitted to start, it became clear that the United States was insisting on the right of airlines on the London–New York route to make a competitive low-fare response. This came with the 'Standby' and 'Budget' fares introduced by Pan American and T.W.A. (and British Airways) at the time of the Skytrain commencement. However, by this time, events were becoming bound up with the new push of U.S. aviation policy, with the domestic deregulatory trends being promoted on to international services as well. In consequence, an agreement was signed between the U.S. and United Kingdom governments in March 1978 which extended low Standby and Budget fares on to all U.K.–U.S. routes in addition to London–New York. The U.S. then began the signing of a series of bi-lateral agreements with the Netherlands (March 1978), Belgium (October 1978) and West Germany (November 1978). These agreements were of quite revolutionary liberality.

Despite the favourable view generally adopted by the U.K. Civil Aviation Authority to regulatory innovation in recent years, the U.K. is believed to have agreed only with reluctance and under great pressure to the low fares extension of March 1978. The view seemed to be that more experience should be gained with the workings of these fares on the London–New York route before any extension on to other routes took place. However, the bi-laterals with the Netherlands, Belgium and West Germany all included the low-fares/flexible-pricing principle. They permitted much freer market entry in terms of additional gateway points and permission being given for new carriers to serve existing routes (the principle of 'multiple designation' strongly resisted by the U.K.). Each agreement also gave much enhanced competitive opportunities for charter services through an abolition of most of the restrictive conditions pertaining to charters.

The result of these developments has been to ensure that air services over a large part of the North Atlantic are now operating under conditions of considerable economic freedom. Low-fare innovation has been widespread, with the summer of 1979 seeing Standby and Budget Fares offered not only out of London and Amsterdam as in 1978, but in addition from Brussels, Frankfurt and, to a lesser extent Paris. Equally significant, there has been an explosion in market entry, with European carriers operating to an increased number of U.S. gateways (K.L.M., for example, began on Amsterdam–Los Angeles service in April 1979) and U.S. carriers widely permitted to operate to Europe under the principle of multiple designation.

The extremes of change on the North Atlantic in the 1977–9 period have been paralleled by regulatory developments in other markets. Probably of most importance, the role of the International Air Transport Association as a forum for airlines to agree fares and rates has been altered by a combination of internal and external pressures.

I.A.T.A. had become a much-maligned organization during the 1960s and 1970s.[28] It had been criticized, for example, on the grounds that it had become ineffective. I.A.T.A. traffic conferences had become prolonged affairs, often failing to produce any workable agreement between the airlines involved, and then with acute 'compliance' problems where agreements had been reached and airlines did not apply them in the market-place. It had also been said that it operated as an anticonsumerist cartel which kept fares at higher than their natural level. In answering these accusations, I.A.T.A. replied,[29] with some justice, that acting as a price-agreement forum was only a small part of its total activity. The industry as a whole gained substantially from its other work as an airline trade association. In any case much of its role as a price-agreement forum, and certainly its working methods, had been dictated by government policies.

Whatever the correctness of these arguments, the fact remained that by the Autumn of 1977 matters had begun to come to a head. The most powerful factor in this was the threat of the Civil Aeronautics Board to withdraw anti-trust exemption from U.S. airlines, which would effectively have meant their withdrawing from I.A.T.A. *en bloc.*

The result of the pressures was that I.A.T.A. member airlines agreed to the setting up of a Task Force to examine the whole of the working of the Association. This Task Force sat through the winter of 1977–8, with its

---

28 *See*, for example, Pillai (1969), and Boyd-Carpenter (1975).
29 *See*, for example, I.A.T.A. (1974), and Brancker (1977).

recommendations being accepted by a Special General Meeting of the membership in July 1978.

Inevitably, radical attempts to reform an Association such as I.A.T.A. are controversial, and it is by no means certain at the time of writing what the final system for obtaining price-agreements in the industry will be—or indeed if such a system will exist at all. However, some proposals of the I.A.T.A. Task Force have already indicated the certainty that a significant loosening of the controls of the past will be forthcoming. Airlines are being offered the choice of joining I.A.T.A. purely as trade association members, or of participating in these activities and the traffic conferences to agree fares and rates. What this will probably mean in practice is that United States carriers, if they remain members of I.A.T.A. at all,[30] will only engage in trade-association activities. Therefore, all effective jurisdiction of the I.A.T.A. conferences on routes to and from the U.S. could be lost. On such routes, price levels will revert to being decided by a process of agreement between airlines and governments. Current trends in U.S. policies indicate that *that* government at least will be only too willing not to interfere, providing that airlines can be seen to be setting their own prices in a competitive market. However, even on other routes, the Task Force proposals are indicative of greater freedom for airline management. They state that there should be an ending of—always ineffective—attempts by airlines within I.A.T.A. to regulate in-flight servicing and other non-price product components. In the specific area of pricing, allowance is made for individual airline innovation in low fares by giving airlines the right to introduce such fares without rescinding I.A.T.A. traffic conference agreements if this is in response to changing market conditions.

This latter point, whilst of considerable importance in itself, is to some extent merely confirming a trend of recent years. There has been a growing move towards bi-lateral airline/government-based low-fare innovation in markets where I.A.T.A. has already ceased to be effective as a multi-lateral fare-fixing forum. Very good examples of this have been the new low APEX fares introduced between U.K. and Australia by Qantas and British Airways in February 1979.

The main trends in regulation in the middle and late 1970s can be summarized as follows:

(i) a marked increase in interest in the U.S.A. in the operation of the industry under de-regulated conditions, with legislation enacted to ensure an eventual de-regulation of United States domestic services by the early 1980s.

(ii) a fundamental change in the North Atlantic international market, where conditions of regulatory liberality have replaced the former tight control. This liberality has included both pricing and market entry, with

---

30 Delta Airlines Inc. withdrew entirely in November 1978, and Braniff in June 1979.

entry to at least some routes in the market becoming a question of management action once safety standards have been satisfied.

(iii) in remaining international markets, those on routes to and from the United States have in some cases seen a loosening of both pricing and entry constraints, under the push of developing U.S. policy[31]. In other markets, entry controls mostly have remained. For example, the recent Australian review of international aviation policy has had as one of its conclusions that entry should not be granted to further airlines, either scheduled or charter, and that an attempt should be made to concentrate more of the market in the hands of Qantas as the national airline. However, widely now in international markets we are seeing a growing flexibility in pricing, with airlines gaining the freedom to innovate, particularly with new, low fares.

With these three areas of development, we can already point to substantial changes in the regulatory framework within which airline marketing activity takes place. This leads us on naturally to a further range of questions relating to the *future* regulatory environment for airline marketing. Did the years from 1976 to 1979 see the trends towards reduced control progress as far as they are likely to? Will there now be a move in the direction of a re-imposition of regulation? Or has the environment for marketing activity been altered for all time, with further emphasis on even greater freedom?

In looking at the future, there are now a number of pressures which will mean that developments of the last few years may in no sense be seen as an aberration. Rather do they respect fundamental changes of long-term significance to the development of the industry. Of these pressures, perhaps the most important is that of *consumerism*, with the 1970s being notable for the rise of consumerism as an economic and political force. The demand for air travel has a strong emotional element to it. Once a low-fare, de-regulated environment has been introduced on a route, acute consumerist opposition is likely to greet any attempt to remove it. At the same time, when such an environment has come on one route, given the publicity which is likely to greet its arrival, calls are immediately heard from consumers in other markets to the effect of 'why not here?'. This is particularly so in markets where strong ethnic links exist between the two ends of the route.

There can be little doubt that consumerist pressures have arrived at an ideal time considering the state of *product availability*. The subject of product design will be considered in Chapter 5. We shall see then that the early days of the industry were largely based on a product of scheduled services using small, relatively inefficient aeroplanes, low-average seat factors, high-quality in-flight servicing and many other features. These

31 Routes between the United States and Israel are a good example of this, with an extremely liberal bi-lateral between the two countries being signed in August 1978.

gave what was undoubtedly a premium product, but only at penalty of extremely high costs. By the middle 1970s the situation had changed. A generation of aeroplanes had arrived based on efficient high-by-pass-ratio turbofan engines and on the securing of economies of scale through large size. These gave the hope of low seat–kilometre costs, particularly in the case of the Boeing 747 on long-haul routes. At the same time, it became clear that the scheduled service was not the only way in which air services could be operated. Rather, such a service represented only one product alternative. By the mid-1970s, much experience had been gained in the operation of the charter product on the routes where non-scheduled airlines had been granted entry. Also, by this time, Laker Airways Ltd. was extolling the virtues of the no-reservation principle as a further way in which a low-cost product could be supplied. Scheduled airlines themselves had begun to experiment within the scheduled service principle regarding ways in which low prices could be offered.[32] Many of the developments of the last three years can therefore be put down to the rise in consumer consciousness coming together with a progressive refinement in the 'state of art' of product development. Various catalysts—particularly Skytrain— have come to hasten trends which in fact have had a long history in the industry and which would have manifested themselves anyway at some stage. We return to this point in Section 9.1, but for the moment we can point again to indications of a continuing process, rather than one which has arrived suddenly and will disappear equally quickly.

As a final point, *tourism development* must be put forward as a factor which is likely to give a continuation of recent trends. The symbiosis of tourism and aviation has already been discussed. We have seen that international tourism has now grown to a stage where it is one of the world's major economic activities, with further expansion expected. Of all the many aspects of the impact of reduced regulation during the last four years, none has been more important than that it has emphasized the need for low fares to permit the growth of any long-haul tourism destination. Low fares have increased the total numbers of tourists travelling. Even more significantly, they have accentuated the trend towards competition between tourism destinations. Those destinations which have had low air fares to them have undoubtedly gained, whilst there have been more and more pressures on airlines to introduce low fares to give other areas the corresponding advantages.

All the evidence which is currently available suggests that tourism development, like the other explanations of growing regulatory liberality, is by no means a temporary phenomenon. Tourism, to an even greater extent than aviation, is an industry where short-term investment and

---

32 This latter point is especially the case with the APEX form of low-fare pricing, with this being discussed fully in Section 6.2.3.

disinvestment is not possible. The growth of tourism is leading to an investment in hotels and other infrastructure, and to an increase in employment, which will be a permanent feature. Indeed, we saw in Chapter 3 that unemployment is likely to be one of the crucial problems of the world economy during the remainder of the century. Therefore, tourism aspects might be expected to encourage the movement towards a deregulated, low-fare-based environment.

Overall, one can point to consumerism, product development and tourism as all being factors likely to ensure that the regulatory base for airline marketing activity in the future will be very different from the tightly controlled one of the past. However, by no means all the trends point in that direction. It is now becoming clear that a reimposition of regulation might come to be seen as being necessary for a combination of economic and political reasons.

Many of the protagonists of reduced regulation in international services are guilty of ignoring the true nature of the international industry if they believe that, on many routes, free market economics can work on a long-term basis. Aviation has always been an intensely political industry in which nations have acted to protect their own interests. It is probable, therefore, that, once reduced regulation has had several years for its long-term effects to become apparent, those nations whose airlines are shown to be losing under the new freedom will change their policies. They will either try to halt the process by a re-imposition of regulation, or else bolster their airline by subsidization. This will in turn bring complaints of unfairness from the airlines' competitors.

It may be that this possibility will turn out to be less serious than many expect. The factors which we have discussed as leading to de-regulation and the political difficulties of excessive subsidization might support such a view. The widespread ability of governments to bring non-aviation aspects into negotiations on aviation matters may also have a similar effect. However, it may still may have a significance in some markets in slowing or reversing current trends.

Much more likely to be important is the probability that regulatory freedom, despite the consumerist pressures which are bringing it about, may have consequences which work against the consumer's interest. For example, the years 1978 and 1979 were notable for a large investment by airlines in new aeroplanes. Three of the four major airframe manufacturers reported orders more than four times those of 1977. In many respects, such an upsurge in ordering was to be expected. The recession from 1973–6 was a time when many airlines held back on equipment replacement because of serious financial problems. The late seventies have therefore seen a necessity for carriers to begin replacing ageing aeroplanes, particularly with rising fuel costs making the older types uneconomic. At the same time, governments are beginning to impose deadlines which will necessitate the retirement of all excessively noisy aeroplanes during the middle 1980s. Many of today's orders may be seen as airlines beginning the process of modifying their fleets to meet acceptable environmental standards. However, despite these points, there is no doubt whatsoever that airlines are widely beginning a process of expanding capacity—indeed, in view of the traffic increases which occurred in 1978, it would be surprising if they were not doing so.

Such capacity expansion may well prove justified, with deregulation the route to the reasonable levels of profitability which have eluded airlines throughout the history of the industry. However, the nature of industry operations under deregulated conditions emphasizes the dangers which exist. Particularly in the U.S. domestic industry and on the North Atlantic, but to a lesser extent on other routes as well, the reduction in regulatory control has been widely interpreted by airlines as requiring the introduction of new fares at low prices. These low fares have often been notably successful in attracting and generating new traffic. However, both because of the low prices at which new traffic is carried, and because of the dilutionary[33] effects of low fares on traffic which would have been carried by the airline anyway, low-fare innovation has significantly raised break-even load factors.

This, of course, is not necessarily a bad thing—indeed there have been claims that a healthier industry will result from it—providing the higher load factors are achieved, as they widely were during 1978 and 1979. However, de-regulation is placing the industry on a knife-edge of continued economic stability. During the early 1980s, airlines will be introducing new capacity in a market which, because of low fares, has become more and more dominated by relatively low-income leisure travellers. Excessive pressures on airline costs or recession in the world economy resulting in a slowing or ending of growth in real incomes—or both—could have a disastrous effect on prospects of traffic coming forward to fill aircraft sufficiently to secure break-even loads. If in turn it proved impossible to reach break-even points in a low-fare regime, real difficulties might appear if airlines attempted a return to a strategy of higher fares to secure more revenue from market segments with a lower elasticity. As we have seen, the consumerist- and tourism-development pressures for low-fare innovation are increasing rather than diminishing, whilst regulatory authorities such as the U.K. Civil Aviation Authority have by their recent policy decisions[34] made it clear that they will resist attempts to use the regulatory system as a method to allow overcharging of Normal Economy Fare users in order to cross-subsidize losses on low-fare traffic. This resistance to

---

33 *See* Section 6.2.3.
34 For example, airlines have repeatedly been refused permission by the C.A.A. to increase North Atlantic Normal Economy Fares.

higher fares needs to be coupled with the large amounts of multiple entry which have been allowed in some deregulated markets in recent years, with the effect of this in spreading traffic thinly between carriers.

All in all, it is perhaps possible to be optimistic that should a reasonable stability in the world economy continue, the impetus towards greater efficiency which de-regulation is undoubtedly providing will be sufficient to ensure financial health on the part of participating airlines. However, should there be a downturn in the economy, the result could be serious problems of instability. This would especially be so in markets where extensive multiple entry has been allowed. It would be highly unlikely that de-regulation would then be seen as working in the consumer's interest, bearing in mind that money would be lost, that the travel plans of many would be upset and that there would be problems of passengers stranded abroad after completing only the outward leg of their journeys. Questions would also be asked in such a situation regarding the allocation of scarce fuel resources.

The danger of developing instability is important for the future of deregulation. However, there are three other considerations which are also very worthy of mention. The first is that all forecasts of high traffic growth and the achievement of the required break-even seat factors are based on the assumption that sufficient *airport* capacity will be available to handle the large amounts of traffic coming forward.

Airport investment is very different from that of the airlines which use them. Today, no airport operator in the developed world can work without being affected by hostile social and environmental pressures, whilst by their nature airport capacity expansion projects have long lead times. Today anything up to a decade or more can lapse between a decision being made that new capacity is needed, and this capacity becoming available for airline use. De-regulation has come at a time when it has exacerbated a growing crisis in airport provision. The genuine difficulties of long-term planning of airports, and the social and environmental pressures against them, are likely to mean a chronic shortfall in airport capacity in some markets in the future. This will be not so much in runway capacity—though even here some centres such as London are likely to have problems of runway capacity shortages—but in terminal and access capacity. De-regulation has joined with other trends in the industry to reduce the demand for runway capacity relative to passenger demand by hastening the introduction of larger aeroplanes and by increasing average seat factors. However, all these trends are only worsening the crisis in terminal capacity. They ensure both an increase in the total numbers of passengers coming forward and, even more significantly, exaggerated daily, weekly and seasonal demand-peaking.

1978 was undoubtedly the worst year in the history of the U.S. domestic industry for airport terminal handling, as the numerous complaints of both airlines and consumers would seem to testify.[35] In the North Atlantic market the lack of capacity of some of the major gateway airports was emphasized in a way which was hardly necessary for attention to be drawn to their chronic problems. The certainty is that, with long lead times of capacity expansion and the social and political pressures against it, these problems will worsen still further over the next few years. Airport capacity may yet prove the Achilles Heel of industry deregulation.[36]

Very much related to the question of airport capacity has been that of small-community service. Reduced regulation in the U.S. domestic industry has been marked by greatly-enhanced service in the major trunk markets. Indeed, this is as one would expect, with the trunk routes offering access to the largest market potential; this in turn allows the use of large aircraft with low seat-mile costs—something which is becoming very important with wider opportunities for price-competition. However, at the same time, there has been concern that some small communities have lost service altogether, whilst many others have seen their air service reduced to short-haul links to major hub airports, rather than the previous range of direct services. Only time will tell if the U.S. commuter airline sector is able to provide adequate service in the small community markets where de-regulation has been an important factor in reducing the amount of service offered by the trunk carriers.

The final problem of de-regulation we have already mentioned briefly on page 100. This is that the business traveller, whom we have argued may have been well-served by previous regulation, may see his quality of service substantially reduced. High seat-factors may reduce seat availability near to departure time. They may make airport handling even more of a trauma than it already is, whilst in-cabin conditions may be worsened by increased seats abreast and/or lower seat pitches. In pricing and fare construction, interline travel will be made more difficult by a growing tariff complexity, and perhaps even by a breakdown of the co-operative agreements between airlines regarding interline journeys. At the moment, it would indeed seem that many airlines are conscious of these possibilities, with the introduction of the three-class aeroplane being an attempt to safeguard the quality of service offered to the business traveller. We will discuss this development fully in Chapter 5, but certainly, should this concept fail, and perhaps even if it does not, the future will see a significant decline in the quality of service offered to the businessman, with de-regulation at least being partially responsible for this. Indirect effects of de-regulation would then be to encourage the development of the air taxi and corporate aviation sectors of the industry, and to emphasize the fact that the 'consumer interest' in aviation consists of a number of facets, rather than an all-pervading 'interest' in the lowest possible fare.

---

35 *See Travel Trade Gazette*, 22 Dec. 78.   **36** *See* Stuart (1979).

4.3.2 Conclusion—the Future of Regulation

The future impact of regulation on airline marketing activity must, in the prevailing circumstances, be very uncertain. Many of the old arguments for the regulation of air transport are still applicable today, especially those stemming from the international nature of the industry. However, the changes of the last few years have been far-reaching in scope. They have come in response to trends which have a long history and the influence of which is likely to be felt far into the future. Overall, a balanced view might therefore be that airline marketing activity will never be carried on in an environment which is even partially free of government involvement and intervention. However, trends of recent years indicate that the future may see the level of this intervention significantly reduced, especially in the United States where the de-regulation fervour has assumed the proportions of a crusade. In international markets, reduced regulation is likely to remain at least for the time being, particularly in mature markets such the North Atlantic. However, here, any development of major recession in the world economy is certain to bring financial difficulties for airlines and consequences which may widely be regarded as being unsatisfactory from the consumer's viewpoint. In such a situation, many governments may come to face a difficult decision between subsidizing airlines or insisting on a re-imposition of regulation in order to protect them. One would guess that the political difficulties of overt subsidy are likely to mean that a return to tighter regulation will be seen as a more palatable alternative.

Overall, therefore, regulation provides an uncertainty against which to view the processes of airline marketing. Normally one would expect that definition of corporate strategy could lead directly to the planning of the firm's products. However, it is very necessary to acknowledge first that, in aviation, regulation provides a constraint on all product design activity.

5 Designing the Product

Returning to the theoretical marketing model discussed in Chapter 1, it is logical having examined the market and airline strategies to move on to consideration of the design of the product. Our model suggests that in looking at such design work, firms should be attempting to find products which match the consumer demand which has been identified, and which can be offered at costs which allow reasonable profits, bearing in mind the willingness to pay of the different segments of the market. In this chapter, we need to be concerned with all aspects of the airline product, with particular emphasis on the relationships between product characteristics and the different corporate strategies available to airlines.

5.1 What is 'The Airline Product'?

To start this work, it is first necessary to decide whether or not airline service can be considered a 'product' in the marketing sense. We have seen in the discussion of industry regulation that some commentators have argued that the airline business possesses a number of unique characteristics. These set it apart from most areas of economic activity. Other writers have taken a view that aviation is no different from other industries and should be treated by the regulator accordingly.

The issue as to whether or not aviation provides a product which can be analysed in a conventional marketing way is, of course, rather different from deciding if it needs special treatment from the regulator. However, both points can be answered in the same manner. Aviation does have a range of features which suggest that it is separable from most areas of industrial activity. But these features do not prevent the use of a conventional marketing approach in the discussion of product design. The airline product is intangible, amorphous and difficult to analyse. It is, nevertheless, still something for which the consumer is willing to pay money to obtain, something which is capable of satisfying wants and needs, and which has features which will contribute—or fail to contribute—to consumer satisfaction.

Of these product features, some will relate to the *aircraft type* employed by the airline. This will decide line-haul speed (though here the tradeoff between speed and fuel consumption is becoming increasingly important), cabin spaciousness and cabin noise. It may also give an aspect of glamour to an airline's operations if it is using the most prestigious equipment. *Cabin layout* will be important, with the number of seats placed in the cabin fixing the aisle space, seat pitch[1] and seat width, the *schedule* adopted will contribute to the product in terms of route network, flight frequencies, flight timings and availability of interconnections. The relationship between the scheduled amount of capacity and the pattern of demand will decide the *seat accessibility* offered, as expressed by the probability of the passenger being able to obtain a seat near to his preferred time of departure. *On-time performance* will be a crucial product component, particularly to business travellers, as will *in-flight service*. Such features as the quality and variety of meals, the availability or otherwise of drinks, in-flight entertainment, cabin décor and flight attendant service, will all need to be planned. *Airport handling* will also be important to many customers, as will the need to make, and the ease of making, a *reservation*. Finally, *price* will be an aspect of the product, as will the *conditions* pertaining to the use of tickets.

These are the product features likely to be of concern to an airline's passenger customers. For freight users, requirements will differ. Such aspects as *freight ground handling systems, aircraft loading systems and door sizes*, and the existence of a *monitoring and control system* to check on a consignment's progress in its transit, all these will all be important.

In this chapter, it is inevitable that each product component should be dealt with separately, beginning in the next section with the planning of the airline fleet. However, it must be emphasized at the outset that it is the *synthesis* of the different components to build up a total product which matches consumer needs and airline production targets which is so vital. This will be dealt with in the book's conclusion.

5.2 Planning the Airline Fleet

The fleet will be at the core of any product design activity. An airline making the correct fleet planning decisions will have made a first step towards successful operations. One without the right kind of fleet will find that it has a handicap which only exceptional success in other areas will cancel out. But what are the main characteristics of aeroplanes which will be important from a product planning viewpoint?

Central to all measures of aircraft characteristics is the *cruising speed*. Today, virtually all jet transport aeroplanes from which carriers will be

---

1 The distance between the front of one seat and the front of the next forward.

selecting their fleets have cruising speeds in the 500 to 600 m.p.h. range, with the exception of Concorde. On short-haul sectors, an equally important measure will be *block speed*. This is the average speed from chocks-away to chocks-on, taking into account taxiing, takeoff and landing and acceleration and decleration phases.

Along with speed, *payload/range*[2] performance will be central to product design. Aircraft are transport vehicles which have an especially strict maximum weight above which operations are unsafe. This maximum weight is made up by the weight of the aircraft 'ready for service,' payload, and fuel. Payload is the measure of the quality of product available for sale, and is a strong contributing factor in the determination of unit costs of operation. However, given the limits on maximum takeoff weight, no aircraft designer can give attention only to ensuring a large payload capability. Allowance must also be made for the weight of fuel to be carried. A distinction therefore always arises between aircraft regarding the range over which they are designed to operate.

An airline flying only short sectors would be foolish to buy a long-range aeroplane. This would mean investment in the fuel tankage, engine thrust and aerodynamic qualities to lift the large quantities of fuel required for long journeys. Aircraft manufacturers have therefore produced a variety of aircraft types and variants with different payload-range capabilities. Aircraft with a relatively small potential payload will be suitable for airlines flying routes with limited traffic potential and/or where flight frequency is important. Similarly, aircraft with a small fuel-capability will be optimal for airlines operating short routes.

For all aircraft types, however, the manufacturer has generally aimed at a degree of flexibility in the way in which his aircraft is used. A first option he allows is to take up all the payload. Then, however, a proportion of the maximum fuel must be left out in order to keep within the maximum takeoff weight. Alternatively, the airline will be able to use all the tank space to secure long range. However, doing this involves a tradeoff in that the longer range will only come at the expense of reduced payload. Finally, between these two extremes airlines will have a flexibility to trade-off payload against fuel with the aim of achieving the optimum mix for the payload potential available and the length of the route.

In some cases, the nature of the airline product available for sale can be affected by the *fieldlength/range* characteristics of an aeroplane. All aircraft have a minimum distance which they will need for their takeoff run. This is decided mainly by the total weight of the aircraft, its aerodynamic qualities and engine thrust, the altitude of the airport and the prevailing air temperature and wind conditions. Of these variables, all except the aircraft weight are fixed in the short term. Therefore, if an

2 For a full explanation *see* Stratford (1974), pp 56–61.

airline finds itself with a need to operate out of an airport where the length of runway is less than the type of aircraft employed might ideally require under the prevailing conditions, it will have to reduce weight. This is usually done by leaving out fuel, with the airline product thereby affected by the imposition of an intermediate stop in what otherwise might have been a non-stop journey.[3]

In any product design, *operating costs* must be seen as a crucial aspect of any aeroplane. Such costs respond to its aerodynamic and propulsive efficiency, particularly fuel efficiency, the utilization obtainable from it, its payload capability, and the sector lengths over which it is used. However, from a product planning viewpoint, it is not only available operating costs which are significant. Costs per *revenue* seat–kilometre or tonne–kilometre will be a very important measure. These are made up of the costs incurred in the production of every unit of output actually sold by the airline. They will be a function both of available operating costs, and of the load factor as a measure of the proportion of the available output which is bought by customers.

Load factor will be influenced by our final performance characteristic— the *customer appeal* of different aircraft. The question as to whether or not aircraft type has a large influence on the choice of airline made by the customer is an interesting one. It may be that some passengers are unaware of plane type until they actually board their flight. However, a safe generalization is that today, wide-bodied types have a definite appeal over narrow-bodied aircraft. This is especially so on long-haul routes, where the advantages of cabin spaciousness are sufficient to outweigh any disadvantages of lengthened aircraft loading and baggage reclaim times. Equally, some aircraft are known to have an attraction for regular travellers. For example, the VC-10s used by British Airways were a consistant success in this respect due probably to the low levels of cabin noise of an aircraft with T-tail and engines placed at the rear of the fuselage.

Given these five characteristics of aircraft performance, what are the fleet planning decisions which will have an impact on the products airlines make available to their customers? The following decision areas are important:

1. Which Aircraft Types will be Obtained by the Airline?

Apart from the remarks above regarding aircraft type, some further comments on this decision are required. An airline may, perhaps by use of some of the complex statistical models now available, be able to decide

---

3 A good example of the product implications of runway length came with the U.K. government's unsuccessful attempts during 1978 and 1979 to force Air Canada to transfer its services from Heathrow Airport to Gatwick. Amongst its objections to making the move, Air Canada claimed that the runway at Gatwick was inadequate to allow it to operate such sectors as London–Vancouver as non-stop services.

exactly on the characteristics required of the aircraft to be included in its fleet. However, such requirements must be set against the nature of the contemporary world aerospace industry.

Aerospace can be divided into these sectors associated with the production of airframes, aeroengines and components. In each sector, risks are substantial. Large and uncertain investments are required over long periods of time before any hope of a return exists. The possibility of profit depends entirely upon securing a very long production run to ensure the widest possible distribution of development and tooling costs.[4] These characteristics have led to the industry being highly concentrated, particularly with regard to airframes and engines. Today, the manufacture of the airframes of the western world's large transport aircraft is concentrated in the hands of the three American companies of Boeing, Lockheed and McDonnel-Douglas, and the Airbus Industrie consortium of European manufacturers. Aero-engines are mainly assembled by the two American Firms of Pratt and Whitney and General Electric, and in the U.K. by Rolls-Royce (1971) Ltd. As with any industry dependent on long production runs for its economic success, the individual consumer inevitably loses a measure of his supposed sovereignty. Today, no manufacturer can risk making available an aircraft type—or even a variant of a type—which so closely matches the needs of a single customer that it does not have a wide sales potential to other airlines. Therefore all plane selection decisions are to some extent a compromise between the airlines' exact needs and the provision which the manufacturer, using his commercial judgement, is prepared to make.

The second qualifying factor on aircraft selection is that many such decisions are intensely *political*. As noted in Chapter 3, the national-pride aspects of aerospace, its importance to defence capability and its employment and balance-of-payments implications have meant that governments have often become involved in airlines' fleet planning decisions. This has especially been so in those countries such as Britain and France where state ownership of national airlines is combined with extensive involvement in aerospace manufacturing.

As a further constraint, brief mention must be made of *fleet commonality*. For any airline, there are sound economic advantages in minimizing the number of airframe and engine types in the fleet, by the use of such options as having the same engine types on different airframes. Thus for example, both the Pratt and Whitney JT-9D engine family and the General Electric CF6 are available on B747, DC-10 and A300 airframes. Such commonality may be important in comparison with, say, the Lockheed L1011, which so far is only available with Rolls-Royce RB211 engines.

As a final aspect on plane-type selection with which we can deal, note must be made of the relationship between the aircraft manufacturers and the

4 *See* Hartley (1974), p. 68.

airlines. Despite the concentration of the aerospace industry and the incentive for market collusion that this gives, it is known that the world market in aeroplanes operates under intensely competitive conditions. Important factors in selection can therefore be the purchase price offered by the manufacturer, trade-in arrangements on old aircraft, the scheduling of progress payments for the new planes and the nature of performance and spares costs guarantees. Many decisions are known to have hinged finally not on the actual characteristics of two closely-matched aircraft, but on the terms and conditions offered by their respective manufacturers.

Plane selection will have obvious and far-reaching consequences for the nature of the airline product, and there has only been space here to consider a small number of aspects of what is a highly complex decision-area. However, in terms of product design the nature of the product will also be very much affected by a second decision relating not to the type of capacity but to the quantity to be purchased.

2. How Many of Each Type of Aircraft Should be Obtained by the Airline?

Modern aircraft are expensive items of capital equipment. The cost of a long-haul, wide-bodied aeroplane is now in excess of U.S.$50 million. It is therefore important that an airline should not purchase excessive capacity. However, equally, the product can be adversely affected if it purchases only small amounts of capacity relative to demand. If it attempts to cater for demand without any back-up capability, its passengers will be vulnerable to delays whenever technical problems arise. Many airlines, of course, do operate without back-ups and it may be that given the high capital-costs of aircraft and the poor utilization which back-up capacity entails, this is a correct policy. However, it will have an impact on the airline's product through a poorer on-time record. The other reason for examining the relationship between capacity and demand is that of *seat accessibility*. The availability of seats near to flight departure time is a crucial product component in some types of air transport operation. This, however, is a function both of the amount of capacity obtained by an airline and its deployment through scheduling policy. This is thus a convenient point to turn to the second part of airline product design—the planning of the schedule.

5.3 Airline Schedules Planning

Scheduling decisions should position the airline's product relative to the market segments its chosen strategy is designed to exploit. The fleet will in some ways be relevant to such positioning, but it is possible for airlines exploiting totally different segments to do so using identical aircraft. Today, the same aircraft are used by both scheduled and charter airlines.

This is despite the fact that scheduled carriers mostly seem to be attempting some form of the total market strategy discussed earlier, whilst charter airlines concentrate almost exclusively on the leisure segment. However, with the schedule as a product component, it is inconceivable that an airline correctly pursuing a total market strategy should do so using the same type of schedule as one selling only to the leisure market.

Schedules planning involves decisions being made in each of the following areas: the *points to be served* by the airline; the *flight frequency* which will be offered to these points, whether these will be *direct flights or flights with intermediate stops*; the *types of aircraft* from within the airline fleet which will be used on each route; and finally the *timings* of the flights.

5.3.1 Scheduling Decisions

In making scheduling decisions, an airline with an appropriate marketing orientation should be aiming at enhancing the achievement of its corporate objectives. However, in doing this it must accept that there are often conflicts over innovations which will have a favourable impact on traffic and market shares but which have an unacceptable cost. Therefore compromise is of the essence in scheduling.

1. Which Points are to be Served by the Airline?

Decisions on the nature of the network are fundamental to all airlines. However, in practice, such decisions are very rarely made on purely marketing grounds, because of the all-embracing system of regulation characteristic of the airline industry. An airline carrying out a correct study of an appropriate route network should be influenced by traffic potential, the likely extent of competition, and the degree to which the segmentation of the market on each route matches its agreed corporate strategy. Thus an airline basing its operations on the leisure market should choose routes between centres of population and holiday resorts, or with a substantial V.F.R. potential; and an all-freight airline should choose those between points with significant freight-generating capability. The total market airline should aim at a cross-section of routes with mixes of business, leisure and freight potential.

However, beyond these generalizations, any decision to serve a particular point will be bound up with economic regulation. An airline wishing to add a point to its network will be dependent upon government agreement. A scheduled airline will need its government to negotiate the appropriate bi-lateral agreement (in the case of an international operation), and then to designate it as the national carrier on the route. A charter airline, with the still basically different methods of regulation applying to charter operations, will usually rely on foreign governments not objecting to its operation of charter flights. Only in the case of the United States domestic industry, when its planned de-regulation is finally completed, will it be possible for an airline to make a decision to include a point in its schedule, and then proceed directly to the planning of services without a necessary intervening—and often abortive—phase of seeking the approval of governments.

Once an airline has defined a route or set of routes, it is an aspect of interest as to how these routes should be approached. In the literature on marketing theory,[5] two possible strategies are set out as being available to a firm making a decision to enter a new market. Either it can develop its own products for the market, or alternatively within the confines of government anti-monopoly legislation, it can acquire a firm already operating in these markets by a process of merger or takeover. De-regulation in the U.S.A. has been followed by a spate of merger proposals. At least some of these have come from airlines wishing to extend their networks without the problems—and risks—of trying to build up services in new markets whilst still facing intense competition from established operators. However, generally, the scope for using merger as a route acquisition method in air transport has been small. The political nature of the industry has limited the possibilities for true multi-national companies, whilst fears of the unacceptable consequences likely to flow from monopoly have generally made government authorities reluctant to approve merger proposals.

2. Direct Flights or Flights with Intermediate Stops?

This decision concentrates upon a classic dilemma of scheduling. In the earliest days of commercial aviation, aircraft ranges were so limited that anything more than a short route had to be operated with frequent stops for technical reasons. However, today, several aircraft are available which have a non-stop range with substantial payload in excess of 5,000 miles (the B747-200, DC 10–30 and L1011–500). Boeing are now producing a special version of the 747 (the 747SP) with a non-stop range of more than 6,500 miles. The development of aircraft range capability has meant that only for the longest international sectors is an intermediate stop a technical necessity. In all other sectors the inclusion of a stopping point or number of points is a product design decision, ideally carried out purely for marketing reasons. Even on very long-haul routes, it is quite common for marketing considerations to dictate extra stops being included beyond the number which are necessary for aircraft refuelling and to take account of crew hours-limitations.

In any product design situation, direct flights between two points have the great advantage that they will give the fastest possible journey time for end-to-end passengers. Intermediate stops mean delays to such passen-

5 *See*, for example, Kotler (1976), pp. 58–9.

gers. It is rarely possible to complete a stop in less than half-an-hour, and often a longer time than this is needed. Wherever an airline's competitors are offering end-to-end passengers direct flights, there will be strong pressure on it to match them by direct flights of its own. Equally, where an airline is coming new to a route where existing airlines are operating with intermediate stops, then it can be a potent competitive weapon to enter with direct services. Intermediate stops also mean additional payments of airport landing charges, reductions in aircraft utilization, more periods of inefficient aircraft operation at low speeds, and extra costs of airport handling.

Despite these disadvantages, the inclusion of intermediate stops on an airline's routes does bring counterbalancing—and frequently decisive—gains. These relate to the increase in the number of cities which can be served and the frequency with which they can be offered in the timetable. In some cases there may also be advantages, appreciated by a large number of passengers, of the ability to use a particularly attractive duty-free shop,[6] or to take cheap 'stopover' holidays. With market potential, an airline substituting an intermediate stop for a previously direct service will still be able to compete for end-to-end passengers—admittedly perhaps with a less attractive product—but will, in addition, have available to it passengers between the origin and the intermediate point, and the intermediate point and the final destination. Through this extra traffic potential, even the end-to-end passengers may, in some cases, be said to gain in that their lengthened journey times may be compensated for by an improved flight frequency and/or the use of larger aeroplanes with lower unit operating costs.

With the imposition of intermediate stops on an international route, an important additional constraint is the ever-controversial point of Fifth-Freedom rights.[7] For an intermediate stop to have maximum value it is essential that the airline should hold Fifth-Freedom rights between the intermediate point and the final destination of the route. If it does not do so, then much of the marketing justification for the stop will be lost.

3. Flight Frequencies and Aircraft Type

Flight frequencies and aircraft types will decide the capacity that an airline makes available on a route. This in turn is an important variable explaining market share, particularly the share of the business travel market which an airline with a business segment or total market strategy is successful in obtaining.

We have seen in Chapter 2 (Section 2.3.1) that the business-travel segment has as one of its dominant characteristics the fact that a propor-

---

6 Shannon Airport in Eire achieved popularity with passengers for this reason, whilst arguably Amsterdam does have such an attraction today.

7 *See* Section 4.2.1.

tion of demand does not book until near to flight departure time. Even where reservations are made some time in advance, last-minute changes of plan can give rise to a need to alter bookings subsequent to an initial reservation. It is therefore likely that an airline offering a high frequency will gain a correspondingly good share of the available market, since some travellers will begin their search for a reservation with the simple constraint of 'next flight out' or with a definite departure time in mind. Obviously the higher the share of total frequency which an airline holds, the better the probability that it will be the airline which can give a departure near to the preferred time of travel. Equally for the proportion of bookings which come through travel agents, a good flight frequency will mean that an airline is likely to be contacted by an agent when he has a client requiring a particular departure time.

However, implementation of a schedule with a high flight frequency is not the sole key to designing a product which will attract business travellers. Such capacity as is made available must be seen relative to the demand coming forward. It will be of no relevance whatsoever to the passenger with an urgent need to travel that an airline has, say, three flights per day on a given route, if these flights are fully booked and perhaps have been so for several days or weeks before. An airline will therefore only be successful in attracting a high proportion of available business demand if it pays attention to one of the most crucial variables in airline product planning—that of seat-availability relative to demand.

As a principle, no airline will want a flight to take off less than full.[8] All output is instantly perishable at the time of production, with the revenue-earning potential of an empty seat lost forever. Therefore, in an ideal world an airline will place just enough capacity into a market to ensure that seats remain available for sale until shortly before flight departure time, with the final seat then sold so that the plane takes off completely full. However, such a situation is seldom achieved. Demand inevitably shows random, unforecastable variations, with any airline providing enough capacity to meet, say, average demand for a particular flight likely to find that on a good percentage of occasions that flight is sold out well before departure (*see* Shaw and Budd, 1979). Aside from random variations, demand patterns for air transport also show large differences through time. Airline capacity, however, is totally inflexible in the short run. Typically, business travel shows a pattern of daily peaking during the early morning and evening periods, and a weekly pattern of much higher traffic from Mondays to Fridays compared with the weekends. These demand variations can, as we shall see, be reduced to a limited extent

---

8 Though in fact some airlines have in recent years begun to advertise relatively low seat-factors as a positive product feature, particularly in the middle cabin of the new three-class aeroplane concept. *See* Section 5.4.1.

through the use of pricing policy and other measures, but they can never be eliminated entirely. What they mean is that if an airline is to provide a good seat availability on its peak flights, and thereby pick up all the last minute demand,[9] it will have excess capacity at off-peak periods. Perhaps the best situation would be to have some sort of *elastic* aeroplane which allowed airlines always to have the correct size of plane available for both peak and off-peak flights! However, in the real world—and despite the use of such limited flexibility as is available by the deployment of the different sizes of aircraft within the fleet—most airlines find that if they schedule sufficient capacity to meet all demand up to departure for their peak flights, they will have substantial excess capacity at the off-peak. This will mean relatively low average seat factors and very large differences between available and revenue seat-kilometre costs.

The product design implications of this problem of flight frequency and seat availability are immense, and are intimately bound up with the operating objectives and marketing strategy of the airline. For any airline whose principle *raison d'être* is seen as being the maximization of market shares for balance-of-payments or prestige reasons, it may well be the appropriate product planning strategy to offer high levels of frequency and seat availability. This will ensure that all possible demand which might be attracted to the airline will be catered for. However, such a policy will affect the airline's unit cost levels. A high frequency will only be possible if the airline uses relatively small aeroplanes. As we have seen, aircraft size is one of the main variables deciding the level of unit costs. Also, if the airline is to offer seat availability to all passengers who might wish to book or change their plans near to flight departure time, it will suffer from extremely low average seat factors. If seat availability is offered to peak-time passengers, the airline will find itself with a size of aircraft, or a number of aircraft in its fleet, which is far in excess of that required to satisfy off-peak demand.

The solution which is adopted by almost all airlines[10] is that, even if the airline has a corporate strategy involving exploitation of the business travel market, and where therefore seat availability is likely to be an important product component, no attempt is made to give last-minute seat availability to extreme peak-time customers. Instead, the airline accepts that such customers will be involved in a measure of inconvenience as average seat factors rise to a level where last-minute availability becomes unlikely.

Such a policy may lose an airline some business of highly-yielding customers. However, the gain of it is the average seat factors will be

9 A particularly important point here is that all passengers who constitute last-minute demand are likely to be using Normal Economy tickets, and therefore to be extremely high-yielding. *See* Section 6.2.2.

10 Glenn (1972) describes this compromise as being made by Air Canada on the North Atlantic.

higher, and therefore revenue seat-kilometre costs lower. In addition, it may be that the actual loss in traffic will be quite small. All carriers in a given market will be facing the same problems of demand peaking. Therefore, assuming that they too are working to objectives based on profitability, they will be making the identical compromise between seat availability and average seat factors. They will not therefore be in a position to take large amounts of traffic from the first carrier at the peaks. This possibility has been enhanced by the general willingness of regulatory authorities to offer protection to scheduled services,[11] and thereby prevent carriers entering a market in order to provide peak-time services only. However, with the movement towards deregulation, this protection may be less important in the future than it has been in the past.

For the airline which is basing its corporate strategy on the exploitation of the leisure rather than the business market, the aircraft-type/flight-frequency decision is quite different. We have seen in Section 2.3.2 that the leisure market has service requirements where expensive product components in flight frequency and seat availability are unimportant, but that the market is normally price-sensitive. Leisure market airlines—charter airlines in the European inclusive holiday industry are a good example—base their operations on the use of large aeroplanes and in particular on using these aeroplanes[12] at very high average seat factors. Also it seems that, unlike the business traveller on scheduled services, the European charter holidaymaker accepts the use of very inconvenient airport departure and arrival times in return for lower fares. This allows airlines to use night-time arrivals and departures[13] which improve aircraft utilization during the peak summer period and counterbalance the problems of securing an adequate utilization during the pronounced winter off-peak of many leisure markets.

4. Flight Timings

Flight timings make up the last decision-area in planning the schedule components of the airline's product. Obviously decisions regarding the timing of flights must be made at the same time as those related to their frequency. However, it is helpful to separate consideration of frequency and timings for the purpose of this chapter.

With regard to timings, any airline schedule must show at least three features to be as successful as possible in attracting business. It must give *convenient, easy-to-remember timings*. It is a truism to say that an airline must offer departures when people wish to travel, but any airline which

---

11 Section 4.1.2.
12 Though some airlines, of which Britannia Airways in the U.K. is a good example, have instead kept their average size of aeroplane small (the Boeing 737-200) and have based their marketing on an extensive availability of services from regional airports.
13 Within the limits of night-flying restrictions at airports. *See* Section 5.3.2.

fails to do this in a market where a substantial demand exists will be leaving the way open for competitors. Also, and this applies particularly to the business traveller and to bookings coming through travel agents,[14] it is likely that the person concerned will be able to retain in his mind the name of an airline which, say, goes 'every day at 3 p.m.' to a particular destination. He will find such retention much more difficult for the airline which only gives two or three departures per week at differing times.[15]

As a second need, it is important that timings should be *consistent*. We shall see in the next section how difficult the altering of departure timings can be at congested airports. Even where this is possible, such changes have definite costs associated with them in the re-education of travel agents and regular users. Finally, it will be necessary for timings to be *co-ordinated*. Transfer traffic over gateway airports is important to most scheduled airlines today. The best way of ensuring success in attracting transfer passengers is to build up frequencies and co-ordinate flight timings over a particular hub. This will allow the airport to serve the widest set of destinations and reduce to a minimum the waiting times between the arrival of an inbound connection and the departure of outbound services. Failure to do this will result in rival airports and airlines building up their gateway potential, and also other airlines at the initial airport obtaining transfer traffic through more convenient connections. Delta Airlines in the United States, particularly with their Atlanta hub, provide the classic example of airline success based on the co-ordination of timings in a schedule.

It is hoped that enough has been said in this section to indicate that the schedule is a vital product component for all airlines, and that decisions relating to it stem directly from an airline's strategy with respect to the available market. An airline aiming to attract the business traveller will have a schedule in which flight frequency and seat availability are the dominant features, and which costs a great deal to produce. The leisure-segment airline, on the other hand, can operate with a quite different and much more cheaply-available schedule. The total market airline will have to provide the seat availability and flight frequency to attract the business traveller. We shall see later (Section 6.2.3) that pricing policy can then be used as a weapon in securing utilization of off-peak capacity and, in view of the low prices which can be charged for such capacity, thereby offering a product to the leisure market as well. Indeed, it is this ability to use off-peak capacity with pricing concepts such as APEX which gives one of the main aspects of the synergy which should be available to the total market airline.

5.3.2 Constraints on Airline Scheduling

Having looked at the components of the airline passenger product made up

---

14 *See* Section 7.1.1.   **15** *See* R. R. Shaw (1975), p. 497.

by the schedule, it is now essential to examine briefly some of the constraints which affect scheduling activity. Although scheduling contributes greatly to the airline product, it is an area where the freedom of action of management is becoming increasingly circumscribed.

An important constraint is that of *airport use limitations*. On some routes these can dominate scheduling. At congested airports, it is likely that sometimes the demand from airlines for arrival and departure slots will exceed the capacity of the airport to handle flights. Where this is the case, a method must be found of allocating the scarce slots between the competing airlines. At most international airports this is done by a Scheduling Committee, with the International Air Transport Association having a co-ordinating role. If an airline fails to obtain its preferred slot through such a committee, a departure will have to be moved until a slot is available.

Also important at the present time are *night-flying restrictions* on airport use. The noise nuisance of the older generation of jet aircraft and community protest against this has led to a few airports around the world totally banning night-time operations. Many others impose restrictions on the number of night-time movements by the noisiest aircraft. As far as departures are concerned, this limits the timing of flights with a night-time departure. However, with scheduled passenger services this is unlikely to be important, except where a substantial demand might exist for cheap night-time excursion fares. Only for scheduled freighter flights are departure restrictions really a problem, and we shall look at this aspect more closely in Section 5.6. However, night-flying restrictions are a constraint on scheduling even for passenger operations because of the way in which they limit *arrival* times. It may be impossible for an airline to schedule a departure out of a given airport if the timing of the departure means that the aircraft will reach the destination airport when night-time restrictions apply. To add to such restrictions, there is the understandable reluctance on the part of passengers to arrive at a destination airport during dead-of-night periods when public transport connections may be non-existent. Furthermore, there are attempts by the hotel industry to avoid guests either checking-out or checking-in during the night. These factors, therefore, are a powerful constraint on an airline's scheduling of departure times. They are most important on long-haul routes, and especially so on east–west services where time-zone changes add further to the complications resulting from the duration of a flight. On such routes, it is quite common for only very short 'departure windows' to exist.[16]

A third problem with scheduling is that of *industry regulation and inter-airline agreements*. We saw in the last chapter that many of the

16 For example, on routes between London and Hong Kong, the departure window at London lasts for only $1\frac{1}{2}$ hours out of the 24.

intergovernmental bi-lateral agreements covering international scheduled services have in them capacity-controlling clauses. Usually there is also an acceptance that capacity will be equally divided between the carriers from the two countries signing the agreement. Even where such a bi-lateral does not exist, airlines themselves have often entered into pooling and other agreements which limit capacity. Whenever these controls apply, they decide the total amount of capacity which can be operated on a given route; they also often decide, in collaboration with the other carrier, the timings of such capacity as is provided. Indeed, it is probably only in the U.S. domestic market (where such capacity agreements are illegal) that regulation is not a dominating constraint on scheduling.

As a final constraint, it is worth mentioning *aircraft maintenance*, which can provide an increasingly important limitation on the product placed by the airline in the market-place. Today, especially on short-haul routes, aircraft are often maintained under a 'progressive' system. Instead of planes being taken out of service for long periods, all but the most major overhauls are split up into a number of sub-sets of operations. Each sub-set is capable of being performed in a few hours. Maintenance is carried out by the aircraft making a number of frequent short stops at the maintenance base, rather than a single long visit. Such a system carries with it the disadvantages of the costs of repeated set-up and set-down operations, but its decisive advantage is that it can minimize the opportunity costs of maintenance. It allows maintenance work to be carried out at night when there is little chance of a short-haul scheduled aircraft being employed on revenue-earning work. For the scheduler, progressive maintenance systems mean ensuring that an aircraft completes its day's flying as often as possible at the location of the maintenance base, and also that there may be difficulties associated with scheduling for early-morning flights from out-stations.

With this discussion of constraints on scheduling, we are now in a position to move on to the next aspect of the airline product—that relating to the quality of customer service offered to passengers.

5.4 Airline Customer Service

In the last section we have seen that the planning of the airline schedule as a product component should stem directly from the contrasting character-istics of the different segments of the air passenger market. Exactly the same is true with the planning of the parts of the product which relate to customer service.

Customer service is a difficult aspect of airline product design. It is intangible both in its components and in the assessment of passenger reaction to it. However, by way of definition, it can be stated that it consists of all aspects of the product supplied to the customer apart from the aircraft type, route and timing. It therefore includes service at the point of sale, at the airport before and after a flight, and in-flight service. It also, strictly speaking, includes the question of a reservation, but this is such a specialized aspect that we shall deal with it separately in Section 5.5.

It is easy to underestimate the importance of customer service as it does not have a great deal of effect on the total market for air travel. Few people will base a decision as to whether or not they will fly to a particular destination on the quality—or lack—of customer service by airlines.[17] However, customer service will still be vital because of its effect on market share. In the past, under tight regulation, competing scheduled airlines have charged the same fares, except where 'illegal' discounting has taken place. Identical fares mean that any passenger without a tight timing constraint is able to choose the airline with the highest standards of service. This will be done on the reasonable grounds that he will not be offered a cheaper fare in return for choosing the inferior product of an airline where standards are not as good. This has been an especially important consideration in marketing to the business-travel segment, where the passenger is likely to be a regular traveller, and therefore have an opportunity to compare the standards of different airlines. He will also be a good capture for any airline which can secure his patronage because of the frequency of his trips and the high-yielding fares he is likely to use.

With the airline specializing in the leisure travel segment, customer service decisions take on a rather different form, particularly in charter markets where the regulatory system allows for pricing freedom. Here, the airline's presumed ideal of providing the highest levels of service must be tempered by the costs of doing so. This is especially the case in view of the selling channels employed by charter airlines, an aspect which will be dealt with in Section 7.1.1.

For the total market airline, customer service poses especial problems. The need to meet the expectations of business travellers, coupled with a requirement to offer low fares to the price-sensitive leisure segment[18] can lead to problems of equitable provision amongst different classes of passenger.

5.4.1 The Components of Customer Service

Customer service for airline passenger traffic can be divided into four component parts:

1. Service at the Point of Sale

For *any* product, the quality of customer service at the point of sale will be

---

17 However, as was mentioned in Chapter 2, there may be the first signs of this happening with airport and A.T.C. congestion leading to a growing preference for surface-transport-based holidays.
18 *See* Section 6.2.2.

vital to consumer satisfaction. However, it is reasonable to suggest such service as being especially important in air transport, because the customer is not buying a tangible product, but merely an air ticket and the hope of future satisfaction.

For charter airlines, the form of selling channel they have used—either by design or as a result of regulatory insistence—has meant that they have not been responsible for point-of-sale service to the retail customer. Instead, they have wholesaled their capacity to travel organizers, who are then responsible for retail selling. For all other airlines, ensuring adequate point-of-sale service is one of the major product problems of the present time.

Planning for point-of-sale service involves scheduled airlines in three separate operations. Firstly, adequate provision must be made for those members of the public who make their reservations direct with the airline. These customers are in minority for almost all airlines, but satisfactory arrangements for them will involve the airline setting up a system for telephone bookings, and also opening sales offices. Secondly, many scheduled airline tickets are sold on an interline basis whereby a passenger makes one booking for a multi-sector flight involving several carriers. Therefore a point-of-sale system must be set up for the hundreds of airlines around the world which might conceivably wish to make bookings with a particular carrier. Finally and most importantly, airlines must allow for their dealings with travel agents. We shall discuss the airline/travel agent relationship in Section 7.1.1, but for the moment it is important to note that many airlines receive upwards of 70 per cent of their bookings through agents. Therefore, to provide adequately for agent-based selling, airlines must offer training programmes to agency staff, maintain a force of sales representatives to ensure that agents are always well-informed about an airline's services, and set up special reservations facilities for agents.

Of these tasks, there can be special problems for airlines in ensuring an acceptable relationship with the travel-agency industry. In some countries this may involve contact with several thousand firms of widely differing levels of skill and commitment to the airline's product. In addition, both for travel agency outlets and for outlets which the airline runs directly, trends in the air travel market have worked against effective servicing in recent years. As airlines have moved towards low fare innovation in their pricing strategies, so their market has extended to encompass many inexperienced and first-time travellers. Also, for sound reasons, airlines mostly have based their low-fare innovation on pricing concepts which have imposed limitations on ticket usage. They therefore have been faced with point-of-sale tasks involving the computation of complex fares and a great deal of explanatory work when selling to customers unfamiliar with basic aspects of air travel. In consequence, costs of point-of-sale service have risen sharply, with airlines being required to take on additional staff and use extra office space for this purpose, whilst a real risk has developed that the quality of service to the business traveller will be jeopardized. (He, ironically, is normally very familiar with air travel and therefore does not take up a great deal of airline time in the making of bookings.)

2. Service at the Airport

Today, airport service is becoming one of the most congested components of the air travel system. As has been noted, the advent of wide-bodied aircraft has reduced the pressure on airport runway capacity. These have allowed airlines to handle increasing numbers of passengers with only a limited growth in runway movements. However, when coupled with continuing increases in passenger numbers, they have contributed to growing terminal congestion problems because of the marked effect which they have had in increasing the extent of peaking in terminal usage patterns.

The responsibility for airport services varies greatly. At many European airports—indeed widely throughout the world with the exception of the United States—the terminal fabric is provided by the airport operator. Many terminal services, too, are offered by him or his concessionaries. Airline involvement is therefore restricted to staffing the facilities for which the carrier is responsible, with this confined at many airports to check-in facilities and the baggage-handling system. In the U.S.A., on the other hand, many of the major airports—such as Kennedy, New York—have been based on a principle of unit terminals where an airline covers the operation of a whole terminal. This is exclusively dedicated to its services, or to the services of airlines with which it has reached commercial agreements for the subletting of capacity.

With regard to airline activity designed to ensure that a carrier achieves a product differentiation over its competitors, the nature of airports today confines such activity to fairly narrow areas. All carriers have been affected by the growth in airport delays brought about by the increased demands of airport security. At international airports it is likely that all airlines will be constrained by delays resulting from government formalities regarding customs and immigration. Aspects where such differentiation will be possible are (a) in the provision of check-in desks, where (assuming desks are not rationed by the airport operator) airlines must make a tradeoff between a provision which will limit queuing and the costs of both rental and staffing of additional desks, and (b) in the operation of the baggage-handling system. The age-old aviation problems of baggage misdirection, theft and loss do seem to vary between airlines and airports. A heavy investment in staffing here might be expected to bring an airline substantial returns in improving its customer service standard relative to carriers not investing as much.

3. Departure/Arrival Punctuality

The question of departure/arrival punctuality is a crucial aspect of airline customer service. As one would expect, almost all attitude surveys amongst *business* travellers have placed punctuality as the most highly-rated product component. However, even for *leisure* travellers, punctuality has been shown to be only slightly less important. Such factors as the unsuitability of airport terminals as locations for prolonged waiting, and inconvenience to meeters and greeters, account for a distaste for delay which is very strong amongst leisure as well as business passengers.

Airlines face important policy decisions with respect to punctuality. Punctuality can be a factor in plane choice, with some aircraft, such as the DC 9, having an especially good dispatch reliability record. Also, in view of the large variations between U.S. airlines in their punctuality data,[19] it may certainly be that management emphasis on punctuality as a product component can improve punctuality records. However, excessive emphasis on punctuality may mean an airline inconveniences large numbers of passengers whenever connecting flights are late. Also, if punctuality is emphasized in advertising and public relations campaigns, it may mean an increased customer annoyance at delays which are beyond the airline's control, such as those due to poor weather or air traffic control congestion.

4. In-Flight Service

Important though point-of-sale and airport service are to the customer, to a considerable extent aspects of each are beyond the control of an individual airlines. Therefore they cannot contribute a great deal to product differentiation. However, all components of in-flight service will be entirely the responsibility of the airline. We shall see later (Section 7.2.2) that almost all airline advertising campaigns aimed at the business traveller emphasize the quality of in-flight service.

In-flight service has been a problem area to airlines throughout the post-war period. It was accepted by the 1940s that price competition in air transport should be eliminated through regulation. It was then inevitable that airlines should place more and more emphasis on in-flight service in an attempt to secure competitive advantage. Consequently, during the early 1950s, carriers were vying with one another in lavish standards of catering and in the offering of expensive free gifts as inducements to potential travellers. However, in 1952, along with the introduction of so-called 'tourist' class with lower fares, airlines within I.A.T.A. concluded a number of Traffic Conference Resolutions—the 060 Series—which set out agreed standards of service provision. For First Class travellers these resolutions did little more than set down a maximum seat pitch (of 42 inches).

---

19 The U.S. market is the only one in the world where the carriers are required to make public their punctuality data.

However, for Economy[20] Class passengers, the 060 resolutions came to cover every aspect of service. Rules were set down covering the maximum seat pitch allowable (34 inches) and the minimum numbers of seats abreast to be placed in the cabin, with this varying with the size of aircraft. All alcoholic drinks were to be charged for, with agreement on minimum prices. The quality of meals was controlled (detail was set down on the permissible content of all meals, down to abortive attempts to decide on the nature of a 'sandwich'). Also, with in-flight entertainment, headphones were only to be made available to those passengers willing to pay a nominal fee.

The 060 resolutions have not been successful. They have provided potent ammunition for critics of the I.A.T.A. system.[21] It is also difficult to see that they have achieved their presumed aim of significantly reducing or eliminating in-flight service competition. So it is not surprising that the I.A.T.A. Task Force of 1978[22] included as one of its central proposals that these rules should be abolished. Airlines now have far greater freedom to design the cabin service component of their product free of outside interference on international services, as they have always had domestically.

With cabin service, therefore, two problems would currently seem to exist. Firstly, as has been suggested, scheduled airlines are widely criticized for their so-called 'excessive' expenditure on in-flight service. Most scheduled carriers incur around ten per cent of their costs in the passenger service category as shown in Table 5.1. Secondly, there are difficulties associated with securing equity in the provision of in-flight service between the users of differently-priced tickets.

Table 5.1. Expenditure on Passenger Services. Sample of Scheduled Airlines

Airline	1976	Year 1977	1978
		% of total costs	
1. Air Canada	11·4	10·9	11·2
2. Air France	11·6	11·4	11·7
3. Air India	9·5	10·6	11·9
4. Alitalia	10·2	10·3	9·2
5. British Airways	11·1	11·4	13·2
6. Lufthansa	9·1	9·6	10·6
7. Sabena	7·7	8·4	8·0
8. SAS	8·6	9·0	9·7
9. Singapore Airlines	12·4	N/A	12·4
10. United	10·9	11·0	11·4

Source: ICAO Financial Data.

20 Tourist Class was eventually merged with Economy Class following the latter's introduction in 1958. The term 'Coach' is used instead of 'Economy' in U.S. domestic service.
21 For example, Boyd-Carpenter (1975), p. 242.   22 Section 4.3.1.

With 'excessive cost,' such criticisms are most likely to apply to the leisure segment of the air travel market. It is here that demand is price-sensitive, with it being an easy progression of logic to propose that if airlines eliminated in-flight service, ticket prices could be reduced. This would allow customers access to the cheapest possible fares. Extra payments would then be made by those who required meals and other in-flight 'frills.'

Interesting though such ideas are, it is important not to exaggerate the effect which they might have on airline costs. A very high proportion (approximately 75 per cent) of the costs of in-flight service are made up by the staff costs of the cabin attendants. It is currently impractical to suggest an elimination of cabin service, because of the minimum provision of cabin attendants required under industrial safety rules. Attendants perform important functions in assisting at any emergency and dealing with medical and other in-flight problems. All airworthiness authorities currently insist that there should be a minimum number of trained cabin staff on each flight. Therefore a movement towards 'no frills' service can only save the costs associated with meal preparation, in-flight entertainment and the increment of cost of cabin attendants for those attendants provided above the minimum number.

The last few years have seen some interesting experiments with 'no frills' services. The original Laker Skytrain concept was an example of a product where the basic ticket price did not include provision of meals or drinks. However, here it has been notable that the no-frills element has only entailed a reduction of a few pounds in the fare, whilst it is understood that a considerable percentage of Skytrain passengers have still chosen to pay extra to receive in-flight meals.

The question of securing equity in in-flight service is more difficult and is important for the total-market airline aiming at a presence in both the business- and leisure-travel segments. It was suggested in Section 2.3.2 that the business passenger is likely to be drawn to an airline which can provide high standards of cabin service, whilst in Section 6.2.2 we shall note that it is only possible for an airline to participate in the leisure travel market if it provides a substantial number of low fares, in recognition of the higher price-elasticity of the leisure market.

These two facts make up a product-planning dilemma. In the past, the dilemma has been 'solved' by dividing the aircraft cabin between First and Economy class, and then providing the same levels of in-flight service for all in the Economy class cabin. This has perhaps had the advantage of simplicity, but it has brought a number of significant consequences. It has jeopardized the quality of service of those paying very high Normal Economy fares. There have also been difficulties of revenue dilution[23] as formerly high-fare passengers, unable to see that they are receiving

23 *See* Section 6.2.3.

anything by way of a superior product, have switched more and more to the use of low fares.

The answer to this problem now adopted by several airlines, has been to subdivide further the Economy Class cabin in the *Three Class Aeroplane*.[24] The concept here is that Normal Economy passengers should have a separate part of the cabin reserved for them, where a quiet working atmosphere and superior standards of catering can be offered. The rear of the aircraft can then be set aside for travellers using lower-priced tickets, where costs can be reduced by lower standards of meals (or even 'no frills' involving extra payments for meals) and theoretically in other ways as well.

The three-class idea has much to commend it from a marketing viewpoint. It is a recognition of market segmentation and the different requirements of the business and leisure segments. It should also reduce the number of complaints—basically reasonable ones—from business travellers that more should be done for them because of high fares they are paying. However, since its introduction, it has become clear that the idea has limitations which will confine its use to certain situations, and even here will probably mean that it cannot be applied in the pure form which the marketing theorist might hope for.

It is essential with three classes that there should be some form of cabin division, to avoid complaints from discount-class passengers regarding their inferior standard of service. Currently, therefore, 3-class service must be restricted to wide-bodied aircraft where the natural division of the aircraft allow it. However, it will only be possible for the concept to operate effectively where some sort of moveable cabin divider is installed in the aircraft. The problem of the 3-class system is that a subdivision of the cabin which is appropriate for one flight may be inappropriate for another. This is especially so on short-haul routes where the passenger mix on an early-morning business flight will be different from that on a mid-day off-peak service. On such routes, it may be that even if a moveable cabin divider for short-haul aircraft were developed, very tight turnround times would mean that it could not be widely employed. The difficulties of trying to operate three classes on small aircraft without cabin subdivision have already been experienced by airlines in the U.S.A., where some carriers have introduced and then abandoned the three-class concept. Even on long-hauls and with wide-bodied aircraft, however, the three-class concept has had to be modified from its original conception. It was hoped that it might be possible for the rear cabin to have a lower seat pitch and/or more seats abreast than the middle one, something which would reduce the true costs of carriage of discount fare passengers. However, again, problems of differing passenger mix from flight to flight have prevented this being

24 British Caledonian were the first U.K. airline to use 3-class, with the introduction of their London–Houston service in April 1978.

done. Also, hopes that the rear cabin might be genuinely 'no frills' with additional payments for meals have not been realized. For example, British Caledonian began their London–Houston operation in 1978 with such additional payments, but then abandoned the system, it is presumed because of the costs and delays of collecting small sums of money from considerable numbers of passengers very near to flight departure time and because of the difficulties of planning catering provision. A final problem of 3-class has turned out to be the need to offer no-smoking accommodation in each class. This has turned it into a 6-class concept for many airlines, something which has been unmanageable except for flights using the largest wide-bodied aircraft.

Overall, it is reasonable to suggest that the three-class concept can make a significant contribution to airline product design, but that it is unlikely to be employed as widely as the simple First Class/Economy Class distinction has been. Indeed, it may be that eventually a two-class system will re-emerge as First Class is combined with the new middle cabin. It has already been suggested[25] that First class passengers are, despite their high fares, paying well below the true production costs of First Class capacity. A new class somewhat above current Economy Class but below First Class might indeed be the best solution. This is a system which is now being introduced by some European airlines as the book goes to press.

The only remaining point to be dealt with under customer service is that of appropriate service standards for charter airlines. We have already seen how as a result, in some cases, of decisions on corporate strategy, but much more because of the nature of industry regulation, these airlines have almost exclusively concentrated on the leisure segment of the market. They have based their competition on the production of low-cost/low-priced services. As far as intra-European services are concerned, charter airlines' customer service standards are notable for the single class of operation they provide and for the lower seat pitches which they give to passengers (generally 29 inches, but sometimes as low as only 27). It is also accepted that catering standards are lower on charters. For long-haul charter operations, on the other hand, catering provision reaches very high levels. The complete absence of regulatory controls and intense competition have been factors leading to good catering standards and the offer of free drinks on such services as North Atlantic Advanced Booking Charters.

Overall, customer service can be emphasized as vital in airline product design. As always, decision-making for it should follow from a logical process of market analysis and definition of corporate strategy with respect to the available market. Again, as with other aspects, it is the total market airline which has the greatest opportunities but also the chief difficulties in designing this part of its product.

25 C.A.A. (1977a), p. 20.

5.5 Airline Reservations

The final aspect of airline passenger product design with which we shall be able to deal is that of reservations. This is an area where growing arguments have been apparent in recent years regarding appropriate procedures.

The reservations system required by an airline will be decided very largely by the selling channel which it decides to employ. Any airline basing its selling on wholesaling of capacity to travel organizers will have no need for a sophisticated reservations system. This is the situation enjoyed by charter airlines which confine themselves to selling in this way. For scheduled airlines, on the other hand, relying as they do on a mixture of direct selling to the public, selling through travel agents, and acceptance of interline bookings taken by other carriers, a reservations system has been an essential product component. The airline is offering an instantly perishable product in a vehicle which has a fixed capacity. Its customers have, until now at any rate, always been considered unwilling to take the chance of turning up at the airport and finding that capacity is not available for them.

5.5.1 Types of Reservation System

Given the need for reservations, a system must meet three criteria if it is to perform effectively. It must give high quality of service to the customer in terms of accuracy and speed of response. It must serve the airline by ensuring that as small an amount as possible of capacity goes to waste. Finally, it must do these two things in such a way that the costs to the airline (and, eventually, the passenger) are minimized.

To achieve these objectives, three tasks must be accomplished.[26] The system must be able to *store* large quantities of information over long periods of time. A scheduled airline may be operating upwards of a thousand flights a week, whilst some potential customers typically begin making reservations many months before departure. It must be able to *up-date* this stored information as bookings are received, at high speed. Failure to up-date quickly may result in tickets on a flight continuing to be sold, even though it is in fact full. Finally, the system must be able to *communicate* with the thousands of locations where the airline's ticket might be sold, including its own sales offices, travel agents and offices of other airlines.

In the early years of the development of the industry, reservations operations were based on open display of information and manual

26 *See* Jeaniott (1974).

up-dating. However, the expansion in the demand for air travel, together with the arrival of computer technology, has meant that, for large airlines today, reservations activity is almost entirely computer-based. Real-time computers are ideally suited for reservations work. They store information very efficiently, and up-date it instantaneously. Communication is then possible on a world-wide basis using visual display unit and teletype technology, with telephone communication still available for those outlets where the volume of business is not large enough to justify V.D.U. investment. Most large airlines now have their own computer reservations systems, whilst smaller carriers typically will hire capacity from the system of a larger carrier.

At the present time, developments in micro-electronics are beginning which will eventually come to have major implications for the reservations part of the airline product. In the U.K., a system known as 'Travicom' is being introduced. This allows travel agents access to the reservations computers of a large number of airlines from a single visual display unit. Even more radical, the 'Prestel' system developed by the U.K. Post Office may eventually allow individual passengers to communicate directly with the reservations computers of airlines, and to make credit card bookings, through a special adaptation of their television sets. Besides having important customer service implications, systems such as Travicom and Prestel are likely to be significant in the area of the relationship between airlines and the travel agency industry, an aspect which is considered in Section 7.7.1.

5.5.2 The Problem of Airline Overbooking

When designing the reservation part of the passenger product there is one policy decision which must be made by all carriers. Should the airline overbook its flights? If it does decide to do so, how may such a policy best be applied?

To many outside the industry a policy of deliberately offering for sale more tickets than there are places on an aircraft is abhorrent. It leads to occasions where more passengers report for a flight than can be accommodated on it, with awkward decisions then needing to be made as to which passengers will *not* be carried. In fact, however, the question as to whether or not overbooking should be used is finely-balanced both from the point of view of the airline designing its product, and from that of the guardian of the consumer's interest. Consumers can be shown to gain substantially from the correct operation of an overbooking policy.

The reason why overbooking arises as a policy question is the existence of large numbers of *no-show passengers*. All scheduled airlines find that, of the bookings they take, a large number[27] are never kept because passen-

27 13·5 per cent of bookings taken for British Airways long-haul services in 1974–5 (*see* C.A.A. (1976)).

gers do not turn up to use the seats which are reserved for them. There are many explantions for this fact. A considerable proportion of no-shows may be classifed as 'accidental' in the sense that the passenger has every intention of keeping his reservation but is prevented from doing so. Examples of this may be: delays in the airport access system due to car breakdown or traffic congestion; illness shortly before flight departure time; or—very commonly—delays to incoming flights when a passenger is on a multisector journey. Some may also result from communication failures, as when a passenger instructs his travel agent or secretary to cancel a booking, but this is not then done. However, besides accidental no-shows, a proportion must be described as deliberate, as where a businessman who is uncertain as to what time his meeting will end, books flights at different times with different airlines, knowing that only one reservation will finally be used.

To any airline facing a no-show problem, the attractions of over-booking are obvious. Careful monitoring of no-show patterns over a period of time should indicate a level of overbooking on a particular flight which will match the likely extent of no-shows. If all works out successfully, the extent of no-shows will correspond to the level of overbooking, and all passengers who report for a flight will be carried. The airline in turn gains revenue from seats which otherwise would remain empty[28]. Most importantly, the consumer interest can also be shown to be met by correct overbooking. The increase in airline average seat factors which it brings keeps down fares. Over-booking also allows a higher proportion of travellers to get away on the flight of their choice. Without overbooking, when a flight is full, all additional passengers asking for a seat on it will be turned away and will be forced to travel on later and presumably less convenient flights. When departure of the first flight occurs, assuming the normal proportion of no-shows, there will be the ironic situation of an aircraft taking off less-than-full, and passengers who wish to travel on it still delayed at their origin point.

Despite these advantages, there can be no doubting the extent of consumerist opposition to the practice of overbooking. This results from the one unfortunate consequence which it brings. Almost irrespective of the care with which overbooking is managed, the randomness inherent in no-show patterns means that occasions will arise when more passengers report for a flight than can be carried on it. If this happens, a decision must be made as to which passengers are to be off-loaded. There are obvious difficulties in making such a decision, and there have been past accusations[29] of airlines having policies of choosing the 'most logical

---

28 British Airways, when prosecuted under the U.K. Trade Descriptions Act for its overbooking policy, argued that abandonment of overbooking would lead to a 6 per cent fall in its average seat factor—a crucial amount for a scheduled airline—and that this fall would be accounted for by a loss of very high-yielding business.

29 Simon (1968).

passenger'—the passenger who will do the airline little commercial harm because he does not have interconnections and does not look like a regular traveller, and also who appears unlikely to make a vociferous public complaint. In their defence, airlines have pointed to the rarity of offloading situations. In the U.S. domestic market—again the only one where data are publicly available—despite a recent increase, the off-loading rate is still below one in a thousand emplaned passengers. However, the difficulties posed by off-loading and the damage it does to an airline's commercial reputation have led to a great deal of attention being given to alternatives to an overbooking policy.

Probably the most important discussions have centred around the use of no-show penalties for passengers who fail to turn up. It is, of course, a justifiable criticism of overbooking that those who cause the problem—no-show passengers—are different from the victims of off-loading who suffer as a result of its 'solution.' It therefore seems logical that no-show passengers should be penalized by a proportion of their ticket refund being withheld if they have paid in advance, or else their being required to pay a sum in compensation to the airline where advanced payment has not been involved.

No-show penalties have a long history in the airline industry, and indeed on some routes it is still theoretically possible to charge them. For example, the U.S. airline World Airways in its recently commenced 'no frills' Los Angeles to New York service has based the operation on the charging of substantial penalties to no-show passengers.

The theory of the no-show charge is sound—it should both discourage no-shows and provide the airline with compensating revenue when they do occur. However, it has not proved effective in alleviating the no-show problem, particularly with respect to the market of regular business travellers who are the chief offenders. Any airline which tried to charge a no-show penalty to 'accidental' no-shows would presumably be very unpopular, particularly if the reason for no-showing was a late inbound connection with one of its own flights! As soon as one accepts the position that there are *some* no-show situations where a penalty will not be charged, airlines are involved in a highly invidious and time-consuming process of deciding what is acceptable and what is not acceptable as an explanation, and—worse still—which of their passengers are lying and which are not. Also, for sales not involving the advanced payment of cash, there will be acute difficulties in tracing passengers and forcing them to pay a no-show charge. Finally it is only being realistic to say that if one airline decides to impose a no-show charge whilst one or more of its competitors does not, it will lose substantial amounts of business to its rivals, with it being unlikely that the revenue from the no-show charges will be sufficient compensation.

Other approaches to the solution of the no-show problem are equally unpromising. It has been said that airlines could introduce a measure of equity by only booking flights up to the capacity of the aircraft. Other enquirers would be offered reservations, up to an agreed level of over-booking. However, they would be told that theirs were overbooked reservations and that, in the unlikely event of all passengers reporting for a flight, it would be they who would be considered for off-loading. Unfortunately, whilst this idea has the advantage of fairness, it has both commercial and practical disadvantages. If no price reductions were given to overbooked passengers, it would result in a loss of business to rival airlines, despite the truly very remote chance that a seat would not finally become available. If such loss of traffic were avoided—or at least reduced—by the granting of lower fares to overbooked passengers, the airline could end up giving these fares to a high proportion of all those using its services, with a serious reduction in yields. Well in advance of departure time, many flights are overbooked by a large percentage, not because of the likelihood of no-show passengers, but because it is known that many passengers will alter or cancel their reservations prior to flight departure. Wherever passengers are offered—and presumably appreciate—the opportunity to alter or cancel bookings, the granting of lower fares to all those who are at some stage technically overbooked is simply not possible. Finally, the practical difficulties come from the fact that it is one thing to tell a passenger that if off-loading should be necessary he will be the victim; it is quite another to deal with a situation when, very shortly before flight departure time, as the need for off-loading becomes known, *that* passenger is already sitting in the aircraft, with his baggage in the lower hold.

All in all, it may be that a closely monitored and supervised overbooking policy is the best solution to what is a thoroughly unsatisfactory situation. Indeed, in recent years such a view would seem to have been increasingly accepted by regulatory authorities around the world. However, added provisos have been a need for airlines to compensate at an appropriate rate passengers inconvenienced by off-loading, and to give a commitment to fly them to their destination by the next available flight, even if this is by another airline. Compensation is intended both to cover any incidental expenses the passenger may incur and also to act as an inducement to accept delay. There has in fact been considerable academic interest in recent years in the establishment of market prices for off-loading delays.[30] Congested airport terminals may not be the best places to enact bidding or other systems, but the principle that compensation should be fixed at such a level that a passenger in no great hurry to reach his destination finds the compensation offered sufficient to mean that he feels no inconvenience from the delay, is a sound one and probably represents the best that can be hoped for in the circumstances.[31] Certainly, whatever one's views, it is

---

30 *See* Simon (1968, 1970); Falkson (1969); Vickrey (1972).
31 Except, of course, that the compensation is itself paid out of the fares of passengers who by definition have *not* been no-shows!

likely that an overbooking policy will remain a product feature for scheduled airlines for the foreseeable future.

5.5.3 Alternatives to Reservations

The question of designing the reservation part of the airline product has become complicated in recent years by the development of service concepts which do not require one. These concepts include the *Shuttle*, the product bought with the scheduled airline *Standby* fare, and the initial form of the Laker Airways Ltd. *Skytrain*.

The Shuttle concept has a long history in the aviation industry. It was pioneered in U.S. domestic service by Eastern Airlines during the early 1960s. However, it has only been during the 1970s that Shuttles have been introduced into other markets. There is now a great deal of interest in the Shuttle idea, especially for intra-European services.

The principle of Shuttle operation is that the passenger does not have to make a reservation in advance. Instead he ensures that he reaches the airport by the departure time of his required flight. The airline then guarantees to carry all those who have reported for the flight. It is able to do so by maintaining back-up aircraft, which are brought forward for use should more passengers report than can be accommodated on a single plane.

It is easy to demonstrate a large number of advantages for the Shuttle concept. The passenger does not need to make reservations, saving him time and the airline costs. He can pay in advance if he wishes, but he is equally entitled to pay at the airport when he arrives. As the Shuttle is operated by British Airways, passengers are offered a 'pay on the plane' facility. Also, the passenger is relieved of any anxiety about reaching the airport for a given flight. For a businessman whose meeting ends earlier or later than expected, this means that he can always travel by the most convenient flight, without the trouble of attempting to alter reservations near to departure time. For the airline, Shuttle is one air transport concept which totally eliminates the no-show problem with its attendant waste and bad publicity brought about by overbooking. Finally, for both airline and passenger, it brings the opportunity for exploitation of a market for last-minute, unplanned, decisions to travel.

Despite these advantages, the idea of Shuttle remains a controversial one, because of two important problems. In operational terms, the limited use which is likely to be made of back-up aircraft—on many routes they are only employed at morning and evening weekday peaks for business travel—means a very low utilization of both aircraft and crew. For some airlines it has been possible up until now to minimize the extent of this problem by using old, written-down aircraft with a very low depreciation cost associated with them. This has been the case, for instance, with

British Airways Shuttle services. The employment of the older versions of the Trident aircraft family has meant the use of aircraft in Shuttle back-up work which in an economic sense have had no capital cost associated with them. These aircraft almost certainly could not have been sold to another operator at anything except a nominal price. However, the option to use such old aircraft is now disappearing due to their fuel inefficiency and more particularly because of the widespread imposition by governments of bans on noisy aircraft. From the mid-1980s onwards, these bans will mean that Shuttle operations everywhere will have to be based on the use of aircraft having a substantial depreciation cost. Only when this occurs will it be possible to form a true judgement on the effect of Shuttle on airline operating economics.

The other possible drawback of Shuttle is that it represents a fundamental change in the relationship between airlines and the travel agency industry. As we shall see in Section 7.1.1, travel agents have considerable market power. With a traveller using a Shuttle service, it is certainly still possible to book through agents, and it is known that many passengers will do so, particularly those who are using a short-haul Shuttle route as a connecting flight before transferring to another sector. When bookings are made through agents, commission is paid by the airline in the normal way. However, for any passenger using Shuttle as a single sector, end-to-end service, there is little incentive to book through agents when payment at the airport or on the plane is so easy, and no need exists to obtain an advanced reservation.

Until now, the impact of Shuttle operations on travel agents has been limited because of the relatively small number of markets in which Shuttles have been introduced. Apart from Eastern Airlines' operations between New York, Washington and Boston, Shuttle-type services now exist between Rio de Janeiro and San Paulo, and between Madrid and Barcelona, besides a few other markets as well. However, it is the British Airways innovations in the U.K. domestic market which seem likely to cause the greatest controversy, because of the expansion possibilities which exist. Since the initial introduction of the London–Glasgow Shuttle in 1975, Shuttle services have been expanded to encompass London–Edinburgh, London–Belfast and London–Manchester. No one has suggested that Shuttle provides an appropriate concept for all the airline's operations—the crucial need for a dense, regular pattern confines its use to short-haul business routes. However, if the initial Shuttle innovation is regarded as having been successful—and the expansion in the use of the concept must indicate a consensus that it has been—there are several other routes where these conditions are met. Prime examples are the routes between London and Paris (the busiest international city–pair in the world), London–Amsterdam and London–Brussels. The airline has publicly stated that it is conducting discussions aimed at ensuring the introduction of the so-called Euro-Shuttle. If it is successful in doing so, the numbers of passengers who will be using services of this type could mean a significant impact on the revenues of travel agents, particularly bearing in mind the currently high levels of intra-European Normal Economy fares.

Shuttle, because of its guaranteed seat provision, is a way of giving a good service to business travellers and others who require a certainty in seat availability. However, the last few years have also seen interest in air-transport products where a reservation in the traditional sense has not been offered, but where there has been no guarantee of a seat. These service concepts have been aimed at the price-conscious leisure segment of the market, where the absence of a reservation has been intended to allow lower prices.

Interest in this form of no-reservation service began in 1972 when Laker Airways Ltd. made application to the U.K. Civil Aviation Authority for a licence to operate its 'Skytrain' from London to New York. The essence of Skytrain as it was originally applied for was that tickets would only be purchasable on the day of flight departure, by those passengers reporting to the departure airport or (as it turned out) one downtown ticket-selling point. The restrictions on ticket sales were presumably there to minimize the diversion from existing scheduled services, thereby increasing the chances of regulatory acceptance, and also to allow for the lowest costs of operation.

The concept certainly had much to commend it from a marketing viewpoint. The airline was to be free of the need to operate an extensive reservations system and communications network. It would not be saddled with problems of bad debts with all payments made on the spot by cash or credit card. It would not suffer dilution of revenue due to the proration of fares. There would not be a no-show problem. Finally, though the airline understandably was not eager to press the point in view of the support it needed from agents in its other markets, Skytrain eliminated almost all payment of travel agents' commissions.[32]

Inevitably, Skytrain aroused strong controversy, and it was only after a lapse of five years, and as a result of a series of favourable developments in the environment of international regulation, that it finally began in September 1977. When it was introduced, the established scheduled airlines on the route countered by offering their own form of no advanced-reservation service. This was with the Standby fare. This fare could only be purchased on a space-available basis on the day of departure. It was pitched at a level which was slightly above the Skytrain price for a one-way journey, but as it included a meal (which Skytrain required

---

32 A scheme was subsequently developed to involve travel agents with Skytrain to a limited degree.

an additional payment for), there was very little difference in the fare levels.

The Standby concept—later, as we have seen, extended to all routes between the U.K. and U.S.A.—drew cries of protest from Sir Freddie Laker regarding 'predatory pricing,' something which will be considered further in Section 9.1.2. However, whilst one must accept his complaint that the scheduled airline Standby concept was only introduced in order to compete with Skytrain, the concept does make a great deal of economic sense and could have been experimented with earlier. (Indeed, it probably would have been but for the rigidity of the regulatory system covering international services.) The scheduled airline aiming to attract the business traveller is forced to give a good probability of being able to book a seat near to flight departure. In doing this, any airline which makes adequate provision for the peak will find itself with excess capacity available at the off-peak. Even at peak times, the randomness in business-travel patterns may still mean that some seats remain unsold, despite the fact that the airline has been placing the 'correct' amount of capacity in the market-place. Where spare capacity can be foreseen, cheap pricing concepts based on advanced booking—particularly the APEX fare (Section 6.2.2)—can be used to obtain a market for it. However, advanced booking fares cannot be used to deal with seats which remain unsold because of random and unforecastable variations in demand. It does not become clear that the seats *are* unsold until shortly before flight departure time. Here, Standby fares, providing they do not lead to excessive dilution of revenue from last-minute travellers who would have been prepared to buy a Normal Economy ticket,[33] can be extremely valuable. Indeed, the ability to offer them is another example of the synergy between its different products which can be obtained by the total-market airline.

Despite all the publicity attending the introduction of Skytrain and the competing Standby fares, subsequent operations have not been without difficulties. The result has been that Skytrain has now been changed substantially from its original conception. Initial operations proceeded smoothly until the peak period in the summer of 1978. Then, both the Skytrain and scheduled airline Standby offerings were totally inadequate to meet demand on a day-to-day basis. The result was long queues in Central London and downtown New York, and scenes of appalling congestion at what would in any case, at that time of the year, have been heavily overcrowded airport terminals. The immediate consequence was that the U.K. Civil Aviation Authority gave Laker permission to operate a rolling-booking system whereby he was allowed to make bookings on the

---

[33] or become abused in the sense of a passenger buying a Normal Economy ticket in advance, and then turning up at the airport in the hope of getting a Standby. If a Standby is available, the Normal Economy ticket can then be traded in for its full face-value.

next day's and subsequent flights once one day's seats had been filled. However, in in the light of growing competition in what had by this time become a liberal North Atlantic regulatory environment, Laker was granted yet further concessions by the C.A.A. in June 1979. Sales were then permitted through travel agents and passengers could book in advance on any Skytrain flight that they wished to choose and on which seats were available. (*See* Section 9.1.2) Given that this would involve the setting up of a reservations system and the making of large commission payments to travel agents, there was little more than the absence of a First Class cabin to distinguish the Laker-style product from that of its rivals, although in fact its prices remained somewhat lower.

It is difficult to make a judgement as to the likely long-term significance of air transport products which do not feature either an advanced reservation or a guaranteed seat. Both Skytrain and Standby have demonstrated that a market exists of price-conscious travellers who wish to have a flexibility for last-minute travelling and routing decisions, but who cannot afford Normal Economy fares. Skytrain and Standby have been valuable in meeting the needs of this market, particularly at off-peak periods. However, one is bound to say that the large amount of publicity given to Skytrain may have meant that many travellers used Skytrain who could have complied perfectly well with the advanced booking and minimum-stay conditions of Advanced Booking Charters. Also, at peak times, airport congestion has been a tremendous problem, which in the case of Skytrain has only been solved by concessions which have moved the concept well away from a true 'walk-on' service. With the scheduled Standby fare it may be that the best solution is the 'Eleventh Hour' system adopted by British Caledonian on a number of its long-haul routes. Here, Eleventh Hour tickets can be bought at any time in advance, but sales of such tickets prior to each flight are limited to roughly the number of seats likely to be available immediately before flight departure time. Holders of Eleventh Hour tickets are then given the seats available, in order of ticket purchase. Those for whom a seat is not allotted are offered tickets for later flights, or else given their money back. The Eleventh Hour idea offers a product which meets the need of a market segment, which allows the scheduled airline to retain its valuable 'fill-up' capability, but which does not pose problems of airport congestion at peak periods.

With the study of reservations and alternatives to reservations, we have now completed the work on the design of the airline's passenger product. It is now necessary to move on to the question of the design of the product offered to freight customers.

5.6 Designing the Freight Product

Freight is now such an important part of the industry that special attention must be given to the design of the freight product by any airline with an interest in penetrating the freight market. A particular emphasis is needed on aspects where the freight product is substantially different from that offered to passengers.

With the question of freight *capacity*, all-cargo airlines have some difficult decisions to make. The airline basing its corporate strategy purely on exploitation of the freight market must make a choice between using older piston or turbo-prop aircraft,the use of narrow-bodied jet freighters, or investment in wide-bodied aircraft.

In deciding between these alternatives, the freight airline will need to bring in many of the same considerations as the passenger or combination airline. Thus it will need to consider payload/range capabilities of the different aircraft types relative to its route network and traffic flows. It will need data on fuel consumption, field length performance and available operating costs. However, in addition, there are two pieces of data which are unique to freight operations, but which can be crucial in plane choice. Firstly, *cabin door size* and *cabin cross-section* of the main deck of the aircraft will decide the size of consignment which can be accommodated in it. All the narrow-bodied jet freighters—the freighter versions of the Boeing 707, 727 and 737, and the McDonnel-Douglas DC 8—are only able to accept consignments up to 86 inches high through their cargo doors. Stowage in the cabin is complicated by awkwardly-shaped cross-sections. In no case can a narrow-bodied aircraft accept the 8 foot by 8 foot rectangular cross-section of International Standards Organization standard-sized containers. Of the wide-bodied aircraft.[34] the freighter version of the DC 10 is still unable to accept two such containers side-by-side on the main deck, with the B 747 unique amongst civil aircraft in being able to do so.

As a second point, *design density* is a crucial performance-variable of a freighter. Such aircraft do not, of course, only have their weight-limited payload as a capacity measure—they also have a fixed volumetric capacity. If an aircraft only has a limited volume relative to its maximum payload, it can often be the case that an aircraft will become volumetrically full before the maximum payload is reached. Of the aircraft currently in service, the narrow-bodied jets all have serious design density problems,[35] something which can be extremely serious when the industry is largely basing its freight pricing policy on weight rather than volume.[36] The Boeing 747 freighter has a design density which is below that of the 707 by some 30 or 40 per cent, but of course the immense payload/range capability of this aircraft confines its use to the busiest long-haul services.

---

34 There are currently no freighter versions available of the L 1011, and few A 300s have been sold in the convertible configuration offered by Airbus Industrie.

35 *See* Schneider (1973). Further details on the nature of freighter aircraft can be found in Smith (1974), Ch. 2, and (1976).

36 *See* Section 6.3.

All in all, the problems of freighter aircraft may be taken as indicating an eventual need for the design of aircraft exclusively for the carriage of freight, rather than as at present the freight side of the industry using what are essentially conversions of passenger aircraft.[37] However, until now, the development and production costs of a dedicated freighter, coupled with the relatively small size of the market which is likely to be available, have meant that no manufacturer has attempted to produce such an aircraft purely for civil use.

For the total-market airline attempting exploitation of both passenger and freight markets, even more difficult freight capacity decisions have to be made. Such an airline must decide whether or not freighter capacity is to be offered at all. It is one of the aspects of the synergy available to the total-market airline that in providing passenger service it must of necessity make available large amounts of lower-hold freight space. In the older narrow-bodied jets, such capacity may not be of great use because the belly-holds of these aircraft are awkwardly-shaped and comparatively small. Even under the most favourable circumstances of a small passenger and baggage load leaving payload to spare, such aircraft are capable only of carrying a few tonnes of freight, with even then time-consuming loading and unloading problems. It is is the advent of wide-bodied aircraft which has completely changed this situation. The B 747 is capable of taking upwards of 25 tonnes of containerized and palletized cargo in its lower hold, with the DC 10, L 1011 and A 300 families having a freight capability of 12–15 tonnes or even more in some cases.

With such freight capacity in passenger aircraft, it is now a very viable option that the total market airline must consider that it should rely on lower-hold space for its freight provision. Such an option becomes even more possible if lower-hold capacity from passenger aircraft can be supplemented by a limited amount of main-deck capability under the 'combi' principle, and in theory this has much to commend it.[38] Particularly for the airline mainly aiming at penetration of the emergency segment of the air freight market, flight frequency will be a crucial product component and reliance on passenger service will allow this to be largely retained. The airline will also be saved the necessity for investment in freighter aircraft. For scheduled airlines, investment in narrow-bodied freighters has never been financially successful[39] with such aircraft being

---

37 Although Boeing has always claimed that the 747 design was settled upon with equal consideration being given to its use as a freighter, with its initial design coming from a competition for a military freighter which was eventually won by Lockheed with its C 5A.

38 The Boeing 747 is available in an option where the main deck can be used, through the employment of a cabin divider, in a *combination* mode of passenger and freight carriage. Provision of a large main-deck cargo door can still allow such aircraft to accept 8 foot by 8 foot by 10 foot containers, as can the pure freighter version of the B 747.

39 *See* I.A.T.A. (1969).

seen as loss-leaders by many airlines. Investment in the B 747, in several ways a better freighter, involves a very large capital sum. Also, because of its high capacity, there will be a need to concentrate traffic over hub points with a resulting requirement for extensive transhipment and a reduction in direct service between other points.

Despite the appeal of the 'no freighter' idea, trends in the industry indicate that it is only likely to be a viable long-term proposition for airlines with a limited commitment to the freight market; to some customers at least, reliance on belly-holds will reduce the quality of the product. Any shipper of hazardous goods relies on the provision of freighters because industry rules for the carriage of many types of such cargo forbid the use of passenger aircraft lower-hold space for it. Also, to a shipper of large-sized consignments, freighters capacity can be very important. The lower-hold space of the wide-bodied aircraft is capable of accepting reasonably-shaped consignments up to 66 inches in height, but this is well short of the 96 inches maximum height which can be stowed on the main deck of the B 747F. Also, reliance on lower-holds still can leave airlines short of freight capacity, because of the demand pattern shown by air freight. As one might expect, air freight demand peaks strongly at night, following production during the working day, and at the end of the working week, with a pronounced trough in demand on Sundays and Mondays. This demand pattern means that an airline which relies exclusively on day-time passenger departures for freight carriage will be forcing a delay of possibly many hours on to its freight customers. Much of the freight capacity that will be provided in passenger aircraft, therefore, will be wasted from the point of view of the freight shipper because it is offered at times when little freight is moving. However, the airline may find itself chronically short of freight capacity during the Friday-night/Saturday peak.

Besides the disadvantages which apply now to an operation without freighters, there are a number of long-term trends in the industry which may eventually reinforce the need for freighter provision. There are grounds for expecting that on routes with freight potential, freight carriage is likely to expand faster than that of passengers. Routes with freight potential are those with an extensive amount of business travel, and we have seen that communications improvements may mean a relatively slower rate of growth for business trips in the future. It is also likely that the freight departments of total-market airlines will come under increasing pressure from their passenger colleagues over the use of lower-hold space. In the past, it has more or less been accepted that such space has been available for cargo carriage once passengers' baggage and air mail have been loaded. Even here, however, conflicts have occurred as late-arriving passengers have caused cargo to be offloaded because of the supposedly superior revenue-earning capability of using marginal payload for passengers rather than freight. Aircraft manufacturers are now producing variants which are offering airlines a number of possible uses for aircraft lower holds. For example, Lockheed promote the L 1011 with an option which allows either an upper-deck or a lower-deck galley. The lower galley increases the seating capacity of the aircraft, but at the penalty of almost halving the lower-hold space. Other aircraft are on offer whereby part of the lower-hold capacity has been taken up for extra fuel tankage. This increases range but again at a penalty of reduced freight capability. Finally, with the lower-hold space of wide-bodied aircraft already five feet six inches in height, it would only seem to be a matter of time before aircraft become two-deck with some lower-hold space used for passenger carriage. Indeed, Pacific Southwest Airlines of California have already used such a configuration for a short period in the Lockheed Tristar.

With the questions of freight capacity and freight scheduling, it is certain that in the future any airline wishing to make more than a limited penetration of the freight market will only be able to do so by a substantial commitment in the direction of the freight side of their business. The days of basing a freight product on lower-hold space, and on the use of conversions of obsolete passenger planes as freighters, are passing. All airlines hoping for a total market approach face a need to commit large amounts of resources to their freight product.

Such large sums can also be seen looming in aspects of airline's *customer service* for freight. Unlike on the passenger side, inflight service is not significant for freight, except for highly-specialized live-animal cargoes. However, customer service is still very important, for the greatest emphasis needs to be given to ground-handling before and after carriage. We shall see later that almost all airline advertising aimed at diverting traffic from other airlines emphasizes quality of ground-handling. Any airline which fails to make adequate provision for it risks a loss of market share.

Freight ground-handling has posed many problems for airlines. With one or two minor exceptions, air freight has been an expanding part of the airline business and airlines have constantly been faced with a need to try and plan ahead to keep handling capacity up with demand. In addition, air freight has been characterized by a preponderance of small parcel-sized consignments,[40] with acute problems always likely to arise from any attempt to handle such consignments in expensive on-airport locations. Finally, as we shall see, the question of freight handling has become very much bound up with the relationship between airlines and air freight forwarders as marketing intermediaries, a controversy which will be covered in Section 7.3.1.

In the middle 1960s, a number of airlines opted for sophisticated automated freight-handling systems. These were aimed at allowing them to

---

40 C.A.A. (1977b).

continue to handle cargo at airports with better service and lower costs for their customers. Also—one may guess—they were intended to protect the airline's interest relative to the freight-forwarding industry. If carriers failed to retain the ability to handle goods in on-airport locations, they would become totally reliant on forwarders, with a consequent loss of market control. However, very widely, the move towards automated cargo-handling did not prove successful.[41] There were complaints that the systems installed were unreliable, whilst automating the cargo-handling process saddled airlines with fixed systems in an industry where rapid growth and change placed a premium on flexibility.

During the 1970s, many carriers retreated from the idea of automated on-airport handling systems. Instead, the advent of wide-bodied passenger aircraft meant that a high proportion of freight came to be loaded into aircraft in containerized or palletized form. Where this happened, airlines increasingly found the answer to their handling problems in offering concessionary rates to those shippers and forwarders prepared to take the unit-load devices (U.L.D's), pre-load them and present them to airlines in a ready-for-carriage form. This so-called Bulk Unitization Programme has been vital to airlines in rescuing them from intractable problems of on-airport cargo-handling. However, it has brought significant consequences for investment, where airline's requirements for what are expensive aircraft unit-load devices has been greatly increased. The programme also has important implications for the relationship between airlines and the freight-forwarding industry—an aspect to which we return in Section 7.3.1.

Two further points remain to be made with respect to the design of the freight product. The first of these is the controversial one relating to the provision of a *freight reservations system*. Theoretically, a reservation system should be as much a part of the freight product as it is of the product offered to almost all passengers. However, in the past there have been problems associated with offering certainty of carriage with respect to freight consignments. It is not until freight is actually delivered in the airline that it becomes known exactly how many consignments can be placed in the space available, given the variations in consignment density, shape and stowability. Also, rightly or wrongly, there has been uncertainty as to whether a consignment will go on a booked flight because many airlines have been prepared to off-load freight in order to accommodate late-arriving passengers. Today, many airlines do operate a freight reservations system, particularly for pre-booked unit-load devices from freight forwarders, though this latter case really only passes the uncertainty resulting from varying consignment shapes and densities from the airline to the forwarder.

The difficulties regarding reservations give particular importance to the final aspect of the freight product—that of a *monitoring and control system*.

---

41 *See* Smith (1974), p. 134–43.

A passenger who is directed on to the wrong flight presumably will tell the carrier fairly forcefully of the mistake that has been made. However, mistakes with freight consignments may go undetected for long periods, whilst consignees and their agents will have a constant need to be kept informed about the progress of a consignment and when it is likely to be available for collection. A monitoring and control system—usually today by real-time computer—should therefore be an important part of the freight product for airlines.

The design of the freight product is an interesting aspect of airline marketing. The total-market airline having the ability to use lower-hold space in its passenger aircraft is able to offer flight frequency and, arguably, cheaply-available capacity as a way of attempting to penetrate both the emergency and the routine markets. The all-cargo airline, particularly the all-cargo charter carrier, may not be able to offer the frequency of departure to compete in the extreme emergency market, but will have other advantages which will enable it to meet more precisely the needs of the routine shipper. Certainly it would seem to be the case that the rapid growth of freight charter airlines in Europe in recent years can be explained by growing regulatory freedom for charter carriers to design services which meet the needs of a considerable segment of the routine freight market for lower freight rates.

We have now dealt with the important aspects of product design in airline marketing. However, alongside decisions on the product, policy must also be formulated on pricing. It is this extremely controversial aspect to which we now turn.

6 Problems of Pricing

Today, airline pricing is receiving unprecedented publicity. The offer of low fares on some routes has brought complaints from consumer groups regarding those markets where the trend towards low fares is apparently being resisted. Everywhere, airlines are criticized for the inequity and complexity of their fare structures.

In this chapter, emphasis is placed on pricing in its context as a *marketing* decision. Pricing cannot be seen in isolation. It flows directly from market analysis and corporate strategy definition, whilst pricing and product design decisions must be made together rather than sequentially as we are forced to deal with them here. The level of price set will be a crucial factor deciding the usage made of a particular product, especially of those products aimed at price-sensitive segments of the market.

To provide the necessary information, the chapter first of all deals with the question of the criteria which should be achieved by a successful airline pricing structure. In a second section, the structure of passenger pricing employed by the world's main airlines is outlined. We then look at some explanations of why pricing takes on the form that it does. In a final section, we deal with the difficult question of pricing for air-freight services. If the chapter is successful, it will demonstrate how important it is for the person with an interest in airline marketing to be well-informed regarding the *principles* of pricing, in addition to understanding the detail of how airlines actually do price their product.

6.1 Criteria for Pricing

If an airline has as its dominant corporate objective adequate profit-making, the main criterion for pricing policy must be that it should *ensure the achievement of corporate profitability,* both in the short term and, most importantly, in the long term as well. The distinction between short and long term is necessary because the history of the aviation industry is notable for the existence of many price structures which have allowed for enhanced short-term profitability as a result of the innovation of lower fares. However, such fares have often only brought profit improvements because they have generated low-yielding traffic to fill seats that the airline would have operated anyway. The profit picture becomes very different when the long-term questions of capacity replacement and expansion have to be faced.

If an airline's written or unwritten objectives include broader issues than merely profitability, then price structures must aim at ensuring that these are met as well. For example, an airline which is expected to provide support to a national tourism industry will presumably implement a pricing structure which carries with it provision of low fares to allow for tourism development.

However, besides criteria related strictly to corporate objectives, it is very necessary today to emphasize other criteria. For example, *simplicity* —or rather the lack of it—is becoming a major concern of pricing. A complex tariff structure brings many consequences which are especially serious for airlines. Air transport more than any other mode is concerned with interline journeys where fares are combined between carriers.[1] Even for point-to-point fares on a single carrier, complexity in the tariff will involve airlines in costs of staff training, and costs of staff time and passenger delay whilst fares are worked out and the details of the different price options explained. It also means that the tariff becomes highly esoteric with consumers—and particularly infrequent travellers—often not knowing whether the price they have been charged is the correct one or not.

A further criterion for pricing is the important contemporary one of *equity*. Despite the changes noted in Chapter 4, air transport has traditionally been an industry where the forces of competition have been given very limited play. Also, demand elasticities vary substantially between market segments. Therefore, a clear temptation exists for airlines to charge excessively high prices to those market segments where elasticities are low and regulation is tight. This can either be to make excessive profits for themselves, or else to cross-subsidize the offering of low fares to price-elastic segments. It will be an important objective which we shall set for pricing that such situations should be avoided, despite their obvious short-term gains. This is because of the long-term problems they are bringing to the industry in passenger dissatisfaction. They are also meaning that increasing attention is now being given by some government regulatory agencies to ensuring that there is equity in pricing.

As a final criterion, we can add that of *stability*. Constant changes in tariffs involve airlines—and, eventually, their customers—in very high costs of up-dating and re-education, and it must be seen as an extremely important criterion of pricing that price structures should be as stable as

1 *See* Hanlon (1977), pp. 223–4.

possible through time. Indeed, at the time of writing the lack of stability in airline price structures is one of the most serious administrative problems facing airlines and travel agents.

6.2 Scheduled Airline Pricing Policy—Passenger

If we move on from discussion of criteria for pricing to consider the ways in which airlines who actually publish a tariff[2] do price their product, there would seem to be little chance of being able to conclude that our criteria are either being applied or met. The scheduled sector of the industry has scarcely been notable for its high levels of profit (Section 3.2.3), whilst it is now under attack for both the complexity and inequity of its price structure. However, it is hoped that, after outlining the tariff structure in the next section, it will be possible to go on to examine the principles on which pricing should be based. Such an examination will show that the definition of an appropriate passenger pricing structure has become an extraordinarily difficult task for marketing management.

6.2.1 The Structure of Passenger Pricing

Despite the recent problems with the I.A.T.A. system for negotiation of international fares and rates (Section 4.2.1), there is still an underlying consistency in the tariff structures employed by competing airlines and between different routes. On most routes, airlines offer a *First Class fare*. This is available to all customers without conditions, buys the use of a separate cabin in the aircraft with superior service, does not vary with season, and no restrictive conditions apply to its use. The disadavantage from the passenger's viewpoint is, of course, that the First Class fare is very high, with even a surcharge of 20 per cent on top of it for those passengers wishing to use the Concorde services provided by British Airways and Air France. In addition to First Class there is on all routes a *Normal Economy* fare. (The term 'Coach Fare' is applied to this pricing concept in the U.S. domestic market.) This is lower than First Class, but is still extremely expensive by today's standards. In addition, it does vary with season on some routes (notably on the North Atlantic), with a peak-season surcharge then applying. However, the compensating advantage is that again the fare is offered without restrictive conditions and it is available for use on any flight on which a reservation can be obtained.

If pricing were confined merely to the use of Normal Economy and First Class fares, it would certainly have the merit of simplicity. Also, in that

2 Charter airlines, mostly restricted to the wholesaling of capacity to travel organizers, do not offer a published tariff in most cases.

Table 6.1. Air Canada: Price Structure on U.K.—Canada routes (June 1979)

14–60 Day Advance Purchase Excursion Fare (APEX)			22–45 Day Economy Excursion Fares		
From London (return)	*Low*	*Peak*	*From London (return)*	*Low*	*Peak*
	£	£		£	£
Calgary/Edmonton	234·50	292·50	Calgary/Edmonton	278·50	349·00
Gander	153·50	206·00	Gander	201·50	266·00
Halifax	170·00	222·00	Halifax	216·00	280·50
London Ont.	233·00	285·50	London Ont.	277·50	342·00
Montreal	186·00	238·50	Montreal	230·50	294·50
Ottawa	200·00	252·00	Ottawa	244·00	308·50
Regina	234·50	292·50	Regina	278·50	349·00
Saskatoon	234·50	292·50	Saskatoon	278·50	349·00
Toronto	200·00	252·00	Toronto	244·00	308·50
Vancouver	251·50	312·50	Vancouver	296·00	369·00
Victoria	256·50	320·50	Victoria	304·00	377·00
Winnipeg	217·00	269·50	Winnipeg	261·50	326·00

14–21 Day Economy Excursion Fares			North Atlantic Youth Fares		
From London (return)	*Low*	*Peak*	*From London (return)*	*Low*	*Peak*
	£	£		£	£
Calgary/Edmonton	351·00	400·00	Calgary/Edmonton	254·50	294·50
Gander	243·50	292·50	Gander	171·50	206·00
Halifax	265·00	313·50	Halifax	189·00	223·50
London Ont.	346·00	395·00	London Ont.	253·50	288·00
Montreal	288·00	337·00	Montreal	206·00	240·50
Ottawa	312·50	361·50	Ottawa	220·00	255·00
Regina	351·00	400·00	Regina	254·50	294·50
Saskatoon	351·00	400·00	Saskatoon	254·50	294·50
Toronto	312·50	361·50	Toronto	220·00	255·00
Vancouver	375·50	424·50	Vancouver	271·50	315·00
Victoria	383·50	432·50	Victoria	280·00	323·00
Winnipeg	328·00	377·00	Winnipeg	237·00	271·50

Standard First Class Fares		Standard Economy Class Fares		
From London (one way)		*From London (one way)*	*Low*	*Peak*
	£		£	£
Calgary/Edmonton	516·50	Calgary/Edmonton	229·50	267·50
Gander	286·50	Gander	142·50	181·50
Halifax	319·00	Halifax	159·50	197·50
London Ont.	410·50	London Ont.	212·00	248·00
Montreal	355·00	Montreal	178·00	216·00
Ottawa	381·50	Ottawa	194·50	232·50
Regina	488·50	Regina	229·50	267·50
Saskatoon	496·00	Saskatoon	229·50	267·50
Toronto	404·50	Toronto	195·00	233·00
Vancouver	545·00	Vancouver	252·50	290·50
Victoria	547·50	Victoria	259·50	297·50
Winnipeg	464·00	Winnipeg	215·50	253·50

First Class buys a superior service on board the aircraft, it would probably be seen as being equitable between different classes of passenger. However, on almost all routes today, pricing is *not* limited to First Class and Normal Economy fares, as there are usually a number of *Special Economy fares*[3] on offer. These are always lower than Normal Economy—often substantially so, as shown in Table 6.1—but, by way of disadvantage, have restrictive conditions applying to them.

The list of possible conditions pertaining to Special Economy fares is now very long, with each fare usually having one or two of the following conditions:

Minimum stay conditions are set for many fares today. These prevent the user of the special fare from making his return journey at that price before the lapse of a certain period of time. Should the passenger wish to come home before this time is reached, he can, of course, still do so, but he must pay the price of a Normal Economy ticket.

Maximum stay conditions. Besides minimum stay conditions, many fares have maximum stay conditions fixed for them whereby a passenger must return before the lapse of a specified period of time. Failure to do so entails the payment of the Normal Economy fare.

Fares only applying to particular groups. Some Special Economy fares are pitched at very low levels, but can only be used by members of certain groups. An example of this is, of course, the discounts offered to children, which are almost entirely without cost justification.[4] Other examples are the Spouse Fares available on some routes, where a 50 per cent reduction is offered to a spouse travelling with husband or wife using a First Class or Normal Economy ticket; Youth Fares offered to those under 23 (or 26 in some cases); and Student's Fares.

Fares with special booking conditions. Many Special Economy fares confine the offer of lower prices to those who are prepared to conform with certain booking conditions. Most widespread of these fares is now APEX (Advanced Purchase Excursion). This offers low fares to all those who are prepared to book a minimum period in advance (usually 21 or 30 days. There is often also a minimum stay condition applying to APEX fares).

---

3 The term 'promotional fare' is often applied to these, but this in many cases does not give the true purpose of the fare. Today, few Special Economy fares can be seen as being promotional in the short-term sense—much more they must be considered as part of the airline tariff on a long-term basis.

4 Indeed it will cost an airline more to carry a child than an adult where special escorts for unaccompanied children must be provided.

However, other types of Special Economy Fare confine low fares to those who *don't* book in advance. This is the case with the Standby Fare offered by scheduled airlines on the North Atlantic, and also with the IPEX (Instant Purchase Excursion) of many European routes. This latter limits booking to, at the earliest, the afternoon of the day before departure with a need also to use off-peak week-end flights. Recently the IPEX conditions have been eased on some routes so that they only require a stay over a week-end, with booking possible at any time in advance of travel when a seat is available.

Fares only available as part of package holidays. Besides fare types which are offered to the public, many scheduled airlines now sell fares on a wholesale basis. These must be combined with appropriate accommodation before sale to the public. Most important of these are the ITX fare, a low fare available on an individual basis to passengers able to book a package of flight and accommodation, and the S.G.I.T. (Special Group Inclusive Tour). This makes available even lower prices than ITX to travel organizers who are prepared to take the risk of contracting to obtain a minimum group size. The difference between S.G.I.T. prices and Normal Economy tickets is often very large, with instances being quoted (Air Transport User's Committee (1976)) of S.G.I.T. prices which have been less than a fifth of the Normal Economy fare.

Fares restricted by availability. With the advent of deregulation of the U.S. domestic market, many airlines in the States have begun to offer special domestic deep discount fares without any conditions applying to them at all. The only control has been that the number of seats sold on any flight at such low fares has been limited, with those which are available being allocated on a 'First come, First served' basis.

Overall, the mix of First Class, Normal Economy and a wide range of Special Economy fares allows us an initial conclusion that in no sense can the present structure of passenger pricing be called simple—indeed the picture is one of notable complexity. This complexity becomes greater still when the difficulties of constructing fares on multi-sector flights by different carriers are brought in. In addition, the large differences between the highest fares and the lowest may appear to indicate substantial inequity in the structure, whilst there have been complaints over inequity regarding other aspects as well. The U.K. Air Transport User's Committee (A.U.C. 1976) has pointed to the far higher rates in terms of pence per mile which apply to European routes compared with those in U.S. domestic service. Within Europe it points to large differences in rates between routes, a point previously made by Rosenberg (1969) and Cooper and Maynard (1972).

As a conclusion to this section, it would seem that we cannot say that the current structure of scheduled airline fares is meeting the criteria which were set earlier. Scheduled carriers are notable for their dismal profit record, whilst the pricing structure they have employed has been widely attacked as being highly complex, and thoroughly inequitable, with problems of instability now adding to the weight of criticism.

For the moment, it is not necessary to comment on the validity of such criticisms, although it will become obvious later that at least some of them do have a degree of justification. What *is* necessary is that we should look at the principles behind pricing as a marketing decision and discuss how airlines should price their services in order to pursue a correct marketing philosophy. Here a crucial interplay exists between pricing and the structure of the air transport market, the corporate strategies employed by airlines, and the kinds of products which they should be designing to assist in promoting these strategies.

6.2.2 Market Structures as Pricing Constraint

Table 6.2 gives an entirely hypothetical model of an air travel market. In it, the airline concerned is fortunate to have a perfect knowledge of the market. It knows the numbers of consumers in each market segment, their service requirements and their price elasticity of demand as expressed as a maximum amount they are prepared to pay to secure air service between the end points of the route.

Table 6.2. Differential Pricing Between Market Segments Theory

Consumers	'Willingness to pay'	Uniform revenue maximizing price	Revenue under 'perfect' differential pricing
A	£500	£300	£500
B	£450	£300	£450
C	£400	£300	£400
D	£350	£300	£350
E	£300	£300	£300
F	£250	—	£250
G	£200	—	£200
H	£150	—	£150
I	£100	—	£100
J	£50	—	£50
Revenue		£1,500	£2,750
Passengers carried		5	10

This market conforms exactly to the structure outlined in Section 2.3. It divides between passengers—presumably businessmen and wealthy leisure travellers—who are prepared to pay a very high fare in order to travel, and segments of less-wealthy leisure travellers, whose willingness to pay is much lower. It can also be assumed, though initially this will not come into the model, that the market has a typically pyramidal structure, of relatively small numbers of consumers being located in the upper segments and much larger numbers in the lower segments.

How should the airline approach this market? The advocate of simplicity in pricing would see the correct policy as charging the single fare which maximizes revenue. In this case, it is either £250 or £300. (Obviously at this stage we are not considering the implications of segment size.) Any fare, either higher or lower, will reduce revenue below the theoretical single-fare maximum.

Such a pricing policy would have the merits of simplicity and apparent equity, but two very significant consequences would stem from it. Those passengers with a very high willingness to pay would *underpay* relative to their low demand elasticity. The airline would be losing revenue that it might have been able to obtain since passengers would be given a bargain fare well below what they would have considered reasonable value-for-money. The other consequence is that the airline would receive no revenue from large numbers of passengers within the market. Although passengers in the price-elastic segment would part with some money in order to travel, the airline would be pricing above their willingness-to-pay. Clearly, therefore, this single-fare strategy would lose the airline potential revenue, whilst it would be inappropriate for any total market airline wishing to secure as wide as possible a penetration of the available markets.

The theoretical alternative to this *uniform* pricing is shown in the third column of the Table. There, the airline has changed its pricing strategy to a *differential* one, where prices are varied so that each segment is offered a price which matches its willingness-to-pay. Thus, higher prices than the uniform price are charged to the inelastic segments, and lower prices to the elastic ones. Although the model does not show this, it can be expected that conditions will be imposed on the use of the low fares which confine their use as far as possible to consumers with a low willingness-to-pay. Otherwise, excessive *revenue dilution* can be expected to be a problem whereby low fares are used by those from market segments with a much higher willingness-to-pay.

Although Table 6.2 gives hypothetical data, the situation it represents is only an extreme form of the one which exists in the real world. Airline markets are segmented between business and leisure passengers. We have summarized in Chapter 2, Section 2.3 the available evidence suggesting that there are substantial differences in demand elasticities between business and leisure travellers. It is therefore one view of contemporary scheduled airline pricing policy to suggest that First Class and Normal Economy fares are the high fares offered to the business segment, and that the Special Economy fares are aimed at the more price-conscious leisure segment. The imposition of restrictive conditions on Special Economy fares can be seen as an attempt to prevent the revenue dilution which would result from their use by business travellers. Thus minimum-stay conditions of seven days or more applying to them exclude a high proportion of business trips, which tend to be of relatively short duration. Maximum-stay conditions also help to restrict the use of the fares to holidaymakers. Anyone going on a trip longer than a few weeks is not likely to be on vacation. Special advanced booking requirements, again, can be seen as excluding many business trips, as the details of these often only become known shortly before flight departure. Therefore the possibility of advanced booking is excluded. Finally, provision of accomodation with a fare means that it may not be suitable for a business trip, many of which are based on moving around between centres, and in fact may be a way of imposing a minimum-stay condition on the use of a ticket.

The successful use of differential pricing brings many advantages to an airline. It will obtain extra revenue from price-inelastic customers and it gets at least some return from passengers who would not travel by the airline at all otherwise. However, despite these advantages, the use of such pricing remains an aspect of extreme controversy amongst both airlines and consumers. For airlines, the disadvantages are that revenue dilution can become a chronic problem—something to which we shall return later—and that inevitably any tariff structure based on differential pricing will be a complex one. From the consumer's point of view, and entirely as one would expect, the criticism has been that differential pricing is inequitable.[5] It involves the charging of much higher fares to some consumers than to others, with its being 'obvious' that the low-fare passengers are being subsidized by the high fare ones. This argument is also joined by charter airlines, who have claimed that it is quite unfair[6] that scheduled airlines should compete with them on the basis (as they argue) of scheduled services cross-subsidizing losses made on their charter competitive low fares with excessive profits made on the carriage of business travellers at Normal Economy fares. Differential pricing is also supposed to bring dangers to airlines because of the risk that low fares offered to price-elastic market segments will fall 'below costs,' with even such cross-subsidization as does take place being inadequate to prevent substantial loss-making.

This is a formidable display of arguments against differential pricing. It seems almost perverse to say that theoretical arguments can be found to show that, *if correctly applied,* differential pricing can serve the interests of airlines, low-fare passengers and also—and obviously crucially—those who pay relatively high fares as well. However, such arguments do exist, based on an understanding of the structure of airline costs, and we must now deal with them. At the same time, we must bring in the substantial practical

---

5 *See*, for example, Williams (1975), p. 304.
6 *See* C.A.A. (1977a), pp. 29–31, and Hodgson (1979), p. 210.

problems which have arisen when airlines have attempted to bring these theoretical benefits into the real world.

6.2.3 Airline Cost Structures as a Pricing Constraint

It is often said that cost analysis is as much an art as a science, and this is nowhere truer than in the classification of airline costs. However, it is essential that a cost base for pricing is produced, and then used in the definition of tariff structures and price levels.

There are many different approaches to developing such a cost base, but it would seem that a polarization is now developing around two broad groups of methods. These we can call *market pricing within a marginal cost framework* and *product-based* pricing.

Appreciation of the nature of market pricing needs to be based on a classification of airline costs relative to output. Unfortunately 'output' in air transport can have a number of different meanings. It can apply to a seat made available to a passenger (or a unit of space offered to a freight customer), to a flight operated on a route, or indeed to all the flights operated on a route during a given time period. In looking at airline pricing, it has been found helpful to classify the totality of costs by comparing them with the level of output to which they relate. Classification then becomes a marginal one as we look at the costs which will be incurred relative to the unit of output under consideration, if a particular positive decision is taken, which would not have been incurred had an opposite, negative decision been made.

Such a process leads us to a highly arbitrary, but useful, classification of costs into the following four categories.

1. Passenger-Related Costs

These are the costs which will vary around a decision as to whether or not a passenger is carried on a flight which the airline will operate anyway. They are the only costs of an airline which will vary in the extreme short run. They involve the costs of any catering which the passenger does or does not consume. (This merely means the cost of the food itself; a decision as to whether or not a particular passenger is carried will not affect the overhead costs of catering such as staff and equipment.) They may also include the cost of his ticket (again, merely the cost of the ticket itself, since overhead costs of ticketing will not be affected by a decision as to whether or not a particular passenger is carried). An important passenger-related cost (where it is paid) is that of travel agent's commission, with this varying as a percentage of ticket price (*see* Section 7.1.1). Finally, there will be the costs of extra fuel consumed. However, the true proportion of costs which can be said to vary with the decision as to whether or not a seat is occupied on a flight which the airline is going to operate anyway is quite small.

2. Flight-Related Costs

These costs are those which vary with a decision as to whether or not a flight is operated. Most important amongst them will be the costs of the fuel which is or is not consumed, and the airport landing and air-navigation fees which will or will not be paid. Other components will be those of use-related depreciation costs and maintenance costs dependent on aircraft usage.

3. Route-Related Costs

At a level of decision-making related to questions of whether or not a particular route should be operated—this can mean either decisions to begin operations on a route which the airline does not at present fly, or the withdrawal of services from a sector which it *does* currently operate—a much wider spectrum of costs becomes involved. Operating a route may entail the acquisition of aircraft, with a corresponding need to hire flight and cabin crew. Investment may also be required in additional mainte-nance facilities for these aircraft, with the hiring also of extra maintenance staff. Any route will also need investment in station and ground facilities, with recruitment and training of appropriate staff for these. Finally, particularly in the early stages of route development, it will be necessary to incur costs in route-orientated advertising in order to establish the airline's presence in the market.

4. Airline-Related Costs

Despite any attempts which might be made to apportion costs between passengers, flights and routes, it is a realistic view to suggest that there will be some costs in the operations of almost any airline which cannot be broken down in any worthwhile sense. These must therefore be seen as varying only with a decision to operate as an airline. Examples of such costs are those of general and administrative overheads, the costs of a reservations system and general image-building advertising. Whilst ob-viously some attempt at reducing these costs can be made, they are only substantially avoidable for most airlines if a carrier should cease operations altogether.

A classification of costs into *passenger-related, flight-related, route-related* and *airline-related* provides a framework within which one can view the development of airline pricing policies.

An airline beginning operations and having an understanding of the structure of its markets, might initiate a pricing policy based on a single high fare on a given route. This would have as its merits total simplicity and an apparent equity between consumers in that all passengers would be paying the same fare. However, it would have less desirable consequences in that only a relatively small number of passengers would come forward to travel. These would be from the segments comprising business passengers and very wealthy leisure travellers. For all other segments, the high fare would be above the willingness-to-pay, with the consequence that passengers from them would not travel at all, or else would use a cheaper alternative, such as that provided by charter airlines (on routes where charters are permitted). However, any attempt to lower the price to bring forward more price-elastic segments would mean that those segments with a high willingness-to-pay would pay substantially below their maximum price, with a consequent loss of revenue from this source.

For any profit-orientated carrier, basing pricing on a single high fare will bring a number of problems. The small number of passengers coming forward will mean low average seat factors, or else a need to use small aircraft which will be expensive to operate in available seat-kilometre terms. Also, airline service will be confined to those routes where a significant demand from business and wealthy leisure travellers exists. More marginal routes will be uneconomic. Finally, on all routes which *are* operated, the small numbers of passengers will mean only a low level of flight frequency. As discussed in Chapter 2, the fact of high costs and therefore high prices may not be seen as working excessively against the business traveller's interest, given his low price-elasticity. However, flight frequency and flight timings must be seen as prime components of the businessman's product, and the use of uniform pricing is likely to result in a low provision of both.

An alternative to uniform pricing is to move over to some form of differential tariff. To do so, a selection of lower fares will be brought into the price structure. These will attract segments with a higher price-elasticity. Restrictive conditions will then be placed on the use of the low fares in order to minimize revenue dilution.

Such a change will significantly increase the complexity of pricing. It will also invite criticisms of inequity from consumers still required to pay high fares. However, if it works successfully, it can bring consequences which are in the interests of all consumers. This is clear in the case of the price-elastic consumers paying low fares, for an air service will be made available to them at a price which they can afford, whereas none was offered before. However, even for the price-inelastic consumer, a move towards differential pricing can, it is argued,[7] bring decisive advantages.

---

7 *See*, for example, Friedmann (1976), pp. 90–111; Colussy (1977), p. 9.

The additional passengers brought forward will enable satisfactory use to be made of larger aircraft, with low unit operating costs. In the extreme case where an airline has invested money in buying large aircraft, but where passenger loads with a single high fare are inadequate to ensure profitability, differential pricing can bring in extra revenue at an increment of cost which is only equal to the passenger-related costs of the additional passengers. However, even where such excess capacity is not available, the larger number of travellers can allow the use of aircraft of such a size that they force down the levels of seat-kilometre costs for all customers. As a second advantage, extra passengers can be used by the airline to justify increased flight frequencies, particularly at off-peak times. These passengers can also make an extension of the airline's network worthwhile. Routes which have some high-fare travel potential, but not enough to ensure viability for an airline restricting itself purely to pricing for such traffic, can be served under a system of differential pricing. Finally, extra passengers, even if they are paying low fares, allow for a wider distribution of airline-related overhead costs.

All in all, a persuasive *theoretical* case can be made out that differential pricing offers advantages to all consumers. Low-fare passengers are offered a service at a price they can afford. High-fare passengers, despite the apparent inequity of a price structure based on differential pricing, can be said to gain with the two crucial product components of flight frequency and route network. The fact that differential pricing allows the use of larger aircraft with lower unit-operating costs, and also that it will permit a wider distribution of an airline's inflexible overhead costs, can mean that the high-fare passenger would pay *more*, not less, if low fares were not offered to bring forward price-elastic market segments.

However, despite these theoretical arguments, a growing disquiet has been apparent during the last few years over the actual working of differential pricing in practice.[8] The real world has not allowed the theoretical model to work in the way that it should do to benefit both the providers and all classes of user of airline services. This has been for a number of reasons.

Firstly, revenue dilution has been a chronic problem. There has been a need, in consequence, to impose ever-tighter conditions on Special Economy fares in order to reduce it. Critics have suggested that these conditions have now become highly arbitrary and discriminatory, with the minimum- and maximum-stay singled out for special attention in this respect.[9] Furthermore, in many situations, differential pricing has worked almost too successfully, if its aim is seen as being to bring forward large numbers of passengers. We have seen in Chapter 2 that most air transport

---

8 *See*, for example, Civil Aviation Authority (1977a); Air Transport User's Committee (1976).
9 *See* Hanlon (1977), p. 225.

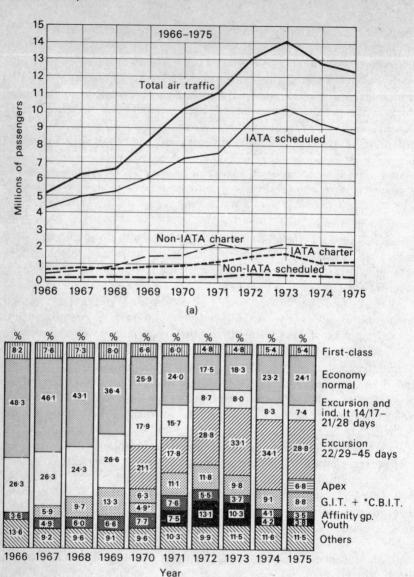

Figure 6.1 (a) Total North Atlantic passenger traffic (1966–1975)
(*b*) IATA North Atlantic scheduled services—passenger distribution of fare type 9 (1966–1975)

The distribution of IATA North Atlantic scheduled passengers by fare type over the period 1966–1975 is illustrated by this chart. In absolute numbers normal fare traffic has increased only marginally, while the major growth has occurred in the promotional fare categories. (Source: *IATA New Review*, Sept. 1976.)

markets have a pyramidal structure. Relatively small numbers of consumers are available when high prices are offered, and much larger numbers at lower fares. Therefore the effect of offering a low Special Economy fare has often been to lead to a rush of demand to use it. In the short term, this may have excellent results of a sharp rise in airline profitability due to the incremental revenue being set against only a small increment of cost. However, in the longer term, the consequence can be financial disaster. When large numbers of low-fare passengers come forward, the effect may be to fill up space available on the aircraft which the carrier already has in service. In turn, this jeopardizes its ability to offer last-minute booking facilities to business passengers, given that most of the generated traffic will be in the leisure segment and therefore likely to book—and fill available space—long before flight departure time. The loss of late booking capability will threaten the airline's competitiveness in the business-travel segment, for late booking possibilities make up a crucial product component for the business passenger. To regain this competitiveness, pressures are likely to build up within the airline for additional capacity to be placed into the market-place—capacity which is, however, only being justified by very low-yielding Special Economy fares. The end result can be that an airline reduces its average yield per passenger, whilst the pressures to maintain flight frequencies and seat availability for the business segment mean that average seat factors do not rise commensurately. In total, therefore, differential pricing does not enhance profitability as theoretically it should, but instead leads to serious financial problems.

The difficulties resulting from revenue dilution and excessive generation of low-fare traffic are perfectly illustrated in Figure 6.1. This covers pricing on the North Atlantic between 1966 and 1975. During this time, the number of passengers on the route more than doubled. However, crucially, average seat factors did not rise. Indeed, seat factors at the end of the period were slightly lower than those at the beginning. It is this fact which makes the lower diagram of the structure of fare usage on the route of particular interest. At the beginning of the period, the route gave a good example of differential pricing working successfully. A large proportion of travellers was using high-yielding First Class and Normal Economy fares. These were being usefully supplemented by a range of Excursion and Special Economy fares, presumably aimed at market segments with a higher demand-elasticity. However, by 1973, a combination of revenue dilution from existing passengers and a substantial generation of new low-fare traffic had completely changed the pattern of fare use. More than three-quarters of the passengers were using low Special Economy fares. In the absence of a rise in average seat factors and—as it happened—with an inadequate reduction in available seat-kilometre costs, the consequence was that the reasonable financial performance of 1966–9 had changed to one of serious and sustained loss-making: the route presented a classic example of one where the use of differential pricing had gone disastrously wrong.[10]

The difficulties of controlling differential pricing in the real-world environment of the industry and the actions taken by airlines to extricate themselves from these difficulties have led to most of the criticisms of passenger pricing made in recent years. Once an airline is employing differential pricing, it is by no means easy to state what action is appropriate if the structure leads to loss-making. If the problems are caused by the offer of low Special Economy fares which result in dilution and excessive generation of low-yielding traffic, it may not be an answer merely to raise significantly or even abolish these fares. The fact of a high price-elasticity for leisure air travel may mean that, at higher fares, some travellers do not make their journeys at all. More realistically, on routes where the regulatory system has allowed the development of charters, higher scheduled fares will lead to a transfer of traffic from scheduled to charter services. Where an airline has committed resources to the carriage of a particular amount of traffic, loss of some of this business, even if it is relatively low-yielding, will result in worsening of the carrier's financial position in the short-run.

Given the limited possibilities for raising the low fares as a solution to financial problems, the temptation has been to opt instead for increases in the high fares in the structure, especially the Normal Economy price. Raising the Normal Economy fare will bring increased revenue, without large losses of passengers. At the same time, the way in which regulation of air transport has developed has meant that, whilst on some routes at least there is extensive competition between scheduled and charter airlines for low-fare traffic, price competition has largely been excluded at the Normal Economy fare. There have therefore been many accusations[11] that airlines have used price regulation through I.A.T.A. to push up the Normal Economy fare, and that they have especially done this on routes where there is limited competition from other airlines and the control of the I.A.T.A. carriers is total.[12]

Whatever the validity of these arguments with respect to past airline practice, they highlight a difficult dilemma for airlines and regulators alike. If carriers consistently engage in a policy of raising Normal Economy fares relative to lower fares, there must come a point where the advantages of differential pricing to the high-fare payer—particularly that it allows for the use of larger aircraft with lower seat-kilometre costs—are more than outweighed by the extent of overcharging. When this point is reached, there must be cross-subsidization existing in its truest sense.

---

10 *See* Friedmann (1976) for a full discussion of the problems of the route during this period.
11 For example, Williams (1975).   12 *See* Cooper and Maynard (1972).

The problems associated with market pricing in a marginal cost framework—that it is very difficult to control and that it can truly become 'unfair'—have been important contributory factors to the development of a new philosophy of pricing. This philosophy—initiated in the United Kingdom by a series of separate innovations—we can call *product-based pricing*. Instead of the former emphasis on varying prices and tightly restrictive conditions in a marginal cost framework, there is now a growing interest in the relationship between customer needs and the long-term costs of product provision to meet these needs. This, it is claimed, can give an equitable basis for pricing.

The effects of this change may not be dramatic. It has, in many cases, shown up a good deal of logical justification in the old pricing practices. However, it does mark an important philosophical development in viewpoints on correct airline pricing policy.

The principle behind product-based pricing[13] would seem to be to relate the different airline prices and the conditions pertaining to them to identifiable consumer needs and price elasticities. At the same time, the products governed by the different prices must, as far as possible, be separated, with the products designed in such a way as to give a relationship between correctly-allocated production costs and price levels.

Several examples are now available where such an approach can be tested in practice. Thus the user of the Normal Economy fare will usually be a business traveller requiring the expensive product components of high flight-frequencies and low average-seat-factors to allow for last-minute booking. A correct cost allocation will therefore apportion to the Normal Economy fare user a high amount of capacity costs[14] and the costs of empty seats in a low average-seat-factor operation. Available research has suggested that, on some routes in Europe at least, costing methods such as these can produce a considerable cost justification for the level of Normal Economy fares, even though these fares were presumably set without reference to such specific cost information. However, on other routes even this apportionment of costs fails to justify the level of the Normal Economy fare, with accusations therefore of cross-subsidization.[15]

Product-based pricing concepts can also be used to justify the levels of many of the Special Economy fares as well. Thus it has been argued[16] that the very low levels of ITX and S.G.I.T. fares on intra-European scheduled services cannot be seen as merely discriminatory pricing to compete with charter airlines. Rather they are low fares with a good measure of cost-justification if the correct cost-allocation procedure is used. Thus,

13 Given its most thorough examination, though not described as such, in C.A.A. (1977a).
14 Arguably an additional allocation of cost should be made over and above actual costs of capacity provision to take account of the need to use small aircraft to allow for the 'schedule convenience' of high flight-frequency/small-aircraft operations. *See* British Airways (1977).
15 C.A.A. (1977a, p. 20).   16 British Airways (1977).

S.G.I.T. costing should be based on very high average seat factors and the use of cheap-to-operate large aircraft, as flight frequency and last-minute booking are of little relevance to the leisure passengers who use S.G.I.T. Also, S.G.I.T. should bear none of the airline's cost of commission payments. It is capacity which is available only on a wholesale basis to travel organizers who are responsible for commission to travel agents.[17] Similar arguments apply to the costs of reservations and advertising, with correct costing relieving S.G.I.T. of any burden of these.

Probably the best product-based justification for a low fare comes with the APEX concept. APEX was pioneered by the former B.O.A.C. during the late 1960s and early 1970s, and has been widely introduced by many airlines in the easing regulatory situation of recent years. APEX is a fare concept based on advanced booking and prepayment—with a cancellation penalty—in return for low fares. It meets market requirements in that it is aimed at a market segment where price elasticities are normally high, but which usually does book well ahead anyway. The advanced booking requirement is therefore not a discriminatory condition, but rather conforms to known market needs. However, in cost terms it brings airlines decisive advantages which allow a strong cost-justification to be given to the low fares available under the APEX concept. Thus advanced payment helps the airline's cash flow and eases its bad-debt problems. Advanced booking allows the carrier to pursue a policy of space planning in the use of capacity. Thus if an airline is to provide adequately for the needs of its business passengers for peak-time trips, it will have considerable spare capacity at the off-peak, given that most costs incurred for peak provision will not be avoidable in the short-run. Space planning for APEX passengers will allow such passengers to be directed towards off-peak flights where they will not jeopardize the service quality offered to business passengers. Alternatively, it may be possible to make a provision for APEX passengers on all flights, particularly with the use of large wide-bodied aircraft, with merely more space allocated to APEX passengers on off-peak as compared with peak flights. However, the cost justification can be retained by a correct space-planning policy which ensures that all space which is allocated to APEX passengers is operated at a very high average seat-factor to counterbalance the low yields. This latter possibility is now seeing its ultimate development with the separation of low-fare passengers through the three-class cabin concept, where differences in catering provision and other service standards are added to the advanced booking requirement as product-differentiating characteristics.

Fare concepts such as APEX point to future directions in correct airline pricing policies. In the future environment for the industry, it is unlikely to be possible for airlines to pursue the old pricing practices. Instead,

17 *See* Section 7.1.2.

important criteria for pricing will be the need for a pricing concept to combine with a product type to make up a package which meets a definable consumer need. This must be done at a price which the market segment at which the package is aimed is prepared to pay, and without the price being significantly above the long-run costs of capacity provision. In such a situation true equity in the price structure will be demonstrable, without airlines being prevented from offering very low fares to those segments whose product needs can be met, under correct costing techniques, at low costs.

Despite the intuitive appeal of the product-based model, however, its use is unlikely to be easy or straightforward. It does raise important policy questions on its own account. Many have maintained[18] that the detailed breakdown of costs which it implies is unrealistic, with any apportionment of joint and common costs between product types likely to be arbitrary and misleading. Also, its use will bring into question the flight frequencies and the route networks traditionally provided by scheduled airlines. Until now, whatever one's views on the correctness or extent of cross-subsidization, scheduled airlines have, through the use of market pricing, been able to maintain a viable operation on routes with only a limited business travel potential. Understandably, charter airlines have protested frequently at what they see as unfair competition. With the advent of product-based pricing, the opportunities for airlines to engage in cross-subsidization will be reduced or eliminated. The effect will be to relieve the business traveller of the burden of 'unfair' pricing whereby part of his fare is used to cross-subsidize the carriage of low-fare passengers. However, a possible reduction in passenger numbers may result in a narrow distribution of fixed airline overhead costs. Moreover, we have seen in Chapter 2 that price is not a product component of prime importance for the business traveller. Critics of product-based pricing have therefore suggested that the possible effects of such pricing—a reduction in airline flight frequencies and particularly a withdrawal of scheduled services on routes with only a limited business-travel potential—may be more than enough to cancel out the benefits of any reductions in Normal Economy ticket prices.

The question of the correct way for airlines to price their passenger product is the subject of considerable disagreement at the time of writing. Obviously, where air transport remains regulated, any pricing decision must be a compromise, with a need existing to secure the agreement of governments and often other airlines as well to any changes. However, even within this need, fundamental differences of opinion are apparent. Market pricing can bring benefits to airlines and to air travel consumers. It offers a way of maintaining a large scheduled network in the face of the problems posed by the structure of the air-passenger market and the nature of airline costs. However, there can be no doubt that it has led to

18 For example, Colussy (1977).

practical problems in the real world, primarily because it does not impose sufficient discipline on the management of pricing. Hence the appeal, from a marketing viewpoint, of the product-based approach. Product pricing brings its own dangers and controversies, but for the first time offers marketing management the chance to define precisely mixes of product, cost and price which can meet identified consumer needs in the market-place. It is therefore important that the future should see a further acceptance of its principles and use.

6.3 Scheduled Airline Pricing Policy—Freight

Pricing for air freight involves many of the same difficulties as for passenger traffic, as well as some which are unique to the freight side of the business. We shall therefore begin the work on freight pricing by looking at some of the problems which must be met and solved by the marketing manager concerned with air freight.

6.3.1 Problems of Freight Pricing

Of these problems, the first very important one is that of directional imbalance. We have seen how, although directional problems arise on the passenger side, almost all passenger routes end up approximately direc-tionally balanced when taken over a year. With freight, it is no more than a fortunate coincidence if a directional balance exists, with imbalance by far the commonest situation. Pricing must therefore encompass the need to ensure profitability on routes where there are directional imbalances and where an airline may be wrestling with the twin problems of capacity shortage in the busy direction and wasted space on the return.

Even the statement 'to ensure profitability' is fraught with difficulty on the freight side, for there are problems in finding a cost base for pricing on which profitability calculations can be made. We have already seen that air freight capacity divides into two. All combination airlines have the opportunity to carry freight in the lower hold of passenger planes. However, many carriers also supplement a product based on the carriage of freight in lower holds with one utilizing pure freighter aircraft. The industry therefore has had to devise a pricing structure which is suitable for both lower-hold cargo and cargo carried in freighters.

With the costing of lower-hold freight space, two contrasting viewpoints are apparent.[19] One suggests that the dominant purpose of airline activity is the carriage of passengers. Lower-hold space is merely a by-product of passenger carriage, resulting from the need for aerodynamic aircraft design. It is therefore held to be reasonable that freight should not have

19 *See* Brewer and Decoster (1967) and Miller (1973).

apportioned to it flight costs such as flight crew salaries and airport and air navigation charges. Instead, it becomes worthwhile to carry freight at any price which exceeds marginal costs. These marginal costs are made up by costs of freight selling, administration, documentation and ground-handling and the increment of cost made up by the extra fuel consumed as a result of the weight of freight in the aircraft.

The alternative viewpoint dismisses the by-product approach as likely to result in a gross underestimate of the true costs of freight. It suggests that the correct philosophy is one of *joint* costing, in which freight in passenger aircraft bears a proportion of such costs as those of flight crew and airport landing charges. This principle is based on the proposition that by-product costing may have been appropriate in the days of narrow-bodied aircraft when potential lower-hold payloads consisted of a few tonnes in a small, cramped and difficult-to-use space. However, the advent of wide-bodied aircraft has brought lower-hold capabilities of fifteen tonnes or more, with the B 747 in passenger configuration capable of accepting almost as much in its lower holds as a pure freighter B 707. By-product costing is not correct where such a large amount of payload is involved. Also, as was noted in Section 5.6, more and more alternative uses for lower-hold space are appearing which are involving managements in decisions as to how such space should be deployed.

The final argument against the use of by-product costing is that, given the need for compromise between airlines still necessary in most aspects of air freight pricing, any pricing structure based purely on by-product costs would mean that profitable pure-freighter operations would not be possible. It would clearly then be foolish for an airline with freighters to agree to a price stucture based on lower-hold by-product costs.

Despite the undoubted correctness at a philosophical level of the joint-costing approach, its actual employment presents yet further difficulties which spring from the acute pattern of weekly peaking characteristic of air freight. As one would expect, the demand pattern for freight follows that of industrial production, with a high proportion of all air freight moving at the end of the working week on Friday nights and Saturdays. With any passenger flights which leave at these peak times, a reasonable costing method for lower-hold freight can probably be found, particularly as the use of lower-hold space by the freight department of an airline saves it the costs of the alternative of employing additional pure freighters. However, it is unlikely that the same costing methods will be suitable for passenger flights leaving at the extreme off-peak on Sundays and Mondays. This is a time when the freight department would operate very little capacity if it were free to work purely in its own interests.[20]

20 There is, of course, an alternative viewpoint. This says that a freight department acting in its own interests will need to provide a large amount of capacity to meet its peak-time needs, and that, like all transport operators, it will be unable, in the short run, to avoid the costs associated with peak-time provision. Therefore, it may be appropriate to apportion costs at the off-peak in the same way as for the peak.

Table 6.3. Air Freight rates, July 1978 per kilo

U.K. to Johannesburg:	
Minimum charge:	£15·62
General Cargo {−45:	£3·61
Rates {+45:	£2·71
No. of specific Commodity Rates in force:	20
Example: 4224: (parts of television sets)	£1·74 (for minimum of 1,000 kilos)
Bulk Unitization Rate:	None available

U.K. to Tokyo:	
Minimum charge:	£17·68
General Cargo {−45:	£5·96
Rates {+45:	£4·47
No. of specific Commodity Rates in force:	23
Examples: 44·2: (electrical equipment)	£1·32 (for minimum of 1,000 kilos)
Bulk Unitization Rate:	£1·41 (800 kilos minimum)

U.K. to Sydney:	
Minimum charge:	£17·68
General Cargo {−45:	£6·26
Rates {+45:	£4·69
No. of specific Commodity Rates in force:	2
Example: 6002: (chemicals . . .)	£2·74 (100 kilos minimum)
Bulk Unitization Rate:	£2·65 (800 kilos minimum)

Whatever the correct conclusion on the appropriate cost base for air freight pricing, it is clear that the complexities of costing provide a difficulty in the definition of pricing policy.

The final set of pricing complications springs from the heterogeneous nature of air freight consignments. Freight consignments can vary to an almost infinite extent in shape, size and weight, and ways must be found of taking account of this in the pricing structure. This must be done bearing in mind the fact that many costs do not vary proportionately with consignment size. Costs of documentation are fixed for almost any size of consignment and costs of ground handling on a per kilo basis are generally much lower for large consignments than for small ones. Then again, costs will vary according to commodity type, with some items such as hazardous goods and valuable cargoes needing special handling which involves extra costs and a need in equity to ensure that these costs are recovered from the shippers of the cargoes which cause them to be incurred. Finally, freight consignments vary in the very important aspect of density, with a need existing for decisions to be made as to whether charging should be based on weight, on volume, or on a mixture of the two with high density cargoes charged on weight and low density ones on volume. If this latter policy is adopted, a decision must be taken on the cut-off point between weight and volumetric charging.

6.3.2 The Structure of Freight Pricing

The structure of pricing on most international air freight routes can be divided into five main categories.[21] Similar categories will be present in most domestic markets although the terminology may be somewhat different.

1. General Cargo Rates

General Cargo Rates are available today on all air freight routes. They are applicable to any type of commodity, without the restriction of a minimum consignment size. Their disadvantage is that they are pitched at an extremely high level, as shown in Table 6.3, although some discount is offered for consignments which can take advantage of the weight breaks which exist at 45 kilos, and often at 100 kilos and higher weights as well.

2. Minimum Charges

Again on all routes, General Cargo Rates are supplemented by provision for a minimum charge, which means in most cases that a shipper will never be charged less than the appropriate rate for a consignment of 4 kilos, even though his particular consignment may weigh less than this. On some routes, minimum charges apply at higher weights of up to 8 kilos. There is considerable logical justification in the minimum charge principle given the fact that costs of documentation and customs clearance will be fixed irrespective of consignment size.[22]

3. Class Rates

Class Rates are a further supplement to the General Cargo Rate tariff, again applicable on all international routes. Under class rating certain types of commodity are offered a discount, as where newspapers are always carried

---

21 Smith (1974) Ch. 9 gives a full outline of the principles of air freight pricing.
22 Though, in fact, separate fixed charges are made for documentation and ground handling. In international service, these are made under the so-called I.A.T.A. 512b Resolution in international services.

at half the appropriate General Cargo Rate. Many more commodities are only carried with surcharges under Class Rating, with, for example, surcharges applying to the carriage of human remains, hazardous goods and high-value cargoes.

4. Specific Commodity Rates

Like Class Rates, Specific Commodity Rates are rates which are only applicable to named types of freight. But S.C.Rs in addition show a number of features which separate out this form of pricing as a distinct aspect. Specific Commodity Rates are not set with any reference to the General Cargo Rate. Instead, they are all at a much lower level than G.C.Rs, with in extreme cases Specific Commodity rates pitched at 25 to 30 per cent of the alternative General Cargo Rate. Further, they are only available for named types of freight. However, unlike the Class Rate situation where only a comparatively small number of commodity types are affected, S.C.Rs are offered on a vast number of commodities. There are upwards of 5,000 different commodities represented in the table of definitions prepared by the airlines within I.A.T.A. Finally, an individual Specific Commodity Rate does not have universal applicability. Instead, S.C.Rs are quoted for individual routes on a city-pair basis. Also, a minimum consignment size almost always applies, with few S.C.Rs being offered for consignments of less than 100 kilos, whilst further weight-breaks are available for larger consignments, often at 300, 500 and 1,000 kilos. There are large variations in the numbers of commodity types having their own S.C.Rs on different routes. In some markets, more than 50 commodity rates are in force, whereas in others there are none at all.

5. Bulk Unitization Rates

Bulk Unitization Rates are a comparatively recent innovation, dating from 1969. They offer low unit rates, substantially below comparable General Cargo Rates. Also, unlike Specific Commodity Rates, they are available for all types of freight irrespective of commodity type. Such low rates, however, are only given for freight which is pre-packed into an aircraft Unit Load Device (U.L.D.) which can be loaded directly into the aircraft. These U.L.D's divide into the three main categories of: large containers with an 8 ft by 8 ft cross-section which can be placed in the main deck of the B 747; airline pallets of the standard industry 125 × 88 in. size; and the so-called L.D. containers which are sub-modular to the lower holds of the wide-bodied aircraft.

For Bulk Unitization rating, each of the different types of U.L.D. is set a 'pivot weight.' This acts as a minimum charge, with the shipper required to pay for this weight even if he is unable to place such an amount in the unit.

Thus for the L.D.-3 container which is sub-modular to the lower holds of the B 747, L 1011, DC 10 and A 300 families, the pivot weight is 760–800 kilos, varying slightly according to route. If, on the other hand the shipper has a consignment of sufficient size which is above the pivot weight with a density and stowability which allow it to be loaded into the unit, he will be required to pay an additional over-pivot-weight rate for each kilo. However, this is a concessionary rate at well below the per-kilo rate for less dense consignments, in recognition of the advantages to the airline of carrying high-density freight.

6. Contract/F.A.K. Rates

As the final element in the present structure of scheduled air freight rates, contract rates have been in existence since the Autumn of 1976, and have aroused considerable controversy. At that time, British Airways, taking advantage of reducing regulation on the North Atlantic, announced that it would offer special low rates on routes between U.K. and U.S.A. for those of its customers who were prepared to sign contracts with it which committed them to giving the airline a minimum of 500 tonnes in a year. These rates were to be available on a freight-of-all-kinds basis, irrespective of commodity type, with even further concessions available for pre-unitized freight. However, the British Airways proposal was greeted by strong opposition from its U.S. competitors, particularly the all-freight airline Seaboard World. One may guess that there was particular concern on the part of Seaboard because the B.A. rate levels were so low that they could only be viable based on the use of lower-hold space on passenger flights—in fact on the synergy only available to the total market airline. This space was something that as an all-cargo carrier Seaboard did not have. Also, in response to the B.A. move, other competing airlines have come to offer contract-level rates, but without requiring their customers—principally in this case freight forwarders—to sign a contract. To a degree therefore, contract rating has been undermined, and its future role in international air-freight pricing must remain uncertain. Indeed, at the time of writing it seems that the trend is towards a wider availability of non-contract F.A.K. rates, rather than an expansion of the contract principle.

6.3.3 Criticisms of Freight Pricing Policy

Just as with passenger pricing, airline pricing policy for freight has been the subject of virtriolic criticism in recent years. These criticisms have been that the price structure has been ineffective in allowing for profitability, that it has become complex and inequitable, and that it shows inadequate recognition of market segmentation.

The fact of unprofitability of air freight has come from the consistently poor financial performance of pure freighter operations throughout the post-war period.[23] Until now, many airlines have apparently seen the operation of pure freight aircraft in a loss-leader context. The airline which offered freighter capacity to its customers was more likely to obtain from them traffic which it could carry in the lower holds of its passenger aircraft and, depending on the costing philosophy employed, be seen to be making high profits from doing so. However, we have already examined the arguments (Section 5.6) which suggest that lower-hold freight space may be in less plentiful supply in the future than it has been in the immediate past, with a real necessity for the total-market airline to make a substantial commitment of resources in the direction of freight. This must be with the purchase of wide-bodied freighter aircraft, especially the B 747F. If this does turn out to be the case, a criticism of the price structure that it does not allow for profitable freighter operations would become serious indeed. Of course, the fact that in several ways the B 747 is a much better freighter aeroplane than its narrow-bodied predecessors will make profitability easier to obtain. This is indeed fortunate because of the crucial importance of such profits to the future of the freight side of the industry.

The questions of complexity and inequity in the structure spring mainly from the Specific Commodity Rate element in it. Specific Commodity Rates provide a classic example of discrimination in transport pricing. As one would expect, all the controversies and arguments which normally attend price discriminatory practices are present here.

Commodity rates first began to be introduced in the late 1940s, when it was realized that consignment value-to-weight ratio was a crucial variable in deciding the likelihood that a particular type of commodity would be sent by air. As was shown in Section 2.6.3, the higher the value-to-weight ratio of consignment, the greater are the benefits to be obtained from the speed of air freight and the less the proportionate impact of the freight rate on the final selling price. Progressively it became clear that air freight's market penetration into lower-value consignments was being blocked by the high level of freight rates. However, to lower *all* rates to allow for such market penetration would have meant a loss of revenue from very high-value freight which would have continued to move by air if the old rate levels had remained. It was therefore an attractive option to move over to discriminatory pricing. The old General Cargo Rate structure was retained and aimed at goods with a low demand elasticity. Special low rates were then offered to particular classes of commodity in situations in which a substantial traffic potential seemed to be available. The international airlines established a board through I.A.T.A. to approve Specific Commodity Rates. It became open for airlines either directly or on behalf of

---

23 *See* I.A.T.A. (1969).

their shippers to apply to the Board for the approval of new commodity rates.

As is so often the case, a theoretical justification can be made that such pricing is in the interests of both the providers and users of air freight services—only in practice do the real difficulties arise. In theory, price discrimination should have allowed airlines substantially increased revenue, which, providing in all cases that marginal costs were covered, should have brought benefits to all. Airlines could hope for enhanced freight profitability, whilst shippers taking advantage of the low commodity rates were being offered the chance to use air freight services which otherwise would have been too expensive for them. However, just as with the Normal Economy ticket on the passenger side, differential pricing can in theory work also in the interests of the payer of high prices. The economies of scale of greater output can result in his being provided with a better product at a lower price than would be the case if concessionary rates to price-elastic users were not offered.

Despite these advantages, it has been the management control in the use of differential pricing which has proved to be so difficult—some would say impossible. During the past thirty years, the number of Specific Commodity Rates has increased so rapidly that there are now in excess of 250,000 of them in force in various parts of the world. Clearly, a price structure based on such a proliferation of rates is likely to be complex and unwieldy. There have been never-ending arguments regarding the definition of the commodity types to which particular rates should apply, and it would seem likely that misdeclaration of commodities has been a potent area for I.A.T.A. compliance activity in recent years.

The result of such trends has been that on some routes, commodity-based pricing seems to have moved away from the mutually beneficial situation of the differential pricing model. Indeed, on routes such as the North Atlantic, so many commodity rates are in force that a very high proportion of all freight on the route moves under them.[24] It is therefore virtually certain that revenue dilution is adding to the difficulties of working and enforcing such a complex price structure.

The final blow to commodity-based pricing has been the advent of Bulk Unitization and other low freight-of-all-kinds rates. On routes where a Bulk Unitization rate is on offer, a shipper has a choice of sending his goods under a low commodity rate if this is available or, if it is not, using an almost equally low Bulk Unitization rate. Admittedly in this latter case he may have to make his consignment part of a forwarder's consolidation[25] in order to reach the pivot weight of a unit load device, but the continuing increase in the use of consolidations by shippers indicates that this is not regarded as a major disadvantage. The result has been that the use of

24 *See* I.A.T.A. (1973).   **25** *See* Section 7.3.1.

commodity-based rating has been undermined, with the shipper able to gain a low rate for his freight irrespective of commodity type. Indeed, it has sometimes seemed that the only justification for commodity pricing has been that it has retained a degree of power in airline's hands in comparison with the freight forwarding industry because it has limited the forwarder's ability to build up consolidations of mixed freight. This point is an important one relating to the selling channels employed by airlines for their freight product, and we shall return to it in Section 7.3.1.

A further criticism of scheduled air freight pricing at the moment can be made on the grounds that such pricing largely ignores the segmentation of the air freight market. It was shown in Section 2.6 that it is possible to segment the demand for air freight into the three basic categories of emergency, routine-perishable and routine-non-perishable traffic, and that emergency situations are usually characterized by a very low demand elasticity. Under the present pricing system, it is very often possible for the shipper of an emergency consignment, which will travel by air at almost any price, to send that consignment under a very low Specific Commodity Rate.[26] Equally, it may sometimes be the case that a routine non-perishable shipper may be able to accept a lower service quality than the premium product demanded by emergency traffic—in return for a substantially lower rate. Under present rating arrangements, such an option is not available to him. It is this latter point which makes the scheduled carriers currently as vulnerable to the threat of charter competition on the freight side as they were in passenger traffic during the 1960s. This point has been emphasized by the rapid progress made by freight charter airlines in those countries such as the Netherlands and Luxembourg which have adopted a liberal regulatory stance towards them.

In May 1979, British Airways proposed an experiment in cargo rating which, if implemented, could go a long way towards answering the criticisms made in this section. Instead of the complex mixture of rating concepts previously employed, this airline, on routes where the regulatory systems allows it, has suggested on air freight rating system which is both market orientated and cost-related. The new rating system is based on three tiers of rates. High rates will apply to a premium level of service offered where express delivery is required, a medium band of rates to so-called booked cargo, and then low rates for cargo which the airline will aim to ship as quickly as possible, but for which it reserves the right to impose a delay of up to 48 hours. This latter point is especially important as it allows the airline to offer low rates at a genuinely low cost whereby

---

26 To a degree, the imposition of minimum consignment sizes on the use of S.C.R.s may reduce the extent of dilution from this source. However, the U.K. Civil Aviation Authority in their study of Air Freight Demand (C.A.A., (1977b)) could find little evidence to support a view that emergency traffic consisted of small consignments to a greater extent than did less urgent freight.

freight is delayed from the weekly peak in demand on Fridays and Saturdays into the demand trough which occurs on Sundays and Mondays. Better use of lower-hold space on passenger aircraft on flights which will be operated anyway could add significantly to airline profitability, besides extending the market for air freight into areas of lower-value consignments. It will also mean, that scheduled carriers will counter in advance the threat of charter competition. The advantage of such a structure must also be that it will reduce revenue dilution currently being suffered on emergency shipments.

Despite the points which can be made in favour of the three-tier rating system in theoretical terms, only time will tell if it is workable in practice. There is a real risk that non-profit-based airlines, or those with large amounts of currently underutilized lower-hold space, will come into the market-place and promote their services on the offer of non-deferred service at the deferred rate—in other words that the deferred rate will become the prevailing market price. It would indeed be unfortunate if this did happen, for three-tier rating, coupled with the reducing extent of regulation of the airline industry as a whole, does offer the best hope for escaping from past unsatisfactory practices in the very difficult area of freight pricing.

Both passenger and freight pricing policies currently provide wide areas of controversy. Indeed, it is arguable that there are problems which are so intractable that a perfect solution may never be achieved. However, we have been able to follow our discussion of product design with at least an outline of the principles of pricing. It is therefore now necessary to turn to the next stage of marketing, that of selling the products supplied to potential customers.

7 Selling the Product

In the marketing of any product, selling decisions are centred around two areas. Firstly, the administration of selling through decisions on the *channels* which will be used for it. This means that the firm must decide whether to deal directly with its customers, or else employ the services of one or more of the different forms of marketing intermediary. Secondly, management must decide upon the *communication* policy which it will pursue. Despite the emphasis placed on the strategic, product design and pricing aspects of marketing in this book, marketing only comes to fruition when a firm proves itself capable of communicating effectively with its customers. Clearly, channel decisions will be interrelated with communication ones, but from the point of view of this chapter it will be convenient to separate consideration of them. We therefore look first at the question of selling channels for the air passenger market.

7.1 Selling Channels—Passenger

Figure 7.1 illustrates the different types of selling channel which are open to airlines for their passenger products. It shows that carriers may, if they choose, deal direct with their final customers. Alternatively, they may do this and also rely on other airlines to sell their services to passengers making multi-sector journeys. However, much more commonly, airlines have come to use the different types of marketing intermediary which have grown up. These intermediaries are *travel agents* who specialize in retail selling on behalf of airlines, and *travel organizers* whose function is to buy large blocks of space from carriers, and then re-sell each seat to the public on a risk-taking basis. This can be done either directly or again through travel agents. The use of both agents and organizers raises important issues for airlines, and we must devote considerable space to an examination of their roles.

7.1.1 The Airline/Travel Agent Relationship

Travel agents are the cornerstone of airline passenger selling today. Widely

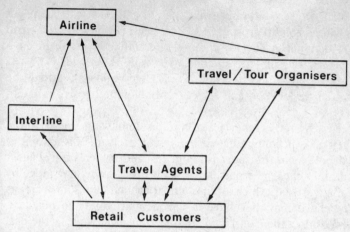

Figure 7.1 Selling channels—air passenger market

within Europe, seventy per cent or more of all airline tickets are sold through agents, whilst even in the U.S. domestic market this percentage is more than fifty.

The reasons for such a domination of selling by agents are not hard to find. They can offer a number of services in a very cost-effective way which are invaluable to both the providers and the users of airline services. Agents save airlines large sums of money through their execution of reservations and ticketing procedures. They can provide information to passengers on such things as airport access systems and visa requirements of destination countries. They also allow the airline to carry out its selling at lower cost because they reduce the extent to which the carrier has to set up and operate its own ticket offices. Today, it is common practice—albeit an expensive one—for most airlines to have a ticket office in the central shopping areas of major cities. For such offices, it is likely that the volume of business coming forward will be sufficient to justify the operation of the office. A location in the most fashionable part of town also has some sales promotional value. However, beyond such busy central shopping locations it would become extremely expensive for an airline to operate a large number of sales outlets purely on its own account. Indeed, such a trend might culminate in the hopelessly uneconomic situation of an airline outlet in a small market centre taking only a few bookings per week. However, without such outlets and without the use of travel agents, potential passengers in such centres would be denied a ready source of tickets, whilst airlines would have to expand their telephone and mail answering systems in order to sell to them.

The advantage which a travel agent has over an airline is that he can sell tickets on behalf of *all* airlines, for travel organizers, and also for others willing to appoint him as an agent for their services. These can include hotels, car hire firms, bus and railway companies and theatres. The result is that agents will be able to prosper in market centres which are too small to allow any individual airline to set up a sales office on its own. As a further advantage, the air travel consumer will be provided with a personalized source of airline tickets (and package holidays) and will be able to go to a single location and select from a comprehensive range of travel products.

Despite these advantages, the fact of airlines employing agents to the extent that they do is becoming increasingly controversial. It is a point of considerable debate in air transport as to the influence which a travel agent has over the airlines chosen by passengers. However, if one may judge by the quantity of advertising which airlines aim at agents, then some carriers at least must believe that they have a considerable ability to persuade passengers who contact them and who are uncertain as to which is the best airline for their needs. This advertising is in many cases, very necessary. It is imperative that, if airlines are to rely on agents for retail selling, these agents should be well-informed regarding the airline's services. However, the fact remains that in any area of marketing activity, advertising by principals to their agents does little or nothing to develop the total market for the product.

The other point about the airline/travel agent relationship is that the agent will require a commission for the services which he performs. This is, of course, an entirely reasonable recognition on the part of the airline of services rendered to it, although interestingly some principals such as theatres do not pay commission but instead leave the agent to secure his income by charging a fee to the retail client. However, difficulties arise because of the competitive aspects of commission payments. In the past, commission levels have mostly been regulated by governments, or, for international services, by inter-airline agreement within I.A.T.A. However, increasingly, override commission payments have become a concern of the I.A.T.A. Compliance Machinery,[1] whilst under the deregulation of U.S. domestic services, commissions by airlines are believed to have risen substantially. It is inevitable that high commissions will bring into question the role of the travel agent and promote the use of alternative products and selling methods which will not entail commission payments at all, or which will at least reduce them.

The role of the travel agent, and the structure of the travel agency industry, is now undergoing significant changes. In recent years, technological developments (referred to in Section 5.5), particularly in the field of direct access to airline reservations computers, have threatened the role of the agent in several ways. For example, the investment now being required from U.K. agents to become part of the Travicom scheme places small

1 *See* Dubash (1975).

agents at a definite disadvantage. Eventually the final development of the Post Office Prestel system may see a revolution in home-based credit card shopping—a revolution which could result in travel agents losing many of the bookings which they now take. The last few years have also seen a series of airline product innovations which again have reduced the role of the agent in selling. The Shuttle concept is one where tickets can be sold at the airport or in-flight with no reference being made to agents at all. The proliferation of the various forms of Standby pricing are again a product which can easily be sold directly by airlines. Finally, and as something with which we shall be concerned in the next section, the most serious threat to the livelihood of many agents is now coming with the development of direct-selling activities by package holiday companies. Many small High Street travel agents in the U.K. are known to derive more than 60 per cent of their revenue from the commissions paid on package holidays, and there is now a real possibility that a large proportion of this revenue will disappear during the next few years.

With the travel agency industry in such a state of flux at the present time, it is indeed difficult to reach conclusions as to appropriate policies for airlines with respect to this aspect of their selling channels. However, the author accepts the inevitability of a degree of conflict between channel members[2] in any form of selling activity, with the existence of such conflicts by no means to be taken as being indicative of an unsatisfactory situation. However, for an airline wishing to make to optimum arrangements for the selling of First Class and Normal Economy tickets to its regular travellers, the advantage certainly lies with a continuing use of travel agents on a substantial scale, providing the carrier obtains a satisfactory share of the market and commission payments are kept within reasonable bounds. However, it is essential that the agency industry must come to appreciate that escalating commission levels, whilst bringing short-term advantages, only hasten the day when it will become correct policy for airlines to review their currently high level of involvement with agents in the sale of these tickets.

With the sale of the lower Special Economy fares, the appropriate policy which an airline should pursue with respect to agents is by no means as clear. Such fares are aimed at a market segment where demand is price-elastic, and where it is becoming important that airlines should be able to go into the market-place with the lowest possible costs. Therefore policy towards travel agents should be decided purely by competition. If the agency industry can prove that, because of the advantages which it holds, it can provide the best outlet for airlines to use, then its long term future is assured. If, however, commission payments rise without compensating advantages coming, then the advent of direct selling by independent

2 *See* Wilkinson (1973).

travel organizers will force all airlines to review the policy of relying on travel agency selling in low-fare markets.

In the U.K., the policy of British Airways towards travel agents would seem to illustrate these points very well. To the outsider it appears that the carrier accepts the long-term need of involvement with the travel agency industry and also the substantial short-term losses which would affect the airline if it tried to reduce significantly the role of agents in its selling. However, various controversial policy decisions in recent years indicate a determination of the part of its management that the airline, as main investment risk taker, must retain a control over the retail market and also, especially in the selling of low fares, ensure that such selling is done in the most cost-effective way. Thus, besides emphasizing in its public statements the importance attached to travel agents, the airline has promoted the introduction of new products such as Shuttle where the role of the agent is reduced. It has engaged in a policy of opening its own sales shops on a large scale in major retail centres, with these shops functioning as high-street travel agents with the vital difference that they are restricted to the selling of British Airways products. Also, it has, in a few cases, provided so-called 'implants' to business houses to look after business travel arrangements presumably in direct conflict with agents, whilst finally it has begun to build up a direct selling commitment in its package holiday business through its wholly-owned subsidiary Martin Rooks Travel Ltd. By these innovations, the airline has assured itself of a role in the resolution of one of the most important policy questions of the present time, and it will be extremely interesting to see the final form which the travel agency industry comes to adopt. Many trends are now indicative of a reducing role for any inefficient or poorly-motivated agents in the years ahead.

7.1.2 The Airline/Travel Organizer Relationship

The use by airlines of travel organizers as wholesalers of their product is, if anything, even more the subject of disagreement than the employment of travel agents. The exact methods of operation of travel organizers varies from country to country, particularly as many governments regulate travel organizers for consumer protection reasons. However, usually, two principal types of organizer can be distinguished. The first specializes purely in air travel by buying large blocks of capacity from airlines, usually on a charter basis, and then re-selling these seats to individual members of the public. The travel organizing activity in the Advanced Booking Charter market conforms to this type. The second gives an expanded role to the organizer in that he does not only buy air travel capacity, but also makes appropriate accommodation and surface transfer arrangements as well. He then combines these elements to make up inclusive holidays, with these then sold in the retail market, either direct or through travel agents.

Table 7.1. Cost Structures of Scheduled and Charter Airlines 1977–78

Cost Category	British Airways U.K. Scheduled Airline £000's	%	Britannia U.K. Charter Airline £000's	%	Monarch U.K. Charter Airline £000's	%
1. Flight Crew, Salaries and Expenses	71,104	6·6	2,828	5·8	1,102	6·1
2. Aircraft Fuel and Oil	221,234	19·8	13,875	28·7	5,829	32·5
3. Maintenance and Overhaul	149,484	13·3	4,623	9·6	2,496	13·9
4. Fleet Depreciation/Rental	83,053	7·4	6,664	13·8	2,740	15·3
5. Landing Fees and Navigation Charges	81,728	7·3	8,504	18·2	1,813	10·1
6. Station and Ground	142,770	12·8	3,128	6·4	1,149	6·4
7. Passenger Services	127,415	11·3	5,335	11·0	1,417	7·9
8. Ticketing, Sales and Promotion	184,966	16·5	76	0·2	73	0·4
9. General and Administrative	22,891	2·0	1,308	2·7	736	4·1
10. Other Operating Expenses	35,008	3·1	1,677	3·4	862	4·8
Total Operating Expenses	1,119,713	100	48,318	100	17,927	100

Source: C.A.A. Annual Statistics.

The use of travel organizers raises pronounced advantages and disadvantages for airlines. The advantages come in remarkably cost-effective selling. Organizers allow airlines to become purely producers of capacity. They are relieved of any burden of unsold space, once organizers have taken their allocation. The Organizer is a risk-taker and it will be he who suffers the short-term problem of unsold seats. Also, airlines will not pay any of the costs of a sophisticated reservations system, of advertising to the retail market, nor of the payment of commission to travel agents. All these very expensive items will be the responsibility of the organizer.

The effect of this limited commitment on the part of airlines to the expenses of selling is illustrated in Table 7.1. The carrier making only a limited use of travel organizers—British Airways—is shown to be spending sixteen and a half per cent of all its costs on ticketing, sales and promotion. The two charter airlines, Britannia and Monarch, who sell all their capacity to travel organizers, incur only a tiny proportion of costs in this category.

Despite these advantages, however, the case for an exclusive reliance on independent travel organizers is by no means clear-cut. The relationship between airlines and organizers is very much affected by the state of the travel market. The cheap travel opportunities in which many organizers have specialized are aimed at a highly price- and income-elastic market segment. It is therefore inevitable that the periodic downturns characteristic of the world economy should produce situations where demand is low relative to (in the short run) an inflexible supply of aircraft seats. In such a buyer's market, organizers are in an excellent position to dictate to airlines over prices and conditions of operation—indeed it will often be essential for them to do so in the interests of maintaining their position in the shrinking retail market. Airlines can then face a difficult situation until the market improves. The other danger of an excessive reliance on travel organizers is that an airline can become committed to serving one particular organizer. Should the organizer then cease trading, the airline can be left in a very vulnerable position. Concern regarding the possible effects of such a collapse on the airline was presumably behind the acquistion by Court Line Aviation Ltd. of the ailing Clarkson's travel organizing company in the U.K. in 1972. However, even such an aquisition could not prevent a catastrophic bankruptcy of the Court Line group in 1974. Hopefully the imposition of tighter regulation of the financial fitness of travel organizers has reduced the risk of such events occurring in the future, but the possibility of them is a factor which cannot be ignored by any airline wishing to decide upon the correct policy to be pursued towards the travel organizing industry.

The degree of advantage and disadvantage attending the airline/travel organizer relationship probably accounts for the process of channel readjustment which is taking place at the present time. One can detect a move towards *vertical integration*, as organizers and airlines both try to secure adequate control both of their operations, and of the retail market. Thus, in the U.K., Britannia Airways (Thomson Holidays) and Monarch (Cosmos) are both now owned by major travel organizers, whilst Laker Airways has set up its own travel organizing company (Laker Air Travel Ltd.) which is responsible for the sale of a high proportion of all Laker products. At the same time, there is now a trend towards *direct selling* by travel organizers. The Danish direct-sell company Tjaerebourg (itself the controller of the Danish charter airline Sterling Airways) began direct-sell operation in the U.K. in 1977 and has been followed by others since. During the summer of 1979, the direct-sell trend gained a major boost with the announcement by the U.K.'s largest travel organizer, Thomson Holidays, that it would set up a direct-selling company, of its own—Portland Holidays—to begin operations in 1980. This is presumably to cover itself against what it must see as growing threat of competition from Tjaerebourg and other direct selling firms. However, it is risking a loss of business for its existing products from an alienation of the travel agency industry. British Airways has again moved to protect its market position by setting up its own travel organizing activity, mainly through its two chief brand names of Sovereign and Enterprise, whilst British Caledonian has developed its Blue Sky packaged-holiday brand. In both these cases, the move into the travel organizing sector would seem to be well-justified, although there is a possibility of offending established independent travel organizers upon whom both airlines are relying for a proportion of their traffic.

Overall, the question of the relationship between airlines and travel agents and travel organizers in the selling channel is in a state of uncertainty. The channel is going through changes as the industry moves towards maturity. What the final form of the channel will be it is too early to say, but it appears clear that we are set on a course towards a much more competitive situation, where no channel member survives by divine right, but only by a demonstration that it can do a particular job in an optimal way from the point of view of the investment risk-taker.

7.2 Marketing Communication—Passenger

Emphasis has already been placed in Chapter 1 on the vital role of communication in marketing. Firms in all forms of marketing are required to make decisions on the size of the communication budget and the distribution of this budget between personal communication, public relations, 'below the line' promotional expenditure and media advertising. For that which is to be spent on advertising, further decisions are required on media location and exposure, advertising content and methods for monitoring advertising success. This section is concerned specifically with these decisions in the context of the air passenger market.

7.2.1 Passenger Communication Policy

Communication costs are substantial items of expenditure for all airlines which do not base their operations on wholesaling capacity to travel organizers. Exact data on total communication costs are obviously difficult to obtain, but from the information which is available on purely advertising expenditure,[3] it would seem that many airlines are spending upwards of five per cent of their total costs on communication with the market. Such a proportion has been criticized as being excessive.[4] However, the fact of regulated competition in the past has reduced the airline's scope for product differentiation in an activity where such differentiation is already difficult. It is widely observed in all industries which face problems in product differentiation that promotional expenditures tend towards a uniformly high level for all participants. This is seen as being the best way of promoting market share. It may well be that a high promotional spending by airlines must be seen as inevitable, particularly in those markets where a tight regulatory framework remains.

Within the distribution of the communication budget, some aspects of passenger selling lend themselves very well to direct representation as a communication technique. Virtually all airlines will need sales representatives to visit travel agents, and also to contact other airlines in pursuit of interline business. These representatives will have as their role ensuring that agents and airlines are informed on service developments, etc., besides performing the normal representative function of keeping the firm's name before the market through entertainment and promotions. Many airlines aiming services at the business travel market will also send representatives to the major business houses, particularly those where an individual manager or department is responsible for all corporate travel purchases.

Rewarding and motivating airline sales representatives conforms to many of the problems referred to in Section 1.2. Rewards involving substantial commission payments might be ideal from the point of view of motivating them to work hard, but it has generally proved impossible for airlines to find an equitable basis on which commission payments might be distributed between employees, bearing in mind the different opportunities available. Also, in any business, representatives have broader functions than simply selling, and commission payments are best for promoting efficiency in those industries—such as insurance—where selling is the dominant part of their work. In industries like aviation, over-emphasis on commission is believed to lead to too much time being spent on selling to new customers and not enough on vitally important customer-relations activity. Whatever the reason, it is generally the case that airline salesmen

3 For example, in *Air Transport World* for July, 1979.
4 *See* Cooper and Maynard (1971), p. 16.

are rewarded on a flat-rate system, perhaps with bonuses for good performance, rather than on a flat rate plus percentage commission on the revenue obtained by the company from the outlets for which they are responsible.

Public relations work is also important in an airline's communication policy. Aviation has an appeal for the general public—and for editors—which renders it exceptionally newsworthy amongst the world's industries. Sound airline 'P.R.' can therefore bring a great deal of 'free' promotion, both of new products and also of the airline's image in general.

However, despite the importance of direct representation and public relations work, there is no airline today which would see its passenger communication policy as being correct without a substantial expenditure on media advertising. Such advertising can be vital in a 'foot-in-the-door' function of ensuring a familarity with the airline's name and reputation on the part of travel agents and business travel managers prior to a sales representative calling. For the markets of the individual businessman making his own booking and the leisure traveller in general, advertising offers the only practicable method of communication. We must devote considerable space to discussion of appropriate advertising policies towards the business and leisure travel segments of the market.

7.2.2 Airline Advertising—the Business Travel Market

As one would expect, the special nature of business travel means that airlines aiming to use advertising to exploit it must adopt an approach in both advertising content and media location which is distinct from that used in the remainder of the market.

With advertising content, it is essential that content should emphasize the particular abilities and merits of the airline, with the presentation of these merits and the reputation of the airline combining to ensure that the advertising content is credible. The advertising, too, must be marketing-orientated, based on an understanding of consumer wants and needs and a demonstration of the ability of the airline's product to meet these needs.

With regard to ways of achieving appeal in advertising to the business traveller, clearly *product differentiation* will be central as the airline shows its superiority compared with its rivals. However, there is a strictly limited number of ways in which product superiority can be demonstrated. Unlike almost all other industries, airlines in the past have been unable to advertise on the basis of *price*. The fact of regulated competition has meant that their published prices have been identical. Even today, where reducing regulation in some markets is allowing airlines to begin to indulge in price competition, the fact that the business-travel market is not usually thought to be price-sensitive will limit the value of advertising content based on price, with only the so-called 'independent' business traveller likely to be attracted to an airline purely because of low prices. Where an 'ad.' is designed to obtain traffic through travel agents, mention of low fares could actually be a tactical error in view of the impact of such fares on commission levels.

Besides a lack of opportunity to emphasize price, *airspeed* is of little value as a differentiating characteristic. Competition mostly takes place between airlines flying only a small number of aircraft types which travel at an almost identical speed. Only the advent of Concorde has allowed differentiation on the basis of higher air speeds to be resumed, but here the small number of aircraft in service has meant that only a few carriers have been in a position to take advantage of this. Finally, direct references to *safety records* are not possible in airline advertising, despite their relevance to the nervous passenger. Mostly airlines have followed agreements to avoid advertising around safety. Safety is therefore given only a soft sell through mention of such aspects as maintenance procedures and the skill and experience of flight crews.

With the virtual exclusion of price, airspeed and safety, it is remarkable the extent to which differentiation in airline business travel advertisements can be narrowed down to only a few product characteristics. Of these, *route network, flight frequency and availability of inter-connecting services* are mentioned in a high proportion of ads. with, on longer haul routes, emphasis also placed on situations where the airline is giving *direct flights* without intermediate stops. *Flight timings*, too, can be emphasized, especially where an airline can point to advantages such as having the first flight of the day to a particular destination. Then again, *aircraft type* can be mentioned, with the use of this tending to increase at times of technological innovation in the industry. However, even today, where on long haul routes at least, the changeover from narrow bodied to wide-bodied aircraft is well-advanced, airline ads. do make a great play on 'wide-bodied comfort' and similar phrases. *Departure/arrival airport* can become very important in particular situations, as in the U.K. at the moment where intense advertising of the merits of Heathrow and Gatwick Airports is done by those airlines using each airport. *Punctuality* has been emphasized by those airlines wishing to promote a high reputation in this product component—T.W.A. is currently a good example—although excessive advertising around this point may make passengers particularly restive when unavoidable delays do occur. *Ethnic affinity* is used by airlines from countries where the national culture allows promotion of such affinity. A good example is Japan Airlines, whose advertising and promotion are very much based on the traditions of eastern hospitality. Ethnic affinity in advertising can hopefully have the effect of encouraging the nationals of the airline's home country to use it, on the principle of 'a taste of home' in distant places. However, much more it is used to promote the airline to foreign nationals, whereby the emphasis on ethnic affinity is supposed to

give novelty and unusual quality to a flight. *Patr...*
in airline advertising, as with the British Airway...
Finally, almost all airline diversionary advertising ...
traveller includes reference to the *quality of in-flight ...*
emphasize cabin spaciousness and comfort—as, for ex...
doing at the time of writing in publicizing its decision ...
seating density on its DC 10s—the quality of drinks and e...
and, over and over again, the attributes of the airline's ste...
particular aspect of customer service promotion at the moment ...asis
by airlines on the advantages which the Three-Class service con...pt offers
to the business traveller.

With the question of media location for advertising to the business
market, there are a number of standard groups of location which are
employed by almost all airlines. Business magazines such as *Business Week*
and *The Economist* are used, as are daily and Sunday papers of an
upmarket readership, especially those with a financial bias. There are also
a number of non-business upmarket magazines in which airlines can
advertise and reach the class of executive likely to be an air traveller. In the
U.K., *Punch* is a good example of this. With regard to other media,
television has the great advantage that real impact can be given to the
selling message through the use of colour, sound and movement. However, for advertising to the business traveller there are problems because of
the high costs, the need for repetition to ensure that the message is driven
home, and also that many commercial television programmes are not
watched by the narrow market segment which is likely to contain a large
number of regular business travellers.

With the similarities between the services of different airlines and the
strictly limited opportunities for product differentiation which this implies,
it is perhaps inevitable that most advertising to the business traveller
should appear repetitious and unimaginative. However, during the last few
years we have seen the beginnings of the use of much more creative
promotion to the business market by some airlines. In the past, almost all
advertising to the business market has been diversionary in character, in
that it has had the aim of ensuring that a businessman who is going to make
a trip or series of trips does so by the airline promoting the ad. It has
always been thought that opportunities for true traffic generation in the
business segment were limited by the fact that business trips were made in
response to specific problems and opportunities. This ensured that trips
would be made anyway irrespective of any airline promotional activity,
with the only task of the airline to ensure that such trips as *were* made used
its services rather than those of its competitors. However, in recent years it
has been realized that such inflexibility may be characteristic of the
'fire-brigade' part of the business travel market where passengers are
travelling to deal with urgent business problems, but that there are large

business travel market where generative work is both possible
thwhile. These areas include those of Incentive Travel (referred to
Section 2.3.1), the arrangement of study tours for particular groups of
professional people, and the generation of additional trips by export
salesmen to trade fairs and in a general way for tours of export markets.
Attempts to generate new business travel have therefore been started.
Airlines have also begun to look into the possibility of using creative
pricing as a way of generating more travel, with advanced booking and use
of off-peak flights ensuring a cost relationship with the low fares offered.
In this latter case, however, a careful watch must be kept on generative
activity to ensure that its effect is not merely to dilute revenue from trips
that would have been made anyway.

With selling methods for generating business travel, airlines have not so
far widely engaged in purely generative business travel advertising. The
main push of promotion has been the production of brochures and other
material, with the developmental work being left to sales representatives
having a specific responsibility for major business houses and travel agents
specializing in business travel.

7.2.3 Airline Advertising—the Leisure Travel Market

Despite the importance of business travel, it is in the leisure market that
we are seeing the main innovations in airline advertising at the present
time. Leisure travel has, of course, always been an important part of the
market. However, in the last few years, there have come new airline
products and lower prices, coupled with reducing regulation which is
allowing for faster innovation. These developments have given airlines
opportunities to penetrate further the much more price- and income-elastic
parts of the leisure market. Consequently, a high proportion of expenditure has been devoted to *generative*, rather than to diversionary promotion, in strong contrast to the situation on the business side.

Within this general theme of traffic generation, two specific approaches
in advertising policy can be detected. With promotion of trips by holidaymakers, an airline has an interest in ensuring that as many trips as possible
which are to be made to a destination are carried on its flights rather than
those of competitors. However, equally, there is a requirement that those
people who are intending to take a holiday are persuaded to take it at a
destination which the airline serves rather than at one which it does not.
This can be especially important for an airline's advertising in a foreign
country. In its home base it is likely to have a route network which is
sufficiently wide to allow it a competitive opportunity in most major
holiday markets. Finally, the airline's promotion must be aimed at those
who are not intending to take a holiday at all, or who may be intending to
opt for an inexpensive non-air-based holiday. It must persuade such people

that a holiday on the airline's services is a more desirable way to spend their disposable income than the alternative goods and services which they may be considering.

With advertising to the holiday market, the diversion of passengers who will travel on a route anyway can be promoted by emphasis on much the same kind of product differentiating characteristics which were noted as being appropriate for the business travel market. However, reflecting the different needs of the business and leisure traveller, more attention probably needs to be given to the comfort and service aspects, and rather less to route-network/flight-frequency. For the generation of new passengers the standard method is that of *destination advertising*. The airline tries to attract attention by pictures of the destination calculated to show how it can match up to the particular wants and needs of those reading the ad. Then, when attention has been gained, dialogue can be used to sell both the destination and the services of the sponsoring airline.

Appropriate locations for this kind of advertising presents an interesting question. Unlike with business travel advertising, airlines have mostly avoided weekday morning papers. These are read at times when people are scarcely likely to be in a receptive mood for subtle holiday adverts. Instead, weekend papers are favoured, as are magazines, especially of the sort likely to be read by those planning a holiday (the U.S. magazine *Travel and Leisure* is a good example of this). Again, T.V. advertising can have real impact because of sound and movement, particularly for exotic locations advertised in winter-time, but is likely to be prohibitively expensive in many cases. The advent of lower fare concepts has allowed airlines to move some way down-market in their advertising of leisure travel, a point emphasized by the increasing proportion of occasions on which ticket price is made a major feature of a holiday/generative ad. However, for any airline in the long-haul market it is still likely that, even with new low fare products, fares will still be high enough to exclude from the market all but the highest income groups, and up-market advertising will still therefore be the rule.

With advertising to the V.F.R. market, further developments must be brought into an airline's advertising policies. We have already noted in Section 2.3.2 that the visiting-relations market consists largely of grandparents visiting their grandchildren. It therefore has characteristics of being relatively old and of having a high proportion of first-time or very-infrequent travellers who are likely to suffer considerable anxieties over the possibility of making a long air trip. It is also a market which is extremely price-sensitive, with a large proportion of potential travellers who have always assumed that air travel was too expensive to allow them any possibility of travelling.

Given these characteristics, advertising approaches to the V.F.R. market are now well-established. Any airline with V.F.R. potential on some of its routes will attract the prospective customer's attention through a picture of an emotional and happy family re-union. The objection of almost every potential passenger—that air travel is expensive and that there is no possibility of being able to afford it—is then answered by an emphasis on the low fares which have become available. Anxieties over the making of the trip can be soothed by mention of the comfort, convenience and service which the airline provides. Exactly this approach has been used by airlines such as Air Canada, Qantas, Air New Zealand and British Airways, which have opportunities to participate in V.F.R. markets, with considerable success.

With the question of media locations for V.F.R. advertising, it is clear that this type of promotion has moved airline advertising locations further down-market than even before. Middle-market press and magazines (notably women's magazines) have been extensively used, especially those which are liable to be read at times which are propitious for the planning of the sort of trip which is being encouraged. Television, despite its cost, has a particular attraction here as a way of reaching exactly the target market segment at a time when people are likely to be relaxed and in a receptive mood for the kind of promotion which V.F.R. advertising is designed to give.

With questions on the overall success of an airline's advertising policy, many criteria for judgement are put forward in standard references on advertising practice.[5] However, in the search for evaluative criteria, the following questions are appropriate. Firstly, is the ad. *located* in such a way that it will reach the target market segment? Secondly, is it a *marketing* ad., concentrating on consumer wants and needs which the airline can meet? Thirdly, is the ad. likely to *attract the prospect's attention*? If it is, is the selling message then persuasively put across, in a *credible* way? Does it have elements of *uniqueness*, which the airline's rivals will not be able to match? Finally, does the ad. *close the deal* of getting the prospect to take appropriate action on the basis of what he has learnt? Of course, all advertising must also contribute to the promotion of the appropriate *corporate image* of the sponsoring airline, a point to which we shall return in Sections 9.1.2 and 9.1.3.

7.2.4 Other Commmunication Techniques

The use of sales representatives for direct communication with customers and media advertising constitute by far the greater part of airline's communications expenditure in the selling of the passenger services. However, there are other aspects of selling which are analagous to the 'below the line' promotional expenditure widely employed in other industries.

Here, *agent's educational trips* are a continuing part of airline selling. The aim of these is laudable enough, in that an airline offering a trip to one of its major destinations to a travel agent is likely to reap benefits of a

5 For example, Kotler (1976), pp. 347–74.

better-informed agency industry. It will also ensure that its name is kept before agents for all the services which it operates. However, educationals are expensive to mount, and there have been accusations that they have become less cost-effective than they used to be. Some airlines have now gone as far as to offer educationals to agents only on a fee-paying basis, with even the nominal fees charged in such cases having the effect of restricting those attracted to a trip only to staff with a genuine interest in its educational value.

Much the same considerations apply to the question of travel for staff from other airlines, although here the aim is to stimulate sales of interline trips rather than travel-agency bookings. However, the offer of such trips usually also brings reciprocating offers, with the effect of increasing the value of the travel concessions which are so important in bringing staff into the industry and retaining them in it.

As another promotional technique, *travel clubs* provide an interesting phenomenon of the last few years. In the U.K., several of the airlines operating in V.F.R. markets have set up their own reunion clubs, either singly or in combination with other airlines. British Airways are now involved with clubs which are operated in their U.S.A., Canadian, Australian and New Zealand markets, all of which have a large V.F.R. component. In all these markets, clubs operate which require payment of a nominal membership fee.[6] In return, members are offered a number of services such as those relating to visa formalities, passports etc., and also information about travel opportunities. From the airline's point of view, the carrier obtains a cheaply-available mailing list for its products. It also has a way of tackling the main problem of exploiting the visiting-relations market—the uncertainty and anxiety felt by many passengers with regard to making a long air trip. However, as a less publicized advantage, a considerable proportion of the business which airlines are now closing as a result of the V.F.R. clubs is believed to be obtained direct, without the intervention of travel agents. This improves control over the retail market and reduces commission payments.

There has only been space in this section to deal very briefly with airline advertising, and there are many interesting questions which remain uncovered. However, it is hoped that enough has been said to demonstrate that the theme of the book of a logical process running through market analysis, strategy definition, product design and pricing, continues into the field of marketing communication. The communication policies of an airline basing its strategy on exploitation of the business travel market will be quite different from one aiming at the leisure market, whilst the total-market airline will have the difficult task of designing a policy which promotes its interests with the leisure traveller without jeopardizing the

6 A period of free membership has been allowed following the setting up of each club.

corporate image of a high-quality airline which it will need if it is to exploit the business market successfully.

7.3 Selling Channels—Freight

With the freight side of the industry, decisions on policy towards selling channels are just as important as with the passenger market—perhaps even more so. With the freight business, the most important relationship is that between the airlines as providers of capacity and firms which, although in the past often known as freight agents, are now usually given the generic name of *freight forwarders*.

7.3.1 The Airline/Freight Forwarder Relationship

Despite the present-day importance of the forwarding industry, defining the forwarder and his role presents some difficulties.[7] It is probably easiest to do so in terms of the functions which forwarders carry out on behalf of airlines and shippers. They are first of all *sales agents* for airlines, and a nominal commission of 5 per cent is paid to them on the revenue which they produce. They have important functions in *surface transport* with collection and delivery services operated on behalf of shippers on a fee-paying basis. They have *documentation and customs clearance* functions, preparing documentation for export and undertaking customs formalities for imports. Finally, they have an increasingly important *ground handling* role. The structure of air freight rates (Section 6.3.2) has always allowed forwarders to engage in *consolidation* activities. The existence of weightbreaks in the tariff structure—reasonable on the basis of the lower unit costs of handling large consignments—allows a forwarder to gather together from his shipper clients a number of small parcels bound for a particular destination. He then combines them together as a single large consignment which is carried by the airline at a significantly lower total price than would be the case if the small consignments were sent individually.

The importance of consolidation has increased still further with the advent of *unitization* as a very important function of freight forwarders. We have seen in Section 6.3.2 how the Bulk Unitization rating programme has led to airlines offering substantial discounts for shipment of goods which are pre-packed ready for carriage into aircraft unit load devices (U.L.D.s). However, the structure of Bulk Unitization rates with their

---

7 The U.K. Institute of Freight Forwarders defines a forwarder as 'Anyone engaged in forwarding as generally understood'. *See* National Economic Development Office (1972).

high pivot weights has meant that it has usually only been freight forwarders with their consolidation services who have been able to build up the consignments of sufficient size to take advantage of Bulk Unitization rates on a regular basis. In addition, aircraft U.L.Ds have special handling requirements—they should not be forklifted—which means a significant investment in scissor-lift and other equipment for any firm hoping to handle them properly. It is, of course, the forwarder rather than the shipper who has the best chance of dealing with sufficient units to ensure a satisfactory utilization of this equipment.

With this wide range of functions, it is not surprising that freight forwarders should have assumed a role in the industry which is important to shippers and airlines. From the shipper's viewpoint the documentation, customs clearance, and collection and delivery services are very useful. For the shipper who is only using air freight on an irregular basis for emergency shipments, reliance on the forwarder can save large amounts of investment in equipment and staff which could only be poorly utilized. Also, for the shipper of small consignments, the forwarder's consolidation services allow access to much lower rates than could be obtained direct from the airline, with often very little loss of service quality. However, it is the airlines for whom the forwarding industry has become even more important.

The work of forwarders in documentation and collection and delivery saves carriers a large investment in back-up facilities. Indeed, there are sound reasons for thinking that airlines could only carry out these tasks at higher costs than forwarders do. With unitization, it would not be an exaggeration to say that the advent of forwarder unitization activity has rescued airlines from a potentially disastrous situation.

The increasing use of pure freighter aircraft during the 1960s, and then the introduction of wide-bodied types during the 1970s has meant that a high proportion of all airline's freight traffic has come to be loaded into aircraft in unitized form. At the same time, airlines have faced the perennial problem in their freight activity of the domination of small consignments with a high proportion of all consignments of 100 kilos or less.[8] There have also been difficulties of handling increasing amounts of cargo in congested on-airport locations. We have noted in Section 5.6 that airlines widely attempted to solve these problems by the construction of automated ground handling systems at airports, and that these proved in many cases to be a bitter disappointment. Bulk unitization rating has proved to be the salvation of many airlines' cargo product.

Despite the powerful and indisputable case which can be made for the gains which forwarders bring to airlines and shippers alike, there is still considerable unease about the forwarder's role in the industry.

---

8 *See* I.A.T.A. (1969).

As one might expect, given the advantages which the use of forwarders brings to shippers, a high proportion of all air freight passes through forwarder's hands. In many countries this proportion is in excess of 80 per cent. However, unlike the travel agency industry which is still fairly dispersed, the forwarding business is now highly concentrated. This is because of the capital investment required by forwarders to handle containers and the fact that a large forwarder can build up bigger and more frequent consolidations to a wider range of destinations. In the U.K. market now,[9] more than 44 per cent of all air freight traffic passes through the ten biggest forwarders. Indeed, many of the largest forwarders are now acting as wholesalers, bringing in traffic from small forwarders on an agency basis to add to their consolidations. It is also suspected that co-loading agreements between forwarders increase the degree of concentration still further.

With this structure, it can still be correct policy for airlines to rely totally on forwarders—bearing in mind the immense advantages which the use of forwarders brings. However, the prerequisite must be that the high degree of market power which forwarders have is used in the airline's interest. This will mean that an airline should not find itself experiencing sudden changes in its market share due to actions of forwarders switching traffic between airlines. If it did so, it would be a wholly unacceptable situation, bearing in mind that the capital commitment made by forwarders is tiny in comparison with the immense sums now being spent by airlines on the purchase of widebodied freighter aircraft. It will also mean that the forwarders as a whole must come to accept a market development role of not only competing amongst themselves for traffic which will move by air anyway, but also attempting creative selling of air freight against surface transport. The fact that many air freight forwarders are owned by organizations with dominant interests in surface transport might lead one to suspect that they might not be totally willing to do this, although it is accepted that in mose cases air forwarders are allowed to pursue an independent policy by their parent companies. However, the freight forwarding industry can only expect to retain the dominant place it has in the air freight business if it works actively in market development.

There are already signs of the beginnings of change in the policies of some airlines. During 1978, the Scandinavian carrier SAS announced that it had purchased a controlling interest in Sweden's largest forwarder, thereby greatly increasing its hold on the retail market. This event may be the start of a long chain, as airlines accept a need to back-up their investments in freighter capacity with a more certain control of the retail market. If they do so, then in turn we may see an acceleration of the reverse trend which is also beginning now of freight forwarders taking a

9 *Airtrade*, August, 1979, p. 17.

substantial investment stake in the industry by beginning to operate their own aircraft under the reducing amount of regulation at the present time.

7.4 Marketing Communication—Freight

Communication activity on the freight side of the industry divides between that designed to divert traffic going by air from other airlines, that aimed at diverting traffic from surface transport, and that made up of attempts to generate entirely new flows of goods.

7.4.1 Air Freight Communication Policy—Diversion from Other Airlines

Diversionary activity for air freight differs in several important respects from that for air passengers. It is believed that, on the freight side of the industry, a significantly higher porportion of the retail market is prepared to leave routeing and carrier decisions to the intermediary. It is therefore necessary that diversionary selling activity should be directed to the forwarding industry and the largest retail customers. Because it is a highly concentrated market, selling can conform to the 'industrial marketing' model of Section 1.1. Communication activity thus consists mainly of direct representation by salesmen, and all airlines wishing to be competitive in the freight market have to keep a large number of salesmen in the field in order to ensure that their selling message is constantly before the forwarding industry.

As with any industrial marketing, advertising assumes a comparatively minor role in this type of freight selling. Such advertising as is undertaken is designed merely to put across a simple selling message regarding the sponsoring airline's services, with this usually confined to either the airline's route network/flight frequency, or the care and reliability of its ground handling.

It is a point of some interest as to which level of staff such advertising should be aimed at. As has been noted earlier, the demand pattern for air freight peaks heavily at night, with therefore a feature of the industry being that it is largely staffed by shift workers who are almost entirely male, and concentrated in the younger age ranges. It may be that, in many forwarding companies, routeing decisions are often left to be made at night, as consignments arrive at the warehouse, and when senior management of the firm are not at work. Therefore the main functions of advertising must be to reach the junior levels of staff, at forwarder's main offices and at their regional offices, whom the salesman is unable to contact on what are hopefully, his regular visits. The content of such advertising usually reflects this aim. It is of a basic and often suggestive kind. In terms of media location, it is concentrated in the weekly and monthly trade press read by junior forwarding staff.

7.4.2 Communication Policy—Diversion from Surface Transport

In strong contrast to the comparatively straightforward selling task of diverting existing air freight traffic from other airlines, the task of diverting goods which it is intended should go by surface transport to being sent by air freight instead is one of the most demanding tasks in airline marketing. It is one where many different approaches have been tried, often with only limited success.

The fundamental problem is that the airline is setting out to sell a high-class, quality product against a much cheaper alternative. It will often be the case that in trying to promote air freight as against surface transport, the air freight salesman will be attempting to persuade the prospective customer that it is correct policy to increase his transport budget by a factor of four or five times, or even more. Naturally this puts a heavy burden of proof onto air freight, and it has become clear that only a skilful and well-informed salesman has any chance of success.

In order to demonstrate the merits of air freight, it has been usual for airlines to use the technique of *Total Distribution Cost Analysis*, referred to in Section 2.6.3. This has involved an acceptance of the higher direct costs of air freight in comparison with surface transport. However, it has had as its basic argument that if total costs of distribution are taken into account, air freight can often be the cheapest solution. This is due to savings in the areas of packaging, insurance, damage and inventory and warehousing costs, the better cash flow which air freight can give, and the opportunities for comparatively risk-free test marketing which it provides.

To put across this message, an airline must rely on direct representation by salesmen, with these salesmen sent out either with a preplanned questionnaire to be completed with the shipper's help, or else a computer-based model which can be used to demonstrate the superiority of air freight directly.[10] In addition, the work of salesman will usually be backed up by media advertising. However, with such advertising, the approach and the locations are quite different from that aimed merely at diverting existing air freight traffic from other airlines. The approach, as one would expect, usually emphasizes the merits of air freight compared to surface transport, rather than just the merits of a particular airline. In terms of media location, advertising is placed so that it is likely to be read by senior executives in general management, rather than by shipping staff.

The use of Total Distribution Cost Analysis is a controversial part of airline selling, and it remains the case that many airlines do little or no

10 *See* Smith and Garnett (1975).

creative selling of this sort. Indeed, of the airlines operating in the U.K. market, British Airways and Lufthansa are amongst the few which undertake extensive promotion of the T.D.C. principle.

The reasons for this apparent lack of interest are not hard to find. As with any creative selling, use of T.D.C. is likely to cost more than merely diverting existing air freight traffic. Even where success is achieved, the competitiveness of the freight market is such that there is a high risk that another airline not engaging in creative selling will come along and take the resulting traffic. However, the main reason is that problems have been encountered in the use of the technique. Salesmen have found that, in many companies, the basic data on the firm's distribution operations which are necessary for a convincing analysis have not been available, with firms reluctant to admit their own ignorance to the salesman. Even where the admission is made, a need then arises for a laborious data-extraction process, usually of necessity carried out at the airline's expense. In many companies, too, the management structure turns out to be a difficult one as far as securing the acceptance of the T.D.C. message is concerned. Despite the vital importance of the shipping function, many firms assign responsibility for it to a junior executive,[11] whose control is only over a narrow part of the company's operations. Where an air freight salesman is forced to talk to the shipping manager, he may be asking someone who is comparatively low in the company hierarchy to fight a major corporate battle to have the transport budget increased by four or five times. This will be in order to reap benefits in the areas of packaging, insurance, inventory and other costs, which are probably quite outside the shipping manager's sphere of influence. It would hardly be surprising if the executive in question decided against making the effort to secure the necessary changes, particular as the air freight salesman would in many cases be attempting to prove that past decision-making on transport modal choice had been wrong.

In some companies, of course, these problems do not apply, in that distribution organization has been centralized so that one executive has overall control of all the sub-functions of distribution. This executive is then in an excellent position to make the trade-offs which are necessary to make a success of air freight distribution. Where such an organizational structure does not exist, however, airlines are forced to try and make the best of the situation by the tactic of advertising to top management of the firm, in the business/quality press that such executives are likely to read. It is hoped that this will produce instructions from above to the shipping manager that the use of air freight should be investigated. However, even when such an instruction is obtained, a final difficulty appears because it is one thing for an air freight salesman to demonstrate the merits of his

11 *See* Davies and Gray (1979).

product for a company setting up a new distribution system: it is quite another to persuade a firm with an existing surface-based system to switch to air freight. In order to reap the full benefits of air freight it will be necessary for the company to abandon its overseas warehousing, with problems of disinvestment and staff redundancy, and with real difficulties of re-establishing the system should air freight fail to bring the expected benefits. It is therefore risks such as these which, when added to the normal factor of corporate inertia, make the diversion of surface transport traffic into the air a difficult and challenging part of air freight marketing.

7.4.3 Traffic Generation in Air Freight Marketing

We have seen how, on the passenger side of the business, attempts by airlines to generate entirely new traffic flows in which they can participate is becoming important as a part of marketing. With air freight, such generative marketing has so far been less significant. This is partly because of a slower pace of innovation and also because in all markets an option to use cheaper surface transport exists. Consequently, most worthwhile traffic flows will have been brought forward by surface transport even if air freight has previously been too expensive.

However, there are now signs that some airlines may be beginning to awake to the possibilities of generative marketing, particularly for perishable traffic. An airline can approach a producer of perishable goods, and put to him the possibility of selling his products in distant markets where they will have scarcity value, with the aid of air freight. Where such an idea is accepted, it can bring the airline the advantage of additional traffic—provided its competitors do not come along and steal the traffic which is generated—and traffic for which the alternative of using cheaper and slower surface transport is not a viable one. It can therefore be expected to be price-inelastic in the face of all but very large increases in air freight rates.

Even in the area of routine non-perishable goods it may be that traffic generation possibilities have not been exploited to the full. Recent signs of experiment in pricing suggest that opportunities to use creative pricing and new products for traffic generation may be arising on the freight side just as they have done on the passenger side. However, within the—admittedly cumbrous—commodity rate system, it has always been possible for airlines to innovate with new low rates if it can be demonstrated that such rates will lead to substantial new traffic flows. Perhaps within this structure we shall come to see a greater emphasis on generative marketing, with airlines promoting the idea further of air freight, and allowing for *test* marketing of goods on a world-wide basis without companies needing to commit themselves to a large and very risky investment in locally-held inventories.

8 Monitoring Performance

With the discussion of selling policies, we have completed work on the different sub-functions of marketing in an airline context. However, before moving on to the conclusions of the book, it is necessary to consider an aspect of marketing which is often ignored, but which is of special importance to airline management. Within the overall airline marketing context, how can top management assess whether or not marketing activity is being carried out effectively?

In many industries, such a problem might not seem to merit much attention, since the monitoring of performance could be easily carried out by comparing the firm's actual performance with its objectives. If objectives are being met—always assuming that they were correct and reasonable in the first place—then the firm is judged to be performing well. If they are not being met, then this is taken as being indicative of a need for corrective action by management.

It is perfectly possible for airlines to use such a system of performance monitoring. Indeed, Pearson (1978) goes as far as to suggest a complete system of airline efficiency measurement based on objectives. However, interesting though such a system might be, it is very important that any method of performance monitoring should take account of two features of the airline industry. Firstly, it is clear from their actions that many airlines are not motivated purely by objectives aimed at profit-making. It is likely to be an aspect of particular difficulty in performance monitoring to find ways of assessing performance relative to non-profit objectives. Secondly, even for carriers which are profit-motivated, performance measurement is complicated by the fact of tight regulation of the industry. Even today, with reducing regulation in some markets, it is perfectly possible for an airline to be, say, producing acceptable profits whilst, under the cover of a blanket of regulation, it is performing very badly. In the short term such a performance may not be seen as being a cause for concern. In the long term, however, the high prices it is likely to engender will be very likely to lead to a build-up of bad feeling towards the airline and a call on regulatory authorities to halt such an abuse of the regulatory system. This kind of situation has now developed in Europe, where the regulated airlines are facing criticisms, rightly or wrongly, from consumerist groups, regulatory authorities and their unregulated charter competitors regarding what is seen as their poor levels of efficiency. Such situations as these highlight the need for all airline managements to find adequate ways of monitoring performance. However, finding such ways has proved an intractable problem in airline economics during the last few years.

8.1 Comparative Cost Data as a Performance Measure

Given the complications introduced into performance measurement by the fact of tight industry regulation, it is a superficially attractive idea to begin by an analysis of airline costs. Even within a regulated framework, an airline which is performing well should be able to produce capacity at low costs, whilst high costs might be taken as being indicative of a need for management action.

There can be no doubt that cost data can be of considerable assistance to the individual airline in performance evaluation. Inspection of the airline's unit cost levels through time may indicate whether or not its costs are rising too quickly relative to its competitors, whilst use of classifications of costs into the departments of the airline responsible for the incurrence of particular costs may show areas of the airline's activity where costs are rising too sharply. A further way of using cost data in performance evaluation comes with the breakdown of costs into their components of capital, labour, fuel, etc. This can, for instance, indicate that an airline's labour costs are rising very quickly, with a need existing for management to look at the possibilities of further capital investment as a way of substituting capital for labour.

Despite the utility of cost analysis as a way of evaluating the performance of an individual airline, analysis of cost data has come to be very contentious in recent years. This is because of attempts to use it to assess the comparative performance of different airlines. Such attempts have become important because of the growing interest on the part of regulatory authorities in the need to ensure equity in pricing. If such a need is accepted, an airline can only price competitively against another if its costs are similar. If they are not, then such pricing is only possible on a basis of cross-subsidization, unless there is to be loss-making. This then means that some consumers with a low demand-elasticity will be overcharged.

With the question of comparative cost data between airlines, some large variations in costs do appear. Table 8.1 gives a comparison of costs between British Airways and Britannia and Monarch, two of the U.K.'s leading independent airlines. It shows that in terms of available seat–kilometre costs, British Airways' costs are very much above those of its competitors. These differences are even more marked if revenue seat–kilometre costs are taken.

Table 8.1. Unit Costs: Scheduled and Charter Airlines

Airline	Cost per available seat-km (pence)		Cost per revenue seat-km (pence)		Seat factor (%)	
	1976–7	1977–8	1976–7	1977–8	1976–7	1977–8
British Airways	18·6	21·9	30·1	36·3	61·8	60·3
Britannia	8·6	10·5	10·1	12·4	84·8	84·8
Monarch	8·7	10·2	11·5	13·4	77·0	76·6

Source: C.A.A. Annual Statistics.

It might at first be thought that, damning though such evidence appears, it should only really concern the British government as British Airways' owners, and those consumers foolish enough to pay the high fares based on that airline's cost levels. Unfortunately the issues are by no means as simple as this. Firstly, almost all air transport markets are still regulated. In many markets, a passenger who has to travel will have no alternative open to him but to use the fares based on high-cost carriers. Secondly, in markets where a degree of competition is allowed, apparently high-cost carriers such as British Airways do compete with their low cost charter rivals in price terms, and it should hardly be surprising that the charter airlines object strongly to what they see as unfair competition.

These two factors have led to a growing interest in the analysis of comparative cost data between airlines. Such analysis has shown that to base *any* conclusions on data as crude as that in Table 8.1 is likely to be totally misleading. Cost data of this sort ignores differences in the operations of airlines, with British Airways a scheduled carrier and both Britannia and Monarch purely charter airlines. There are a number of reasons which can be put forward to suggest that the charter airline is concerned with a product which can be offered at a very low cost compared with a true scheduled product.

A first area of likely cost difference is that of *station and ground costs*. A scheduled airline will operate over a wide route network. Also, particularly on short-haul routes, it will need to have a concentration of flights around the pronounced peaks of business travel. In addition, scheduled airline customers normally show a reluctance to use inconvenient arrival and departure times in the very early morning and late evening. Charter airlines, on the other hand, can operate in a concentrated way over a comparatively small route network, and can further improve the utilization of station and ground facilities by taking advantage of the general acceptance on the part of charter passengers of inconvenient timings. This acceptance can also be very useful to airlines in improving *aircraft utilization.* Charter airlines are almost always able to gain a higher utilization than scheduled carriers, except perhaps at the off-peak winter season when the demand patterns for leisure air travel mean that utilization may fall.

As a further area of cost difference, *catering standards* are still often poorer on charter flights. Many tour operators, particularly those aiming at very price-conscious market segments, still prefer to keep catering provision to a low level. Scheduled carriers on the other hand, particularly in their services to business travellers, find that in-flight service is an important product component, with a substantial loss of market share likely to result from a reduction in its standards.

Cabin configuration can also have a notable effect on costs. Charter airlines operate the cabin of their aircraft in a single-class configuration. This is in contrast to the scheduled carrier which divides capacity between First and Economy or Coach Class and gives greater seat pitch and width to First-Class passengers. Also, as was noted in Section 5.4.1, charter airlines generally only give a low seat pitch to all passengers in comparison with that offered by scheduled airlines. Operation in single class and at a low seat pitch allows charter airlines to carry more passengers on each flight, and thereby force down the levels of seat-kilometre costs.

Despite the importance of all the factors mentioned in explaining cost differences between scheduled and charter airlines, there are two further aspects which are of particular significance. Table 7.1 gave a breakdown of the cost structures of the three airlines under consideration. It showed that, in 1978, British Airways, as the scheduled airline, incurred around 16 per cent of its costs in the category of 'Ticketing, Sales and Promotion,' whereas the two charter airlines showed only an insignificant percentage of costs in this category. The explanation, of course, is that, as previously noted, the British Airways data show up the costs of retail selling, for which the airline itself is responsible. The charter airlines' data, on the other hand, do not include these costs, for these airlines are purely concerned with the wholesaling of capacity to travel organizers. It is the organizers who must then incur the costs of advertising and promotion to the retail market, the costs of a reservations system and the costs of travel agents' commissions. Particularly in view of the fact that both Britannia and Monarch are owned by major travel organizers, the absence of these costs from the airline accounts may be seen as being something of a paper adjustment.

The final explanation of cost difference between scheduled and charter airlines relates to the classic product component of *average seat factor.* We have seen in Section 2.3.1 that any airline wishing to maximize its share of the business travel market will only do so if it keeps its average seat factor relatively low. For the leisure market a low average seat factor is irrelevant as a product component—indeed it will be a positive hindrance to the

Table 8.2. Operating Costs per available tonne-kilometre. Sample of Scheduled Airlines

Airline	1976	Year 1977	1978	Airline	1976	Year 1977	1978
1. Air Canada	23·1	22·7	24·0	16. Korean Airlines	17·3	N/A	N/A
2. Air France	29·7*	31·6*	36·4*	17. Lufthansa	32·7*	35·7*	41·0*
3. Air India	26·3	25·8	31·2	18. National	19·5	20·7	22·6
4. Alitalia	29·0*	34·1*	39·0*	19. Pakistan International	25·7	24·6	25·6
5. American	23·4	24·4	26·4	20. Pan American	19·8	20·8	24·0
6. Avianca	31·8*	31·4	N/A	21. Sabena	39·1*	44·3*	50·4*
7. Braniff	23·7	23·1	23·8	22. SAS	36·1*	37·7*	39·4*
8. British Airways	28·8*	30·8*	35·8*	23. Singapore Airlines	27·9*	N/A	30·0
9. CPAir	23·4	22·9	23·5	24. South African Airways	25·5	N/A	27·7
10. Delta	25·6	25·6	27·4	25. Swissair	34·6*	37·4*	41·0*
11. Eastern	28·9*	30·5*	33·0*	26. Thai International	23·2	37·2*	35·5*
12. El Al	26·0	24·6	26·4	27. Trans-World Airlines	22·0	23·5	25·6
13. Finnair	38·9*	39·2*	N/A	28. United	23·7	24·3	24·8
14. Japan Airlines	26·5	29·1*	37·3*	29. Varig	28·0*	28·9	29·9
15. KLM	29·1*	31·1*	36·3*	30. Viasa	26·0	29·9*	27·8

Mean 1976 = 26·8; Mean 1977 = 29·0; Mean 1978 = 31·3; *above mean value for year.
Source: ICAO Financial Data.

leisure traveller in gaining his prime need of a low ticket price. Because of the variations in the importance of average seat factor with the different market segments, it is the case that the scheduled airline will have to operate at a relatively low seat factor, whereas charter airlines can offer very high average seat factors without their competitiveness being jeopardized. Table 8.1 shows marked differences in the average seat factors of the different airlines. The high seat factors of the charter carriers account for the greater differences between the airlines in revenue as opposed to available seat–kilometre costs.

This list of possible explanations of cost differences between scheduled and charter airlines does not invoke questions of comparative efficiency, at least in a narrow sense. It means that any attempt to decide on comparative efficiency levels between scheduled and charter airlines purely on the basis of crude cost data is fraught with danger, and most unlikely to lead to supportable conclusions. Indeed, in the U.K., the Civil Aviation Authority and British Airways have carried out research which suggests that a very high proportion of cost difference between scheduled and charter airline can be explained away by these methods, to the extent that on some routes a 'like with like' comparison shows virtually no difference between scheduled and charter costs (Civil Aviation Authority (1977a)). Whilst there are aspects of such work which must remain contentious, it is indicative that more is needed than simple cost data for a performance comparison between scheduled and charter airlines. This is because of the strong contrasts in the type of product which each airline offers.

Such a conclusion is beyond argument for scheduled/charter comparisons, but it does raise interesting possibilities for comparisons between scheduled airlines. If scheduled and charter airlines have differing costs which can be explained to a large extent by their contrasting products, it follows logically that cost data should be a valuable aid for performance evaluation between all airlines supplying a scheduled product. Two possibilities exist: either scheduled airlines will all show roughly the same levels of cost for producing their product, or else there will be large cost differences. If these differences exist, will they therefore be explicable in terms of efficiency variations?

Table 8.2 gives data on the operating costs of a sample of scheduled airlines, and it is very clear from this that the picture is by no means one of uniformity. Large cost differences are apparent between the airlines, with some airlines consistently above and some consistently below the year-by-year averages.

Unfortunately, it is almost as dangerous to use such data to draw conclusions about the comparative efficiency of scheduled airlines as it was in the case of the scheduled/charter comparison. There are a great many explanations of cost difference between scheduled airlines besides that of efficiency.[1] *Route network* is the first of these.

---

1 For a full outline of these explanations, *see* Sarndal and Statton (1975).

Any scheduled airline having a network of long-haul routes has every opportunity to obtain lower seat-kilometre costs than one with only short average stage lengths. Long hauls should mean a better aircraft utilization because of a lower incidence of airport turnround periods, less time of inefficient aircraft operation during taxi-ing, landing and take-off, and, normally, lower payments in airport landing fees. Also, an airline with a dense, regular demand pattern on its routes will have opportunities to fully utilize committed resources and to make use of larger aircraft with lower unit operating costs.

Input costs will also be very important in deciding an airline's cost structures, with substantial variations around the world in the costs of fuel and labour, in particular. Any airline having the benefit of low input costs should also, in turn, show low unit costs. The airline with expensive inputs will suffer from high cost levels, with only a limited flexibility available to act efficiently by optimizing its resource mix.

Then again, *hidden subsidies* are a very important part of the international airline industry which can distort the cost picture. Some international airlines, for example, are not required to pay landing and navigation fees to their controlling governments, whilst many have been offered cheap loans out of government funds. Such hidden subsidies may not necessarily be wrong—in terms of national objectives they are probably quite correct—but they will distort any attempt to produce valid costs comparisons between scheduled airlines.

As a final point, *exchange rate fluctuations* must be considered. Comparative cost analysis is dependent on the use of a common unit of currency in which all costs can be expressed. In the past, the unit used has almost always been the United States dollar. However, in recent years, the U.S. dollar has been amongst the world's most unstable currencies, and it has often been the case that what seem to be changes in the comparative efficiency of different airlines are no more than reflections of the exchange rates of the countries of the airlines concerned compared with the U.S. dollar.

There are many other factors which might be invoked to explain cost differences between airlines. However, it is hoped that enough has been said to show that whilst cost data may be useful to the management of an individual airline in monitoring performance through time, they are of very little value in any attempt to undertake analysis of an airline's performance relative to its competitors. There are many factors which can be put forward as being likely to explain cost differences aside from any question of comparative efficiency. In addition, it has been realized that performance evaluation must take account of a wide range of aspects relating to an airline's operations, not simply its production costs. Over the last few years, therefore, it has been a major area of research in air transport to attempt to isolate measures which give a comprehensive picture of all aspects of airline performance. Unfortunately, devising such measures has proved to be a difficult problem.

8.2 The Use of Ratio Data in Airline Performance Evaluation

If it is accepted that measures of performance are needed and that the use of crude cost data is not an adequate way of providing such a measure, then there is a great attraction in the idea of management ratios as comparative performance indicators. Ratios offer the chance of a reasonable basis for comparison of different carriers, together with the opportunity to bring in a wide range of aspects of performance in addition to crude operating costs.

Unfortunately, however, it is very difficult to decide upon a single ratio, or even a small number of ratios, which give an adequate picture of performance. Many very commonly-used ratios have embodied in them exactly the same limitations as comparative cost data, with the likelihood that differences between carriers are explicable in terms of differences in the carrier's operating conditions, rather than differences in comparative performance. Good examples of such measure are available tonne-kilometres per employee (or dollar of labour expenditure), and departures per employee. With A.T.Ks per employee, there is every opportunity for an airline having a long average stage length to show high figures compared with one operating only short sectors. Exactly the opposite applies to the question of departures per employee, where the large numbers of departures achieved by a short-haul airline will generally be more than enough to cancel out the effects of the greater numbers of staff which such an airline must employ. In both cases, results will also depend on the extent to which airlines subcontract their support functions. With available tonne-kilometres per unit of fuel consumption, whilst this would appear to be a perfectly adequate way of assessing efficiency in the use of fuel, the long-haul airline will have pronounced advantages over the short-haul, especially if it has the dense traffic which allows the use of large fuel-efficient aircraft. The short-haul airline will generally need to operate smaller planes because of a requirement to maintain flight frequencies, and will incur a high fuel consumption because of inefficient aircraft operations during landing and takeoff phases.

The difficulties of finding simple individual ratios which function adequately as performance measures has led to considerable statistical ingenuity in developing measurement techniques which can meet a criterion of giving fairness between airlines despite intrinsic differences between them in their operations. Morrell and Taneja (1979) propose value added per unit of resources employed as a unifying measure of performance. They claim that this will take account of the different resource needs of carriers according to their type of operation, and allow a genuine performance comparison. Despite the undoubted usefulness of this idea, it is one essentially borrowed from other industries which operate under competitive conditions. It seems inevitable that the effects of regulated prices in the aviation industry must produce distortions in any 'value added' measure, with substantial differences existing in air fares between different routes, differences which cannot always be related to differences in resource commitment, or to the operation of market forces. Pearson (1976) attempts to overcome the limitations inherent in any single measure by postulating—reasonably—that airline efficiency is a multi-faceted phenomenon, and that many ratios will be necessary to compare efficiency in all its aspects. He takes a sample of European airlines, and compiles tables of the comparative performance of each airline under a wide range of ratio and other variables. A picture of the overall performance of each airline is then gained by the use of multiple regression models which measure the extent of the influence of each variable. Where residuals from the regression equations show a large variation from 'expected' values of a particular measure, they are taken as indicating that the airline is performing either less well or much better than its competitors in terms of efficiency.

Pearson's work has been heavily criticized by the U.K. Civil Aviation Authority.[2] The C.A.A.'s solution[3] to the problem of efficiency measurement is to suggest a route-based analysis, whereby airlines are compared not on a global basis of their entire operations, but rather in individual routes where two airlines are competing directly in producing an identical product. There is certainly merit in this idea, in that it will reduce the problems of 'like with like' comparisons. However, there will be limits to the scope of the analyses which can be undertaken. Problems are also likely to arise because of variations in cost allocation techniques between routes and also because a route comparison may mean a situation where the analyst is comparing the best route of one airline with the worst route of another. Whilst such comparisons may be indicative of appropriate action for regulators, they may not have great value for the airline manager with a need to monitor performance over a wide network.

With regard to the overall question of performance evaluation in airline marketing, if this chapter has seemed to be negative in merely pointing out the shortcomings of past approaches it is because we are dealing here with a very difficult problem. In the future, it is going to be incumbent upon all airline managers to monitor performance closely. Reducing regulation and growing concern on the part of governments with regard to efficient

2 *See* C.A.A. (1977a), pp. 37–41. This source gives a comprehensive critique of many past approaches to airline efficiency measurement, and the interested reader is referred to it for a full discussion of the problem.
3 *Ibid*. p. 20.

resource utilization are just two of the reasons why this will be necessary. The best hope for effective monitoring lies in the closest possible definition of objectives and then a monitoring of the performance of the airline relative to these objectives. If objectives are formulated correctly, then the opportunity is there for at least a reasonable control to be maintained. However, with the question of inter-firm comparisons, which can be so valuable in other areas of economic activity, then it is inevitable that wide differences in the operations of airlines will mean that *any* comparisons will be of only limited value. A need will always exist to inspect the measures which are used in such comparisons and to make the attempt to take account of the fact that a part—probably a large part—of the observed differences will be explicable in terms of contrasts in the operations of the airlines concerned rather than in terms of their comparative efficiency.

With this discussion of performance evaluation, the substance of the book is now complete. It is hoped that by this stage the reader will have an adequate picture of the theory of marketing, and the relevance of this theory to the airline business. We are therefore in a position to move on to the conclusions of the book.

9 The Relevance of Marketing

With the book having ranged so widely, drawing together the different strands to produce an overall conclusion is inevitably difficult. However, in this final chapter, it is intended to do two things. In the first section, we shall demonstrate the application of the principles discussed to three case-studies of industry policy problems. This will, it is hoped, provide initial evidence of the potential value of marketing theory to the airline industry. In the second section, these case studies are followed by the detailed conclusions, where the main points from each chapter are summarized, and comments offered on appropriate directions for airline policies.

We begin now with the first of these case-studies, which deals with the relevance of marketing to the controversies surrounding scheduled and charter services on international routes.

9.1 Marketing and Industry Policy Problems

9.1.1 Marketing and the Scheduled/Charter Controversy

Reference has been made in the book to the persistent arguments throughout the post-war period between scheduled and charter airlines. For many years, scheduled carriers have complained of their being subjected to 'unfair competition' from charter carriers which do not have to accept a public service obligation. However, as was noted in Section 4.3.1, the situation has recently changed. Now charter airlines are criticizing what they see as unfair pricing by scheduled carriers offering charter-competitive fares. It is the theory of marketing which can give a consistent theme to this debate.

We have seen that in the immediate post-war years the world's scheduled airlines based their methods of operation on the offering of a premium air transport product. This gave frequent, regular flights, high-quality in-flight service and a ready access to seats near to flight departure time. It was noted in Section 2.3.1 that these are precisely the kinds of service characteristics which match the needs of a large part of the business travel segment, and of the personal segment as well. With the business segment, the penalty of such a true scheduled service—that it can only be produced at high cost and that, to reflect these costs, prices must also be high—is of lesser importance. Therefore, one can picture the scheduled service as a decisively marketing-orientated concept. It matches the productive capabilities of airlines with the requirements of a substantial market segment to produce results that are beneficial to producer and consumer alike.

However, such a conclusion must not hide the fact that there are other segments of the air travel market whose needs cannot be met by scheduled service in its pure form. For large parts of the market for leisure air travel, the product characteristics of scheduled service are an irrelevance. Also, the high production costs of scheduled operations mean that ticket prices are above those which many potential members of the segment are prepared to pay.

It has therefore been inevitable that charter carriers should eventually come along with a product which could meet these very different needs. Their product involves a full use of capacity with low costs of both production and selling. These low costs are in turn reflected in low prices.

Charters began to be widely permitted on some routes during the late 1950s and 1960s. It was, in retrospect, entirely to be expected that a product which so precisely met the needs of a market segment should prove very popular. Charter traffic grew extremely quickly in the two markets of the North Atlantic and intra-Europe where the regulatory system permitted its existence. In the North Atlantic case, this is shown by the data for the years prior to 1978 in Table 9.1.

Table 9.1. North Atlantic Passenger Travel, 1967–78

Year	Total scheduled traffic (thousands)	Total charter traffic (thousands)	Charters: market share (%)
1967	5,149·8	1,027·1	16·6
1968	5,422·2	1.248·1	18·7
1969	6,173·1	2,279·0	27·0
1970	7,448·3	2,892·6	28·0
1971	7,794·2	3,462·9	30·8
1972	9,782·9	3,713·0	27·5
1973	10,319·0	4,271·8	29·3
1974	9,640·5	3,441·4	26·3
1975	9,082·1	3,750·8	29·2
1976	10,165·8	4,916·3	32·6
1977	10,742·0	5,426·0	33·6
1978	13,090·0	3,480·0	21·0

Source: ICAO Bulletin, May 1979 p. 28.

However, within this framework of growth, it soon became obvious that the charter airlines would themselves have problems. They employed a strategy based purely on exploitation of the leisure segment of the market. This left them vulnerable to fluctuations in the economy which had an effect on their highly income-elastic traffic. It also meant that they faced difficulties of summer peaking in demand. However, in a marketing sense, the growth of charters can be looked at as a new product development to exploit potential market segments which could not be brought forward by pre-existing products.[1]

For a long period during the 1960s and early 1970s, the response of the scheduled airlines to charter development was to argue that charters were subjecting them to unfair competition, and that the answer to the problems which charter growth had brought them was a re-regulation of the industry. This would have resulted in charter airlines coming to accept many of the regulatory constraints applying to the scheduled sector. However, in what a cynic would see as an admission that the charter had isolated an important product/price option, a number of scheduled airlines began to stake their own claim for a place in the new market by forming their own subsidiary airlines to offer the charter product.

Such a situation continued for much of the 1960s in those markets where charters had been allowed. However, by the end of the 60s and through the 70s, we have seen further refinements in the state of the art of airline product development. This time, it has been on the part of the scheduled carriers. For long-haul routes, aircraft manufacturers have developed aircraft of such a size that, although they offer advantages of very low available operating costs, are too large to be filled by the business and wealthy leisure travellers who traditionally have used scheduled services. This is because, with flight frequency an important product characteristic, it has been impossible for airlines to reduce flight frequency and still retain market share. On short-haul routes, whilst some growth in aircraft size has been apparent, the main development has been that there has come an increasing recognition of the fact that if a scheduled carrier is to meet adequately the needs of the business travel segment with its pronounced morning and evening peaking, it will be left with spare capacity in the off-peak mid-day and weekend periods.

It would, of course, be incorrect to argue that there have never been abuses of pricing by scheduled airlines in the face of charter competition. Indeed, in Section 6.2.3, we noted the evidence which suggested that on some European routes, cross-subsidization in its truest sense had taken place. However, this should not be allowed to draw attention away from the fact that the synergy open to the total market airline *does* allow it to offer very low fares quite legitimately, which, if controlled properly, add, rather than detract, from corporate profitability.

1 *See* Schoutt and Costello (1975).

Such fares can come from the pricing of off-peak capacity on routes with a substantial business travel content, and also from the offer of space-controlled APEX and other low fares in the rear cabin of the large wide-bodied aeroplanes. Here, low fares can be counterbalanced by very high average seat factors in the parts of the aeroplane given over to low-fare traffic.

Low fares can also come from the Standby concept where, again assuming proper planning and space control, an airline reserves a proportion of capacity for business travellers who wish to book at the last minute. Given the random nature of business travel demand, there will be occasions when not all this capacity is taken up. Spare seats can then be sold off by the airline near to flight departure time at very low prices. These prices will be legitimate and cost-related, and will give the total-market airline opportunities for further exploitation of highly price-elastic market segments.

The result of this growing understanding of the airline product has been that over the last few years, the competitive relationship between scheduled and charter airlines has changed totally. On the North Atlantic particularly, the scheduled share of the market has risen significantly (as shown in Table 9.1). Therefore, in contrast to the days when scheduled carriers complained of unfair competition from the charter sector, now charter carriers are the ones criticizing the unfairness of the competitive environment.[2] However, what is argued here is that it will be possible for an efficient scheduled airline to offer fares which are charter-competitive and which are quite proper in economic terms. These fares need not come from any attempt by the scheduled airlines to practice predatory pricing, but rather from the theory of marketing and the synergy which is open to the total-market airline to offer capacity at low prices in particular situations.

With the recognition by scheduled airlines of these pricing opportunities, it seems certain that a policy of aggressive price competition with the charter sector will now be pursued. Clearly, it will be necessary for regulatory authorities to monitor this competition. They must ensure that such pricing does not become unfair, and that unacceptable consequences in terms of industry instability or excessive concentration do not result from it. However, lessons from marketing show us that, for all segments of air transport demand to be satisfied, both high-fare/high-quality services and low-fare/low-cost services must be provided. If it is the case that a total-market airline can better offer both kinds of service by a synergistic relationship between the two, it will be difficult to argue that regulatory intervention should prevent this. Indeed, perhaps the most valid ground for complaint from a charter airline would be that regulation of the

2 *See,* for example, Hodgson (1979).

industry prevented it from moving over to a total-market strategy. If in a situation of reducing regulation that option was open, then it would be difficult for an airline which had not taken it to complain of unfair competition from those which had.

The theory of marketing can thus be used to emphasize the principles of the scheduled/character debate. As is so often the case in other industries, the argument centres on a process whereby market needs and the state-of-the-art of product development have advanced together. However, in aviation, innovation of the new products has been slowed by regulation, and the final form of competition probably has still yet to be reached. As the industry moves towards such a stage, it is vital that the strategic options which are open should be fully examined, and that both scheduled and charter managements should decide on a strategy relative to market conditions and their own capabilities. Just as it was undoubtedly wrong for scheduled carriers to put forward their 're-regulation' arguments at a time when the competitive position was against them, so it is now wrong for charter managements to claim immunity from the effects of developments in scheduled product design. Fortunately, there are now signs of a growing blurring of the scheduled/charter distinction, as a number of charter airlines—Britannia Airways in the U.K. and World Airways in the U.S.A. are good examples—take steps to broaden the base of their operations.

9.1.2 Marketing and the Skytrain

As a second illustration of the principles of marketing, it is helpful to turn to the Laker Skytrain. Considerable time has already been spent discussing the Skytrain in Section 5.3.3, but, at the risk of repetition, this concept provides such a good illustration of some aspects of the philosophy contained in the book that it is well worth referring to it again.

We have noted in Section 5.3.3 that the original Skytrain idea was an excellent one from a marketing viewpoint. It was based on the principle of offering a cheaply-available product to a market segment which was believed to be—and has turned out to be—extremely price-sensitive. However, since the introduction of the Skytrain on the London–New York and London–Los Angeles routes, problems have arisen. These have come from the single-market strategy which the concept embodies, and from the nature of the competition which Skytrain has faced.

With regard to the single-market strategy, as originally conceived, the Skytrain only offered a service which matched the needs of the leisure segment of demand, and, to a lesser extent, those of the independent businessman. With the leisure segment, any airline which aims exclusively at it must accept a pattern of pronounced seasonal peaking in demand. The Skytrain has found that, during its first years of operation, demand has indeed peaked in the summertime, as shown in Table 9.2. This was especially serious during the summer of 1978 when the booking conditions then applying to the service meant that long periods of waiting had to be endured by potential passengers.

Table 9.2. Summer Peaking in Skytrain Traffic, 1977–78

Month	Total passengers
October 1977	17,492
November 1977	16,895
December 1977	18,590
January 1978	17,841
February 1978	11,415
March 1978	14,905
April 1978	15,342
May 1978	19,036
June 1978	28,096
July 1978	33,541
August 1978	33,160
September 1978	26,424

Source: C.A.A. Monthly Statistics.

As a further strategic problem, as one would expect with a leisure-market product, the Skytrain must be operated in the face of a demand that is likely to be relatively unstable. Thus, in the summers of 1979 and 1980, the rising value of the pound and inflation in the British economy have led to a stagnation or even a decline in the numbers of visitors travelling from the U.S.A. to the U.K., with this having an effect on the market available to the airlines flying the North Atlantic routes.

The second set of difficulties in the operation of the Skytrain has been that the service has come to face an intensity of competition which (one may guess) even its distinguished innovator may not have anticipated. As has been noted (p. 144), the introduction of Skytrain on the London–New York route in September 1977 was immediately matched by the pre-existing airlines on the route with their Standby fare. Standby was offered at fare levels which were fully competititive with Skytrain. However, this still left substantial opportunities open to the new service. There were those passengers who had genuinely been generated by the appeal of walk-on services and the publicity surrounding them. Admittedly, these passengers were now to be shared with other airlines, but they were still there in sufficient numbers to contribute significantly to the successful start-up of Skytrain. There were also passengers who would have travelled on the route anyway, but who were diverted from pre-existing services. Given the structure of fares, the most likely source of such diversion was

Advanced Booking Charter services, and many initial Skytrain passengers were diverted from this source. Ironically, Laker Airways had had a big involvement in North Atlantic A.B.Cs, and Skytrain therefore merely diverted some passengers from one Laker service to another. The third major source of traffic was a very important one, for it is certain that the innovation of low-fare, walk-on services on London–New York diverted large numbers of passengers from other routes. These passengers had origins or destinations in the U.S.A. or Canada, or in Continental Europe. They completed their journey by taking a U.S. domestic or trans-border flight, or a short-haul flight out of London to the European point.

Since September 1977, there has been a progressive increase in the competition which Skytrain has faced in all its potential markets. The charter airlines, which lost out so severely initially to walk-on competition, have fought back by improving their product. Within a permissive regulatory environment they have successfully argued for a reduction or elimination of the tight conditions which had formerly governed their Advanced Booking Charters. They have also strengthened their product in some cases by combining a charter seat with holiday accommodation (through a travel organizer) to make up packaged holidays, All the time, of course, they have been able to offer a guarantee of a seat which the Skytrain, as initially formulated, could not.

Skytrain also has lost progressively its opportunities for diversion of traffic on to its London–Los Angeles and London–New York routes. In February 1978, the U.K. government conceded the right of all scheduled airlines operating between the U.K. and U.S. gateways to offer walk-on fares, something which was taken up quickly by the airlines concerned (*see* Section 4.3.1). Low fares then came to Southern U.S. gateways such as Houston, Dallas, Atlanta and Miami. These low fares offered the opporunity for travellers from the south to fly direct to Europe at low fares, rather then transferring at New York. Then, through 1978, the U.S.A. negotiated a series of bi-lateral agreements with the Netherlands, Belgium and West Germany which opened the way for the commencement of low-fare services between these countries and U.S. gateways. During the summer of 1979, these low-fare services were available, and will have greatly reduced the competitive opportunities for Skytrain to divert traffic.

The response of Laker to these developments has been to claim that his competitors are engaging in predatory pricing, particularly those who have competed directly with him on New York and Los Angeles.[3] There is clearly a measure of truth in these claims. However, as far as predatory competition is concerned the point has been made elsewhere that the scheduled Standby fare is a synergistic one and can be fully justified under the principles of marketing. It could have been offered by the scheduled

---

3 *See*, for example, *Air Transport World*, November 1977.

carriers on this route long before it actually was. If it is correctly applied, it does offer the chance of 'fair' competition against Skytrain-type services.

The other lesson from marketing theory has been that with both Skytrain-competitive fares out of London and the subsequent growth of competition on other routes, we have seen a classic illustration of the product life cycle. A go-ahead entrepreneur has come along with a good innovative idea which has achieved an initial marketing success. However, it has been this success which has been a strong contributing factor in the growth of competition. Laker as innovator has had no patent protection—no such thing exists in air transport. Also, there has been no benefit for him of a long lead time needing to elapse before a competitor has developed a rival product. In aviation, providing an airline has sufficient capacity available, a new product can often be introduced in only a matter of weeks following a go-ahead decision.

Laker's response to what may be seen as operating difficulties with the Skytrain and the growth of intense competition for the service has been characteristic, and, from a marketing viewpoint, admirable. It precisely illustrates the great opportunities open to, but also the dangers and the resource commitments needed by, any airline moving over from a single segment to a total-market strategy. In July 1979, following a temporary halt to the service during a period of grounding of the DC 10, the Skytrain re-appeared in a quite different format. Instead of the old single-class low-cost operation, three types of Skytrain fare were being offered. The very low fare for a 'walk-on' ticket was still available, although even here the option claimed successfully by the airline was that it should be able to book passengers on the flights of succeeding days if more passengers turned up on a single day than could be accommodated on the walk-on allocation of that day. This eliminated the possibility of long periods of queueing even for passengers using the lowest fare. However, in addition to the lowest fare, Laker also offered a somewhat higher fare based on the 21-day advanced booking and acceptance of a minimum-stay condition characteristic of the APEX concept of normal scheduled services. Finally, to complete the transformation, there was a third fare, allowing booking at any time, with the offer of a guaranteed seat and no minimum-stay condition. As the fare level for this class of service was much higher, it was analogous to the Normal Economy fare of traditional scheduled services. As a further point, the new Skytrain was also licensed to carry freight in the lower holds of the DC 10 aircraft which it used.

The new concept of Skytrain opened up important possibilities for the airline. It allowed it to move over to a total-market philosophy of offering products which suited the needs of all segments of the market. In addition, the ability to offer pre-booked reservations should have ensured a greater support for the service from travel agents, given that commission could now be paid to them exactly as with any other airline's operations.

Despite these advantages, one could still foresee problems for the new concept, problems which illustrate how difficult the question of marketing strategy can be for an airline. Laker Airways had no pre-existing reputation for the carriage of business travellers—indeed the success of the airline had been built on the very justifiable reputation it had earned for bringing low-fare travel to the masses. Therefore, it might well be that image-building advertising and communications work would be necessary before a substantial penetration of the business-travel market could be expected. This could in turn detract from the airline's image as an innovative carrier with regard to 'no-frills' low-fare services. A similar problem of a lack of reputation could also hinder the airline in securing penetration of the air-freight market, although here the ability to offer very low rates in what is virtually an unregulated freight market would presumably help. However, the other major change which the new Skytrain meant is that it moved Laker away from a position of operating with very low overhead costs of administration and selling. The advent of a bookable Skytrain committed the airline to setting up a reservations system. The ability of travel agents to participate fully in Skytrain selling increased the commission payments which needed to be made.

There were, of course, criticisms of the changes to Skytrain. The old-established schedule airlines on the route argued that the Skytrain of 1979 was nothing like the original concept for which Laker applied in 1972. However, from the point of view of this book, it provides an excellent illustration of many of the principles and problems of strategy which we have discussed. Indeed, at the time (October 1980) when the book is finally being prepared for printing, we have a record through the summer of 1980 of complaints against Laker Airways from travel agents regarding the poor administration of its booking system (as in *Travel Trade Gazette*, 7.7.80), and yet further changes in the Skytrain concept whereby the fare which can be booked at any time has been substantially reduced, and even the so-called 'walk-on' fare can now be booked at any time up to eight days before flight departure. Therefore, some of the problems noted earlier as being possibilities have indeed appeared, whilst the concept of Skytrain itself is still clearly in a state of evolution.

9.1.3 Marketing and Competition in the U.K. Aviation Industry

As a final illustration of the book's principles, it will be useful to look at the U.K. aviation industry. Perhaps more than in any other country, the operations of British aviation have been affected by the vicissitudes of government policy. Successive changes in the regulation of domestic air transport services,[4] in competition policy for international routes,[5] and in

4 *See* Gwilliam and Mackie (1975), pp. 333–45.
5 *Civil Aviation Policy. Cmnd.* 6400, 1976.

the institutional arrangements for the state-owned sector,[6] have all combined to give an inconsistent background to the industry, an inconsistency which has been increased by seemingly never-ending arguments regarding the aircraft selection policies of the state-owned airlines.

During the 1970s, one theme at least has been consistent—complaints against British Airways. British Airways was set up in 1973 as a result of the merger between the pre-existing B.E.A. and B.O.A.C. Since then, the airline has been criticized for gross overstaffing, poor service, slow progress in implementing an integrated organizational structure,[7] and finally and most recently as a 'most inefficient airline' by the U.K. Civil Aviation Authority.[8]

It is no part of this section to argue that these criticisms are invalid—some of them self-evidently are—although it would be an interesting study to decide how much blame should be attached to the management of the airline, and how much to archaic traditions of labour relations widespread in the British economy. However, it may be a useful sideline to note that in recent years the planning function of the airline has seemed to offer a very good example of the philosophy which this book has tried to embody.

During the winter of 1977–8, it became clear that the world aviation industry was arriving at a period of transition. Reducing regulation in some markets began to offer opportunities for innovative action. At the same time, British Airways was facing immense problems of fleet replacement. Many of its aircraft were old and less than ideal for its purposes, having been bought as a result of arguments between B.E.A. and B.O.A.C. and successive governments over fleet planning policies. In addition, it was certain that the airline would have to replace all its aircraft by 1986 with the exception of its B 747s and L 1011s, because of the government noise legislation which will ban all the older and noisier planes from 1986 onwards. These aircraft would in any case have become very fuel-inefficient by the mid-80s. The overall feet replacement cost was seen as being something in the region of £2 billion.

From the point of view of the marketing theorist, such a time provided an ideal moment for the airline to examine its strategy for the future. It responded by undertaking a major planning exercise aimed at plotting the airline's course up to the 1986 noise deadline and beyond. Obviously, the results of this exercise have mostly remained confidential, but a careful monitoring of the public statements of the airline's executives[9] does allow the outsider to glean something of the major decision which was taken. It is worth dwelling on this at some length, for it does illustrate the marketing philosophy of matching the opportunities offered by the mar-

6 *See* Thomson and Hunter (1973), pp. 53–115.
7 U.K. Select Committee on Nationalized Industries, 1976.
8 Following a public hearing into proposed increases in U.K. domestic fares in March 1979.
9 For example, in *Air Transport World*, February 1979, pp. 54–9.

ket-place with the strengths and weaknesses of the firm. The major conclusion which would seem to have emerged from the study is that the airline is fully and finally committed to what we have called the total-market philosophy. It is to attempt to improve its hold on the business-travel segment traditionally the preserve of the scheduled airlines. It is also to try to participate fully in the carriage of low-fare, price-elastic traffic from the leisure-travel segment, as well as increasing its success in the air freight market.

Such a strategy has a considerable number of advantages for the airline compared with the alternative which was presumably evaluated, of being a 'premium product' airline aiming only at the business-travel segment and the wealthiest leisure travellers. It will maximize the numbers of passengers which the airline will carry, giving the best opportunities to improve its currently low labour-productivity. It will give it a base in each of the major market segments and offer the best opportunities to participate in industry growth wherever it comes. It will protect its interests in the U.K. aviation industry by a direct competition with smaller but dynamic independent carriers such as Laker. Finally, in terms of the arguments presented in the book, it offers the airline the chance for synergistic relationships to be developed between its products which should give it good competitive opportunities.

Just as we have suggested in theory, this total-market strategy presents great practical difficulties along with these opportunities. The airline is committing itself to the design of products which match the needs of all market segments, without the situation developing where adequate provision to one segment jeopardizes services offered to another. This will present a major task, particularly if reducing regulation affects the degree of competition prevalent in the industry. However, even if it does not, the growing interest on the part of the Civil Aviation Authority in pricing matters is likely to mean that one traditional way for scheduled airlines to provide for both the business and the leisure travel segments—the offering of low fares to leisure travellers against a background of accusations of cross-subsidization from the business segment—will be ruled out. However, even here the initial signs are promising. The airline is devoting considerable research into offering a genuinely different product to the business segment, particularly by the wider introduction of the three-class aeroplane concept. It is also looking at many possible ways of reducing the true costs of carrying low-fare passengers, to enable it to meet the prime need of a large part of this segment for the lowest possible ticket price for a reasonably comfortable journey.

One is only too well aware of the cynical remarks which can be made about the British Airways strategy—that the airline is giving too much attention to looking too far ahead, and not enough to its immediate problems. It has also been seen as a late convert to the cause of low fares, with this idea now being pursued with the messianic zeal which often marks the late arrival on the scene who has ground to make up (although in fact B.A. and its predecessor B.O.A.C. have a long history of interest in lower fares, especially with its development of the APEX concept). However, one can see here an attempt to plot a strategy which meets market needs, which is responding to the opportunities and threats facing the airline from the external environment, and which matches the identified strengths and weaknesses of the firm.

The three illustrations given in the chapter so far do, it is hoped, confirm the relevance of marketing to the analysis of the airline industry's problems. In a book of case studies now in preparation, it is hoped to expand on this relevance to a much greater depth. However, for the moment, it is now necessary to move on to the overall conclusions to this book, by analysing the usefulness of marketing to the policy problems faced by airlines at the present time, and those which they are likely to face in the future.

9.2 Airline Marketing—The Future

Anyone who is working in commercial aviation is concerned with an industry which has grown at a remarkable rate. From tiny beginnings, the world's airlines are now carrying more than seven hundred million passengers each year, many millions of tonnes of freight, and are earning around $70 billion in revenues. Such a situation could only have been achieved by an industry which has had opportunities open to it on a massive scale, and also a supply of the entrepreneurial talent capable of exploiting these opportunities.

Yet aviation has never been free of problems. Almost since the inception of commercial air services, arguments have raged over such issues as air transport regulation, the extent or correctness of subsidizing airlines, and the environmental impact of aircraft operations.

We come now to the most important section of the book when an attempt is made to consider the future of airline marketing. In this section, we need not spend a great deal of time on the opportunities open to airlines. If growth is considered a desirable objective—which by the airlines themselves at least it presumably is—then the opportunities open to airlines remain immense. We have noted the appeal of air travel to those who are already existing customers of the industry, favouring carriers with the continuing prospect of repeat purchases. It is also apparent that, as possibilities for air travel reach new markets in developed and developing countries, these possibilities are enthusiastically taken up. In the future, social and economic trends will result in increased leisure time becoming available to many. Without doubt, therefore, in addition to the substantial markets already developed, the future areas for growth are very large indeed.

However, despite these opportunities, it is impossible to view the future without a measure of unease, because of the extent of the problems which the industry now faces. It is certainly possible to argue, for example, that airline growth is not to be encouraged, because of the demands on resources which aviation makes. Even if the correctness of such growth is accepted, then there is an immense range of problems which must now bring into question the possibilities of it being realized.

The remaining task of the book is therefore to look at each of the problem areas and suggest appropriate courses for future action. This will involve the inclusion of the personal opinions which have, for the most part, been kept in the background in the earlier sections. It is, however, emphasized that these opinions represent no more than a bulletin on what is always a constant evolution in thinking. Indeed it is hoped that their most valuable function may be to stimulate discussion following the book's publication.

In order to begin this part of the conclusion, a summary will be given of each of the earlier chapters, together with a statement of the main policy problems covered and conclusions reached. Then a statement of view will be given regarding each problem area, together with any necessary qualifications to such a view.

Chapter 1 of the book did no more than give an outline of the theory of marketing. Its main relevance to this conclusion will come at the very end of the book, and consideration of it will be deferred until then.

In the first part of Chapter 2, a description was given of the structure of air transport's markets. It is hoped that this section has demonstrated the value of the concept of market segmentation, and that it is possible to produce a reasonably consistent classification of the airlines' passenger and freight markets. The second section of this chapter dealt with future market growth prospects. In it, some of the most fundamental problems relating to airline marketing arose. It is now necessary to consider these problems and to provide a commentary on them.

The first point which any discussion of market growth prospects must consider is the question as to whether or not such growth should be encouraged, or indeed whether it should be actively discouraged or stopped. The main arguments with regard to these issues are those related to the resources consumed by aviation, and to its wide effects on social ties and the proliferation of 'tourism blight' of previously unspoilt areas.

The resource argument springs mainly from aviation's consumption of fuel, and its use of scarce land resources for its airports, with the attendant problem of loss of amenity through aircraft noise.

Of these arguments, the one regarding aircraft noise is the easiest to deal with, as a new generation of aircraft is now being introduced which will mostly markedly reduce the levels of airport noise, and should therefore calm the amounts of—entirely resonable—community protest against excessive airport noise levels.

The points regarding oil and land consumption—and tourism blight —are more difficult, and need to be considered carefully. However, practical points regarding the importance of aviation and tourism in the economies of many countries and their employment situations are ones which cannot be ignored. Also, despite some commentators' criticisms regarding the effects of excessive mobility, there can be no denying the fact that travel is an extremely attractive product to many people. To impose some artificial limit to growth would presumably mean confining the consumption of this commodity to what is still a small élite of the world's population. Such a policy would be most unlikely to be politically acceptable. Finally, the author at least does not discount the value of aviation in improving international communication and understanding—indeed this may be its most valuable contribution.

With regard to a policy on growth, the overall policy for the future must be one of balance. It will be seen as being correct policy by the vast majority of actual and potential users of aviation that continued growth should be allowed. However, increasingly, these users must be prepared (to a reasonable degree) for their convenience to be reduced, if such a reduction will lessen the wider social impact of aviation. A very good example of this will come with regard to the land requirements for airport development. As noise declines as a major issue in airport planning, it will be more than counterbalanced by a rising concern regarding the massive urbanization and regional planning impact of airports. A very obvious policy option here would then be to move some passenger-processing (especially for low-fare passengers) to already-urbanized areas, with declining inner city areas likely to be suitable. Passengers would then have to accept a measure of inconvenience and also a greater use of public transport in their airport access journeys.

Overall, the balance of what is a very difficult argument comes down on the side of allowing a further, strictly controlled growth of aviation. What, therefore, is likely to be correct policy for airlines regarding the next question dealt with in Chapter 2, that of the availability and price of aviation fuel?

Overall, the book has taken the view that there will be sufficient fuel to meet aviation's needs in the medium-term at least, with the main justification for such an opinion being the readjustments in the production of and markets for energy which high prices will cause. The major problems for air transport with respect to aviation fuel are certain to be temporary—and uneven—shortages, and a continuing escalation in price.

With regard to policy for the future, clearly aviation cannot rely on other energy users to make readjustments—it must respond as well. However, there are large areas where a response will be possible. Thus we have looked at the opportunities for the accelerated introduction of fuel-efficient aircraft. Also, operating procedures related to such aspects as aircraft taxiing may yield substantial savings. Eventually, chronically high fuel prices must surely give an incentive for wasteful air traffic control delays such as those now being experienced in Europe to be alleviated by investment in the development and installation of new technology.

Overall, therefore, there are substantial savings which can be made, and the only appropriate policy for the future must be that every aspect of aviation's operations—largely built up during an era of very low fuel prices—must be re-examined. Indeed, even such a hallowed practice as duty-free purchases being made on departure could yield significant savings in fuel if such purchases were instead permitted on arrival. In the next few years, therefore, airlines can greatly improve their position as fuel consumers, and the actions taken by many carriers to counter the rapid rise in fuel prices experienced during 1979 and 1980 offers encouraging evidence that such a transformation will come about.

Fuel was one of the factors used in Chapter 2 to reach a conclusion that the future will see a steady increase in aviation's cost levels. With regard to the other factors likely to affect the future of costs, the main comments which one would wish to make on the future of technology were included in Section 2.8.2. However, more needs to be said on the question of user charges as another factor mentioned in the chapter, indicating an increase in airline costs as being the most likely future situation.

In Section 2.8.2, it was noted that user charges for airport and air traffic control services were amongst the fastest rising costs for all airlines, as governments everywhere attempt to eliminate subsidization of these services.

To talk of appropriate 'policies' for airports and A.T.C. may not be very helpful to airlines, in that they have no choice but to pay the charges levied on them by governments—though even here there is some opportunity to influence policy by lobbying. However, the wider issues raised by the user charges debate are immense, and well worth a brief comment here.

Overall, it is unreasonable for a mature industry such as aviation is rapidly becoming to expect its infrastructure to be provided on a basis of subsidy. This is said despite the full recognition of the fact that aviation can bring wide benefits to an economy and might at least have a case for subsidy. The political problems of overt subsidy are becoming too severe, particularly in the light of many governments' acceptance of an economic philosophy requiring limits to be placed on public spending. However, one's greatest concern is over the efficiency of airport and A.T.C. provision. Monopoly power has never been thought of as being conducive to low costs and efficiency in any area of economic activity, and there is little reason for thinking that the provision of aviation infrastructure is likely to be any different in this respect. Therefore, with the massive increases in airport and A.T.C. charges which are forecast for the next few years, monitoring the efficiency of airport and air traffic control provision will become an important policy task for government and airline alike.

Overall, our conclusion in Chapter 2 was that airlines are, in the future, likely to face cost levels which are rising as steeply as those in most other industries. Indeed, it may well take actions along the lines set out above to make sure that the cost situation is no worse than this.

Such a trend in costs clearly makes future growth prospects stemming from socio-economic factors of vital concern to airlines.

Of the aspects which were mentioned in Chapter 2, there *are* some where appropriate policy actions might have some effect. Thus, with the point about communications technology and its effect on business-travel growth, advertising the virtues of personalized discussions could certainly be useful. Also, corporations with sufficient resources might see it as a prudent business diversification to match airline investment with investment in businesses concerned with the new technology. With the future of leisure travel, airlines are already engaging widely in 'destination' advertising to boost holiday traffic, and in the kind of generative V.F.R. advertising discussed in Section 7.2.3. By both these methods, airlines may be able to reduce the impact of rising cost levels in slowing growth, by encouraging consumers to maintain or increase the proportion of their expenditure devoted to air travel. Finally, a sensible policy in V.F.R. markets may be to aim to develop ethnic links into future holiday traffic, to counterbalance any tendency towards a falling-off in V.F.R. potential.

To a degree, of course, airlines must accept the market potential which is available to them. However, as regards future policies, it is hoped that Chapter 2 has shown that, by the strictest attention to costs, plus the use of creative marketing techniques, a significant impact on the market will be possible. This will be especially so if the correct policies can be brought to bear on product design—something which we shall consider shortly.

However, before looking at product design, attention must be given to the material covered in Chapter 3. The first part of this chapter dealt with the structure and characteristics of the airline industry, and the nature of the different objectives which are available to be pursued by airlines. As far as policies are concerned, this section should have emphasized successfully the complexities and interrelationships which stem for airline operations, and the fact that airlines cannot form their corporate objectives without considering the wider implications of their activities.

These wider implications are crucial to the discussion of strategies, with which Chapter 3 was concluded. This section noted four possible types of strategy, those aiming at the business-market segment, the leisure segment, the freight segment, and a 'total-market' solution aiming at all three.

For future policies, decisions on strategy are at the core of successful airline marketing. Carriers must decide on which type of strategy they are to adopt, and also the detail of how the strategy is to be implemented. As far as the type of strategy is concerned, then it is one of the major challenges of the future that many indicators in the industry suggest the 'total-market' approach as being the most appropriate. Such an approach offers the best opportunities for established airlines to defend themselves against their rivals, whilst the high capacity of the wide-bodied aircraft is giving the total-market airline crucial advantages because of the synergistic relationships which can be obtained between its products. However, despite the undoubted theoretical correctness of the total-market approach, its adoption in principle still leaves airlines with crucial policy decisions to make. In particular, there is no more vital decision for the future of many airlines than the decision of how far 'down-market' to go in pursuit of leisure traffic. Aiming at very price- and income-elastic low-income travellers is probably the best way, at the moment at any rate, for airlines to protect themselves against the consumerist lobby. It also opens for airlines a market of both actual and potential users which is of immense size. However, this market is likely to be price-sensitive and any airline trying to exploit it will be faced with an intense price-competition and low yields. Also, it is a market which is likely to be unstable, especially during times of economic recession. Finally, providing products which match the needs of the low-yielding leisure segment may jeopardize the airline's image amongst higher-yielding business and up-market leisure travellers.

At the time of writing, there would seem to be the most fundamental disagreement between airlines on this aspect of strategy. Indeed, amongst European airlines, Lufthansa and Swissair are very good examples of carriers which, although unquestionably pursuing a total-market strategy, have so far shied away from the large commitment to low-fare innovation which would allow an effective penetration of the low-income part of the leisure market. Also, in the U.S. domestic market, it may well be that the currently better financial position of some of the regional and local service airlines comes from their concentration on high-yielding markets, whilst the trunklines have engaged in a fiercely-competitive battle for low-yielding traffic.

Clearly, decisions on the family of strategy to be selected, and the particular interpretation of that strategy to be used, should depend on the circumstances of each airline. However, despite the current threat of recession and all the problems that this will bring, the author has not changed his view that, for the majority of well-established, large airlines, a strategy aimed at the widest possible penetration of all market segments is the only strategy likely to offer protection from predatory competition. It should therefore be evaluated carefully as a basis for planning.

In Chapter 4, we dealt with the regulation of air transport. If this has been successful in providing the knowledge needed by the marketing executive with respect to this vital subject, it should have emphasized the extent to which governmental regulation constrains marketing activity in aviation, and that there are a number of sound reasons why this should be so. However, equally, the chapter will have shown regulation as being an area where significant changes have come about in recent years, and an area which forms the focus for one of the major policy debates in aviation at the present time, Clearly, therefore, it is necessary for all involved in airline marketing to have a view on the nature of correct regulatory policies.

As the de-regulation debate matures, it is becoming clear that three factions (at least) are discernible. The United States government's view has remained inflexibly at the end of the de-regulatory spectrum for the past four years. Equally, at the opposite end of this spectrum, we find the opponents of de-regulation: those who are critical of the consequences of reduced regulation in those markets where it has been allowed, and those who are determined to prevent its introduction in those markets which remain tightly regulated. In between these two extremes one may place those looking for a more balanced position of attempting to encourage freer competition in those markets where it is believed it will prove practicable and beneficial. The stance adopted by the U.K. Civil Aviation Authority would conform to such a view.

In looking to provide commentary on de-regulation, the author is first of all conscious of the difficulties involved, and is the first to admit that his own thinking on the matter is still evolving. However, such a description would probably fit many of those with an interest in commercial aviation, so it does not preclude the offering of at least preliminary remarks on some of the regulatory developments of the last few years.

The first comment that it is worth making is that recent years have shown the domination of what many would see as restrictionist views in many countries of the world. Such events as the Special Air Transport Conferences held by I.C.A.O. in 1977 and in the Spring of 1980 have proved to be sounding-boards for the many countries which (often reasonably, given their own situations) advocate the continuation of tight regulatory control over the industry. It is therefore clearly wrong to anticipate a move towards greater economic freedom in large parts of the world.

However, such a view should not be allowed to end the de-regulation debate, because those markets where reduced regulation has arrived, or may reasonably be expected to arrive in the future, are also the largest in terms of industry output. Thus reduced regulation has been shown to be a worthwhile topic for discussion as far as U.S. and Canadian domestic services are concerned, for international services on the North Atlantic, and for intra-European services. Taken together, these markets make up around 80 per cent of the tonne-kilometres performed by the world's airlines. In none of these markets is it acceptable to say that reduced regulation is 'not possible' for *a priori* reasons. Clearly, therefore, arguments about regulation cannot be dismissed or ignored.

To evaluate the correctness of reduced regulatory control over the industry, it is first necessary to emphasize some of the extremely serious consequences which have appeared in those markets—notably the North Atlantic and U.S. domestic service—where reduced regulation has come about. In both these markets, the main trunk routes have seen an explosion in market entry to the point where the 'excessive competition' arguments noted in Section 4.1.2 may be beginning to be appropriate. At the same time, in the U.S. domestic market, concern has arisen at the loss of service to small communities. Also, the U.S. trunkline carriers have seen the high profits they recorded during 1978 and the first half of 1979 decline very substantially, in some cases to the extent of large losses being made. Passengers have almost certainly suffered through a growing complexity in airline tariffs, and by reductions in standards of telephone-answering by airlines. To try and overcome these problems, U.S. airlines have been hiring large numbers of ticketing and reservations staff, but of course then only at a penalty of a substantial increase in their indirect operating costs. Such costs have also been increased by the rapid rise in travel agents' commissions which de-regulation has seen. As a final criticism of moves towards reduced regulation, such actions have been described as being in direct conflict with a policy of fuel conservation. Escalating fuel prices and shortages are placing an emphasis on conservation, with free market entry leading to increased fuel consumption.

This is indeed a formidable array of arguments to support a reimposition of regulation where it has been relaxed, and a determination to ensure that it is retained in such markets as those for intra-European scheduled services where no relaxation has so far come. Yet an alternative interpretation can be given to most of them, with these alternatives most certainly needing to be considered by the marketing executive.

To deal first with the point of about de-regulation leading to foolhardy market entry and eventual profit declines it was always certain that an industry such as the U.S. domestic one, which has been very tightly regulated, would go through a difficult and painful transition process once greater freedom arrived. Such a transition may well take several years before a mature, less-regulated state is reached. Thus, between 1977 and 1979, the U.S. domestic industry moved from a situation where no new U.S. airline, other than the established trunkline carriers, had been designated on a trunk route since 1933, to a situation where a large degree of freedom of entry was possible. Far from it being surprising that the industry has had difficulties in making this transition, it would have been astonishing if this had not been so. However, the fact of this transition period cannot of itself be used to argue that de-regulation should not have taken place. Indeed, it may well be that de-regulation is merely meaning that airline management are having their mistakes found out in a way which did not happen before. This, in the author's view, would be an appropriate opinion in the case of Braniff Airways, a U.S. trunk airline which has experienced severe financial problems. This airline embarked on a massive expansion programme in the comparatively stable economic environment which followed de-regulation. However, such an expansion left the carrier particularly vulnerable to the recession and rising costs which have now affected its operations.

The point about de-regulation leading to low profitability can be answered further by looking at the performance of the U.S. trunklines during the 1973–5 recession. Tight regulation most certainly did not save the airlines from severe loss-making then, and there is little reason for thinking that it can (in itself) do so during the recession of the early 1980s. Indeed, there are at least some reasons for thinking that reduced regulation has *helped* the airlines prepare for the onset of recession. It has allowed for easy route withdrawals so that networks can be trimmed. It has permitted a faster rate of fare increase to price-insensitive travellers. Finally, intensive price-competition may have reduced the extent to which, with the leisure market, airlines have fallen into the trap of believing that fare increases to price-elastic travellers will improve a carrier's financial position. If the increase merely drives away traffic, then its effect is, of course, likely to be exactly the opposite.

Arguments about the effect of de-regulation on service to small communities are undoubtedly worthy of discussion, in that there are many well-documented examples of where a reduction in service has taken place. However, criticisms that de-regulation has caused a withdrawal of the trunklines from small community service are misplaced. Rather, it should be seen as a distortion of the old *regulated* environment that these carriers had a presence in the small community markets in the first place. It is most unlikely that a carrier geared up for the scale of operation necessary for trunkline operations will be equally successful in providing the flexible, small aircraft operation needed in small community markets. There is every possible reason to think that the small community markets vacated by the trunkline airlines will be taken over by the commuter sector of the industry. If this does indeed happen, then it must be seen as a major point in favour of de-regulation. Any policy which allows airlines to fly in the markets to which their pattern of operations is most suitable must be in the carriers' corporate interests, and in the interests of the majority of consumers.

The point about de-regulation being incompatible with a rational fuel conservation policy is again a difficult one, and to an extent hangs on the degree to which one regards leisure travel by air as a frivolous waste of resources, or as a right which should be made available as widely as possible. However, the crucial argument regarding fuel conservation is that under the old regulated regime of U.S. domestic service, a great deal of fuel was, in a sense, at least, 'wasted,' because, as we have seen in Section 4.3.1, the lack of price competition led to a concentration on competition in capacity and frequency, with the result that average seat factors widely fell below 50 per cent.

A possible way of reducing this waste in the future might be to reimpose regulation, and to stop excessive capacity competition by the use of the capacity-controlling mechanisms widely employed in the bi-lateral agreements covering international aviation. However, as will become clear below, such a situation would be less than ideal, whilst there must be considerable doubt as to whether or not it would be possible under U.S. Anti-Trust laws. Under de-regulation, airline average seat factors have risen substantially as passengers have come forward to use the low-fare offerings which have been made. Although such high seat factors may have been against the business traveller's interest because of their effect on seat accessibility, they allow one to reach a conclusion that de-regulation has permitted an increase in the consumer satisfaction derived from each gallon of fuel burnt by the industry. This should be seen as one of the major gains of reducing governmental control of competition.

The final argument regarding regulation is the most important, but also the most difficult. Whether one accepts it or not depends partly on one's experience of the workings of bureaucracy. However, the author's experience and reading lead him to believe that it is both correct and important. It is included here in order to provide a stimulus for debate.

Aviation is, of course, by no means unique in having regulated prices. In the U.K., examples of situations where price competition is largely restricted include the commissions asked by estate agents on property sales, the fees asked for many professional services and the rates of interest paid by building societies. Studies of the working of such industries where price competition is limited[10] provide analogies which are instructive as far as the aviation industry is concerned. It is very clear from these studies that the absence of price competition is very commonly associated with a slow rate of innovation of new developments, and an inexorable rise in costs. This increase in costs is due to expenditure on non-price competition, and also to a tendency—apparent in any organization—for bureaucracy to expand to absorb budgeted revenue. Once this has happened, a situation arises when the argument is produced that the regulated prices cannot be

---

10 An example of an investigation into professional service fees without price competition is the study of surveyor's services published by the U.K. Monopolies Commission in 1977. *See* U.K. Monopolies and Mergers Commission (1977).

reduced because the firms in the industry are only making low profits, and that these low profits are indicative of the fact that there is no consumer exploitation. However, it has been regulation which has provided the environment in which costs have risen to absorb revenues.

If these analogies *do* apply to the regulated sectors of aviation, then reducing regulation must have a final crucial role. It must be seen as a way of forcing innovation on any airline which might otherwise be reluctant to develop its operations. It must also be seen as offering the main hope for airlines being in a situation where costs have to be kept down in order for carriers to remain competitive and job security in the long term ensured. The pace of innovation in aviation markets where free competition has been allowed—such as the North Atlantic compared with the South Atlantic, and the leanness and efficiency of airlines in competitive markets such as those for European inclusive-tour charters—provide unquantifiable but telling evidence in favour of such a proposition.

As an overall summary of view on the regulation debate, one is well aware of the criticisms which can be made of the de-regulatory trends of recent years. One must also acknowledge the continuing validity of many of the arguments which can be made in favour of continuing tight regulation of the industry. Yet I am still some distance from being swayed from a view that the correct policy from the consumer viewpoint at least is a policy that aims at giving the freest play to competitive forces for as long as possible in the mature aviation markets where this is politically feasible. This will mean in U.S. domestic service, the North Atlantic, and intra-European networks. Even from the position of airline marketing adopted in this book, a very plausible argument can be put forward that such a policy will be in the interests of the majority of airlines as industry participants in such markets. In the less developed world, however, the maintenance of a much tighter regulatory framework will be necessary for a mixture of political and economic reasons.

Moving on to perhaps less weighty, but still important, matters, Chapter 5 considered the detail of product design in the industry. Overwhelmingly, what should be seen as the most significant point from this chapter is that product design should in no sense be seen as either an isolated or random process. In a properly-planned business, it should stem directly from the study of market needs and from the strategy adopted by the firm relative to the available market segments.

For the future, airline product design decisions are even more important than they have been in the past. For any airline with a business or total-market strategy, product planning policy must ensure that products are offered which match the needs of the business segment. This will mean that decisions will be especially important with respect to scheduling and customer-service policy. However, for the leisure segment of demand, future product planning is nothing short of vital. We have seen how this segment of demand is price-sensitive, and that the lowering of operating costs will not be available in the future to assist airlines in securing additional penetration of this market. Airlines with an interest in the leisure market must therefore ensure that the leisure traveller is required to pay for the product features which he requires, and no more. Only in this way will profit-based airlines be able to offer the fares which will allow a further penetration of the leisure segment. Policy for the future must therefore involve an inspection of all aspects of fleet planning, schedules planning, customer service and reservations to ensure that this comes about. Particularly attractive areas for innovation may include the introduction of yet larger aircraft—if necessary at lower frequencies—to reduce still further seat-kilometre costs, a more automated and 'do-it-yourself' approach to airport handling, and a close examination of capacity to ensure that the leisure traveller is not required to pay for the seat accessibility which in almost all cases he does not need.

Chapter 6 dealt with airline pricing, and should have emphasized what a complex decision-area pricing has become, with an active debate in progress at the moment between the proponents of market-based and product-based pricing. As regards future policies, the author's hopes are firstly that the correctness of the product-based approach will be accepted. Then, important areas for future attention must be to attempt to ease the problem of tariff complexity, though it must be said that it is doubtful if any correct airline pricing policy can ever be truly simple in the sense of, say, there being a single price to cover all travellers on a route. A further area where work would seem to be particularly necessary is the one of tariff stability. It is very important that in the future airlines should succeed in reducing the frequency of changes in tariffs, and also that they should investigate the use of advanced methods of communication, such as the U.K. Prestel system, in order to ensure a better and faster dissemination of fare changes to sales outlets.

Chapter 7 considered a wide range of problems of airline selling. Most of the points regarding communication with potential customers are, conceptually at least, non-controversial, in that they should spring directly from a study of the structure of aviation's markets, and the agreed corporate strategy. However, a comment well worth making for the future is that airlines, like all organizations, must be wary of committing excessive resources to communications expenditure. Advertising agencies—and, indeed, an airlines' own advertising and promotion staff—have a clear interest in a high level of promotional expenditure. However, the best advertisement for any airline's services remains a correctly-designed product, with such a product then having the additional benefit of lending credibility to any advertising undertaken.

The main policy issues in airline selling are undoubtedly those related to the role of travel agents, travel organizers and freight forwarders in the industry. Though (as has earlier been covered) the exact role of each of these types of marketing intermediary is different, appropriate policy with respect to each of them is the same, and can be discussed as such. With each of them, there is nothing intrinsically wrong with airlines being heavily dependent on intermediaries. Indeed, there is clear evidence of the value of intermediaries because of the work which they do on the airline's behalf—work which the carriers could only do themselves at higher costs. However, as was emphasized in Sections 7.1 and 7.3, the vital qualification is that the intermediary's market power is used in the interests of the airline as investment risk-taker. As regards policy for the future, then it is entirely correct for airlines to use intermediaries, but, at the same time, they must be able to demonstrate that they do not totally rely on them. Support has already been given to British Airways' policy in this regard. This airline is making full use of intermediaries, but also, by such expedients as its travel shops, implants and direct-selling holiday companies, is showing that it has a capability for carrying out a large part of its own retail selling in the future if a situation arose where its market share fell to unacceptably low levels. As far as the future of agents and forwarders is concerned, then an appropriate view would be that the competent, responsible firm has nothing to fear—indeed it is to be hoped that the future will see an increasing partnership between such firms and airlines. However, the agent with poorly-trained staff and little commitment to the creative selling of air transport must realize that in the competitive world of the 1980s he must either improve his operation or face an unlamented disappearance.

Chapter 8, it is hoped, can stand alone as emphasizing the real difficulties which attend the monitoring of performance in airline marketing, whilst the first section of this concluding Chapter 9 has given three case studies which demonstrate the relevance of marketing theory to the discussion of some of the industry's policy problems.

A summary of each chapter, and commentary on the policy issues raised, moves us near to the end of the book. However, still the most important policy recommendation remains to be given. The book, it is hoped, has shown the logical consistency of a marketing approach for the conduct of airline business. It is this approach which gives us the key to the final, vital recommendation.

Despite the immensity of the problems it has overcome, the airline industry has in many ways been fortunate during the first seventy-five years of its existence. A readily-available market, falling resource costs, rapidly-improving technology and a generally favourable treatment from governments are at least four factors which support such a view. However, we are now arriving at a cross-roads where none of these factors are likely to apply in the future to the extent which they have in the past. Resource costs are now rising rapidly, whilst the era of very large reductions in operating costs of the industry's technology may be coming to an end. Finally, it would be true to say that in many respects the relationships between airlines and governments are more strained now than they ever have been, with governments bowing to consumerist pressures, and asking for ever-increasing payments in user charges.

In such a changing environment, what will be the characteristics of successful airlines of the coming, difficult, period of the industry's development? It is the basic thesis of the book that these airlines will be the ones which adopt a marketing approach. These airlines will devote the initial stages of their planning to obtaining a thorough understanding of the actual and potential markets open to aviation. Only this can form an adequate basis for their activities. They will then formulate objectives which reflect their corporate situation. These objectives will be translated into a strategy, derived by a combination of a knowledge of market opportunities and the perceived strengths and weaknesses of the firm. Finally, the strategy will lead to a logical process of product design, pricing, and selling, to ensure its implementation, with a constant effort, too, to monitor performance in the execution of the strategy.

There is nothing revolutionary or 'difficult' about such a proposition. Indeed, its correctness is obvious. It has therefore been one of the major criteria for the writing of the book that the material in it should be kept simple, and what is essentially a straightforward message made comprehensible to all as a foundation for further study. If it has been successful, the reader should have been taken to the point where he is familiar with the basis of the marketing approach to airline operations. I now hope that as many as possible of those reading the book will feel stimulated into further research and reading to add to the initial contribution which should have been made. I then look forward immensely to discussing the ideas put forward with as many as possible of those with a concern for this vital and fascinating industry.

A Note on Sources

A number of references have been included in the text, to assist those who would like to read further on any of the topics covered.

For those readers in the U.K., most of the source material can be found at the library of the Civil Aviation Authority at CAA House, Kingsway, London WC2 B 6TE, (telephone 01-379-7311). The library is open to visitors on weekdays from 10.00 until 16.00.

For those who are not in the U.K., it is expected that university and other libraries will have available the main books and journals. In case of any difficulty, however, it is suggested that those who are interested in a particular source should write to its publisher.

For sources where a problem arises, and which are regarded as especially important, readers will be welcome to contact the author at the City of London Polytechnic, 100 Minories, London EC2 M 6SQ. He will be pleased to supply specific information on the source, and to indicate where it might be ordered or obtained.

References

ADAMS, J. G. U., London's third airport, *Geogrl J.*, **137**, 468–505 (1971).

AIR TRANSPORT USER'S COMMITTEE, *European Air Fares* (London, 1976).

ALLEN, R. G. D., *Statistics for Economists* (London, Hutchinson, 1966).

ANSOFF, H. I., *Corporate Strategy* (London, McGraw-Hill, 1965).

ASHTON-HILL, N., *The Needs of the Business Traveller* (*Mimeo*, 1978).

BAILEY, R., *Energy — the Rude Awakening* (London, McGraw-Hill, 1977).

BAKER, M. J., *Marketing — An Introductory Text*, 3rd edn (London, Macmillan, 1979).

BARFIELD, N., A perspective of commercial airliner programmes for the 80s and 90s, *ICAO Bulletin*, 32, no. 2, 14–16 (1977).

BELL, M. L., *Marketing: Concepts and Strategy* (Boston, Houghton Mifflin, 1972).

BOYD-CARPENTER, Lord, The contribution of civil aviation to the economic strength and well-being of the U.K., *Aeronaut. J.*, **78**, 181–4 (1974).

BOYD-CARPENTER, Lord, Where is U.K. Civil Aviation Going?, *Chart. Inst. Transp. J.*, **36**, 239–43 (1975).

BOYD, H. W. and MASSY, W. F., *Marketing Management* (New York, Harcourt Brace, 1972).

BRANCKER, J. W. S., *IATA and What it Does* (Leiden, A. W. Sitjhoff, 1977).

BREWER, S. H. and DECOSTER, D. T., *The Nature of Air Cargo Costs*, (University of Washington, Graduate School of Business Administration, 1967).

BRITISH AIRWAYS, *Civil Air Transport in Europe* (London, 1977).

BRITISH AIRWAYS, *British Airways and the Business Traveller* (London, 1978).

BROOKS, P. W., The development of air transport, *J. Transp. Econ. Policy*, *1*, 164–83 (1967).

BRUTON, M. J., *Introduction to Transportation Planning*, 2nd edn. (London, Hutchinson, 1975).

BUSINESS WEEK, *A Study of Recent Air Travellers* (New York, 1979).

CABRAL, L. F. R., Fleet planning for profitability, *Air Transport World* (Oct., 113–17) (1978).

CAMALICH, A., *Requirements of the business traveller*, Presentation to International Civil Airports Association Conference (Guadalajara, 1976).

CAVES, R. E., *Air Transport and its Regulators* (Cambridge, Mass., Harvard University Press, 1962).

CHRISTOPHER, M., *Marketing Below the Line* (London, Allen and Unwin, 1972).

CIVIL AVIATION AUTHORITY, Annual Report 1972/73 (1973).

CIVIL AVIATION AUTHORITY, *Origins and Destinations of Passengers at the London Area Airports* (London, CAP 363, 1975).

CIVIL AVIATION AUTHORITY, *Airline Overbooking* (London, CAP 381, 1976).

CIVIL AVIATION AUTHORITY *European Air Fares — A Consultation Document* (London, CAP 409, 1977a).

CIVIL AVIATION AUTHORITY, *Air Freight Demand* (London, CAP 401, 1977b).

CIVIL AVIATION AUTHORITY, *Domestic Air Services — A Review of Regulatory Policy* (London, CAP 420, 1978).

CIVIL AVIATION AUTHORITY, *Passengers at the London Area Airports in 1978* (London, CAP. 430, 1980).

COLTMANN, D., *Air freight*, in Wentworth, F. R. L., Ed., *Handbook of Physical Distribution*, 261–279 (London, Gower Press, 1976).

COLUSSY, D., Travel facts, policies and other myths, *IATA Rev.* (8–12 Sept. 1977).

COOPER, M. H. and MAYNARD, A. K., *The Price of Air Travel,* Hobart Paper 53 (London, Institute of Economic Affairs, 1971).

COOPER, M. H. and MAYNARD, A. K., The impact of regulated competition on scheduled air fares, *J. of Transp. Econ. Policy*, **6**, 167–75 (1972).

DAVIES, G. J. AND GRAY, R., The export shipping manager in the U.K., *Int. J. Phys. Distrib. Mater. Mgmt*, **10**, 51–67, (1979).

DAVIES, R. E. G., *Airlines of the United States since 1914* (London, Putnam, 1972).

DEPARTMENT OF TRADE, *Report of the Working Party on Discounted Air Fares* (London, HMSO, 1978).

DOGANIS, R. S., Air transport — a case study in international regulation, *J. Transp. Econ. Policy*, **7**, 109–33 (1973).

DOUGLAS, G. W. and MILLER, J. C., *Economic Regulation of Domestic Air Transport* (Washington, The Brookings Institution, 1974).

DRAPER, G., *Regulation and Consumer Needs* (Washington D.C., Air Transportation Research International Forum, 1978).

DUBASH, A., Additional skills and authority acquired to check malpractices, *IATA Rev.* (4–5. Sept. 1975).

EDWARDS, Sir Ronald, *British Air Transport in the Seventies*. Report of the Committee of Enquiry into Civil Air Transport. Cmnd. 4018 (London, HMSO, 1969).

ELLISON, A. P. and Stafford, E. M., *The Dynamics of the Civil Aviation Industry* (Farnborough, Hants, Saxon House, 1974).

FALKSON, L. M., Airline overbooking: some comments. *J. Transp. Econ. Policy*, **3**, 352–4 (1969).

FRIEDMANN, J. J., *A New Air Transport Policy for the North Atlantic* (New York, Athenaeum, 1976).

GERSHUNY, J., *After Industrial Society? The Emerging Self-Service Economy* (London, Macmillan, 1978).

GLENN, C. H., Factors to be considered in airline scheduling, *Can. Aeronaut. Space J.*, **18**, 149–56 (1972).

GREATER LONDON COUNCIL, *Tourism — A Paper for Discussion* (London, 1978).

GREEN, J. H. T., *United Kingdom Air Traffic Forecasting* (London, Department of Trade, 1978).

GRUMBRIDGE, J. L., *Marketing Management in Air Transport* (London, Allen and Unwin, 1966).

GWILLIAM, K. M. and MACKIE, P. J., *Economics and Transport Policy* (London, Allen and Unwin, 1975).

HAMMARSKJOLD, K., *International Air Transport, Tariffs and Trade* (London, Royal Institution of International Affairs, 1978).

HANLON, J. P., The international air passenger tariff, *Chart. Inst. Transp. J.*, **37**, 221–6 (1977).

HARTLEY, K., A Market for Aircraft (Hobart Paper 57) (*London, Institute of Economic Affairs*, 1974).

HODGSON, W. H., The impact of low fares on the air transport industry — views of Monarch Airlines Ltd., *Aeronaut. J.*, **83**, 210–11 (1979).

HOWARD, K., *Inventory Management* (International Journal of Physical Distribution Monograph) (Bradford, MCB Books, 1973).

HUSSEY, D. E., *Introducing Corporate Planning* (Oxford, Pergamon, 1971).

INTERNATIONAL AIR TRANSPORT ASSOCIATION, *The Economics of Air Cargo Carriage and Service* (Geneva, 1969).

INTERNATIONAL AIR TRANSPORT ASSOCIATION, *The North Atlantic* (Geneva, 1973).

INTERNATIONAL AIR TRANSPORT ASSOCIATION, *Agreeing Fares and Rates*, 2nd edn. (Geneva, 1974).

JACKSON, P. and BRACKENRIDGE, W., *Air Cargo Distribution* (London, Gower Press, 1971).

JEANIOTT, P., Computerized reservations systems meet today's needs, *ICAO Bulletin*, **29**, 35–6 (1974).

JOHNSON, K. M. and GARNETT, H. C., The Economics of Containerization, *University of Glasgow, Social and Economic Studies*, **20** (1971).

KAHN, A. *The Economics of Regulation* (New York, John Wiley, 1969).

KAMP, J., *Air Charter Regulation* (New York, Praeger Publishers, 1976).

KEITH-LUCAS, D., Design for safety, *Aeronaut. J.*, **77**, 483–8 (1973).

KOTLER, P., *Marketing Management*, 3rd edn. (New York, Prentice Hall, 1976).

LANE, R., POWELL, T. J. and PRESTWOOD-SMITH, P., *Analytical Transport Planning* (London, Duckworth, 1971).

LITTLE, I. M. D. and McCLEOD, K. M., The new pricing policy of the British Airports Authority, *J. Transp. Econ. Policy*, **6**, 101–15 (1972).

LIPSEY, R., *An Introduction to Positive Economics* (London, Weidenfeld and Nicolson, 1975).

McFADZEAN, Sir Frank, Energy-current and future supplies and prices, *Chart. Inst. Transp. J.*, **37**, 72–7 (1978).

McIVER, C., *Marketing for Managers* (London, Business Books, 1972).

MASEFIELD, P., *Proceedings of 197? Annual General Meeting* (Geneva, International Air Transport Association, 1977).

MILLER, J. C., Optimal pricing of freight in combination aircraft, *J. Transp. Econ. Policy*, **7**, 258–68 (1973).

MILLER, R. and SAWERS, P., *The Technical Development of Modern Aviation* (London, Routledge and Kegan Paul, 1968).

MORRELL, P. S. and TANEJA, N. K., Airline productivity re-defined: An analysis of U.S. and European carriers, *Transportation*, **8**, 37–50 (1979).

MURPHY, G. J., *Transport and Distribution*, 2nd edn. (London, Business Books, 1978).

MUTTI, J. and Murai, Y., Airline travel on the North Atlantic. Is profitability possible?, *J. Transp. Econ. Policy*, **11**, 45–53 (1977).

NARODICK, K. G., An analysis of the frequent business flyer, *European Research, September,* 215–219 (1978).

NATIONAL ECONOMIC DEVELOPMENT OFFICE, *The Freight Forwarder* (London, 1972).

DE NEUFVILLE, R., *Airport Systems Planning* (London, Macmillan, 1976).

O'CONNOR, W. E., *An Introduction to Airline Economics* (New York, Praeger, 1978).

OLINS, W., Corporate identity — the myth and the reality, *J. R. Soc. Arts,* **127,** 208–23 (1979).

PEARSON, R. J., *The Comparative Efficiency of European Airlines* (Paris, Institut du Transport Aérien, 1976).

PEARSON, R. J., Monitoring airline performance, *Aeronaut. J.* **82,** 64–74 (1978).

PERROW, J. A., *Economics* (London, University Tutorial Press, 1971).

PILLAI, K. G. J., *The Air Net* (Grossman, New York, 1969).

PONSONBY, G. J., Transport Policy Co-ordination through Competition, *Hobart Paper,* **49,** (London, Institute of Economic Affairs, 1969).

PUGH, A. T., Pricing in the Air, *Lecture to the Metropolitan Section of the Chartered Institute of Transport* (London, 23 Nov. 1978).

DE RAISMES, G., *Inventory Management*; In F. R. L. Wentworth (Ed.) *Handbook of Physical Distribution* (London, Gower Press, 1975).

RAMSDEN, J. M., *The Safe Airline* (London, Macdonald and Jane's, 1976).

REED, P. W., *Competition and regulation in international aviation — a European view*, Travel Research Association Conference (Sept., 1978).

ROSENBERG, A., *Air Travel within Europe* (National Swedish Consumer Council, Stockholm, 1969).

SARNDAL, C. E. and STATTON, W. B., Factors influencing operating costs in the airline industry, *J. Transp. Econ. Policy*, **8,** 67–88 (1975).

SCHNEIDER, L. M., *The Future of the U.S. Domestic Air Freight Industry* (Boston, Harvard University, 1973).

SCOUTT, J. and COSTELLO, F. J., Charters, the new mode: setting a new course for international air transportation, *J. Air Law Commerce,* **41,** 1–28 (1975).

SHAW, R. (1979), Forecasting air traffic — are there limits to growth?, *Futures,* **11,** 185–94 (1979).

SHAW, R. R., The scheduled airlines in a changing world, *Aeronaut. J.,* **77,** 489–501 (1975).

SHAW, S. and BUDD, L., The measurement of airline seat accessibility, *Air Transport Discussion Paper* **1** (City of London Polytechnic, 1979).

SHOVELTON, W. P., Bermuda 2 — A discussion of its implications: Negotiation and Agreement, *Aeronaut. J.,* **82,** 51–4 (1978).

SHOVELTON, W. P. (1979), Bermuda 2 *et al., Chart. Inst. Transp. J.,* **38,** 289–93 (1979).

SIMON, J. L., An almost practical solution to airline overbooking, *J. Transp. Econ. Policy,* **2,** 201–2 (1968).

SIMON, J. L., Airline overbooking — a rejoinder, *J. Transp. Econ. Policy,* **4,** 212–13 (1970).

SLATER, A. G., The advantages of air cargo distribution in perspective, *Inst. J. Phys. Distrib.,* **4,** 54–67 (1974).

SLETMO, G. K., *Demand for Air Cargo — an Econometric Approach* (Stockholm, Scandinavian Airlines System, 1973).

SMITH, P. S., *Air Freight — Operations, Marketing and Economics* (London, Faber and Faber, 1974).

SMITH, P. S., The future of freighters, *Airtrade*, 21–7 (March, 1976).

SMITH, P. S. and GARNETT, H. C., Total distribution cost simulation model, *Int. J. of Phys. Distribn*, **3**, 355–64 (1975).

SMITHIES, R. M., The changing demand for air transport — the North Atlantic case, *J. Transp. Econ. Policy*, **7**, 231–49 (1973).

SPATER, G. A., The economics of capacity control, *Chart. Inst. Transp. J.*, **36**, 8–11 (1973).

STRATFORD, A. H., *Air Transport Economics in the Supersonic Era*, 2nd edn. (London, Macmillan, 1974).

STRATFORD, A. H., *Airports and the Environment* (London, Macmillan, 1975).

STRASZHEIM, M. R., *The International Airline Industry* (Washington, D.C., Brookings Institution, 1969).

STRASZHEIM, M. R., The determination of airline fares and load factors, *J. Transp. Econ. Policy*, **8**, 260–73 (1975).

STUART, C. R., The impact of low fares on the air transport industry. Views of air carriers — British Airways, *Aeronaut. J.*, **83**, 207–9 (1979).

SWEETMAN, W., B 767 and A 310 — Sisters under the skin?, *Interavia*, **36**, 1025–9 (1979).

TANEJA, N. K., *The Commercial Airline Industry* (Bloomington, Lexington Books, 1976).

TANEJA, N. K., *Airline Traffic Forecasting* (Bloomington, Lexington Books, 1978).

TAPLIN, H. E., Price elasticities in the vacation travel market, *J. Transp. Econ. Policy*, **14**, 19–36 (1980).

THOMSON, A. W. J. and HUNTER, L. C., *The Nationalized Transport Industries* (London, Heinemann, 1973).

THOMSON, J. M., *Modern Transport Economics* (Harmondsworth, Penguin Books, 1974).

UK MONOPOLIES AND MERGERS COMMISSION, *Surveyor's Services. A Report on the Supply of Surveyor's Services With Respect to Scale Fees* (London, 1977).

VICKREY, W., Airline overbooking — some further solutions, *J. Transp. Econ. Policy*, **6**, 257–69 (1972).

WADDINGTON, C. H., *The Man-made Future* (London, Croom Helm, 1978).

WASSENBERGH, A. H., *Aspects of Air Law and Civil Air Policy in the 1970s* (The Hague, Leiden, 1970).

WELBURN, T. H. N., Price and quality in air transport, *Chart. Inst. Transp. J.*, **38**, 345–9 (1979).

WHEATCROFT, S. F, *Air Transport Policy* (London, Michael Joseph, 1964).

WHEATCROFT S. F., Air transport demand 2000 — through a glass darkly, *Aeronaut. J.*, **81**, 366–72 (1977).

WHEATCROFT, S. F., *Demand elasticity revisited* (Paper presented to Travel Research Association, New York, 22 Sept. 1978).

WILKINSON, I. F., Distribution channel management — power considerations, *Int. J. Phys. Distrib.*, **4**, 4–15 (1973).

WILKINSON, K. G., Fuel economy — the next stage, *Flight International*, 227–36, (31 Jan., 1976).

WILKINSON, K. G., The role of advancing technology in the future of air transport, *Aeronaut. J.*, **81,** 185–92 (1977).

WILLIAMS, J. E. D., *The Operation of Airliners* (London, Hutchinson, 1964).

WILLIAMS, J. E. D., Aviation — profit or prestige?, *Flight International*, 303–5 (20 Feb. 1974).

WILMSHURST, J., *The Fundamentals and Practice of Marketing* (London, Heinemann, 1978).

General Index

Accidental no-shows, 139
Accommodation and the tourism industry, 59
Advanced booking (as a pricing condition), 157
Advanced booking charters, 98, 102, 146, 186, 221
Advertising,
principles, 7, 196
airline, 63, 191–196, 201–204, 223
Aerolineas Argentinas, 12, 70
Aer Lingus, 12, 70
Aeromexico, 70, 72
Aerospace equipment manufacturers, 80–81
Affinity group charters, 98
Age structure of population (as a factor explaining air transport demand), 27
Agent's educational trips, 196–197
Air Afrique, 70
Air Algérie, 70
Air Anglia, 83
Air Canada, 12, 69, 117, 124, 133, 196, 209
Air France, 69, 70, 133, 155, 209
Air freight,
market segmentation, 30–40
market potential, 40
product design, 146–152
pricing, 172–181
selling channels, 198–200
communication, 201–204
Air freight forwarders, 150, 151, 177, 179, 180, 198–201, 237–238
Air India, 12, 70, 72, 133, 209
Air Jamaica, 70

Air New Zealand, 70, 72, 196
Air passenger pricing, 155–172
fare structures, 155–159
principles, 159–172
Air Portugal, 70
Air taxi services, 112
Air Traffic Control, 61, 65, 129, 132, 229, 230
Air transport—patterns of growth, 66–67
Air Transport Licensing Board, 96
Air Transport User's Committee, 15
Air Transport World, 78, 190, 221, 224
Air travel market potential, 26–28, 56–61
Aircraft type (as a product feature), 115, 192
Aircraft maintenance (as a constraint on scheduling), 128
Aircraft performance, 115–117
cruising speed, 115
block speed, 115
fuel consumption, 116
payload/range, 116
fieldlength/range, 116–117
Aircraft utilization, 117, 122, 207, 211
Airline De-Regulation Act, 96, 103
Airline-related costs, 163
Airport capacity, 61–62, 111–112
Airport Development Aid Programme, 49
Airport handling, 115, 122, 131
Airport landing charges, 122, 163, 210, 229
Airport security, 131

Author Index